THE

Powers of the World to Come:

AND

THE CHURCH'S STEWARDSHIP,

AS INVESTED WITH THEM.

BY

GEORGE B. CHEEVER, D.D.

NEW YORK:
ROBERT CARTER & BROTHERS,
No. 285 BROADWAY.

1853.

STEREOTYPED BY
THOMAS B. SMITH,
216 William St., N. Y.

PRINTED BY
JOHN A. GRAY,
97 Cliff Street.

PREFACE.

THE present work has its origin in a course of lectures on that mighty phrase adopted as its title, in the solemn passage of God's word in Hebrews, 6: 4, 5, 6—*and have tasted the good Word of God, and the* POWERS OF THE WORLD TO COME. It is, in fact, a practical survey of what is termed in some quarters the Eschatology of the Scriptures; the realities which according to Divine Revelation we are to meet beyond the grave. We are wholly dependent on Divine Revelation for the least knowledge of them; and yet that Revelation has so long rendered them familiar, that they seem possessions of our intuitive experience, or gifts of our Natural Theology. Thousands walk beneath their light without thinking of them, and act by their light, without any acknowledgment of the source from whence it flows, as men walk beneath the stars without lifting up their faces to the heavens, and pursue their avocations by the conclusions of astronomy, without any study of the heavenly bodies.

To know Divine Truth, the object of the soul's pursuit and affections must be the Divine Author of it. This is distinctly declared in that striking passage in Hosea, "Then shall we KNOW,—if we follow on TO KNOW THE LORD." Correspondent with this is that grand passage in the thirty-sixth Psalm, "With thee is the fountain of life; IN THY LIGHT SHALL WE SEE LIGHT." And correspondent with both these passages, and illustrative of them, is the great declaration of Christ, "He that followeth ME, shall not walk in darkness, but shall have THE LIGHT OF LIFE." All true, all living knowledge, derives its life, its power from this personal, experimental, heart-knowledge of God in Christ Jesus. In proportion as communion with God increases, so will increase the knowledge of his Word; while without that communion, though the world were filled with Lexicons, Grammars, and learned expository helps of every kind, and philosophical and theological speculations ever so acute and erudite, the Word would remain a sealed Book, a dead letter. The Word is written for believing hearts as in sympathetic ink; communion with God by the Spirit is that hidden sympathetic fire that makes the letter burn, and reveals its meaning. Therefore, according to Cowper's sweet picture,

Yon cottager that weaves at her own door,
Pillow and bobbins all her little store,

shall have, by the humble prayerful study of God's Word by the Spirit, a knowledge of heights and depths in the Divine intelligence, that the most learned minds have never reached, and cannot appreciate. "I thank thee O Father, Lord of heaven and earth, because thou hast hid those things from the wise and prudent, and hast revealed them unto babes. Even so Father, for so it seemed good in thy sight."

The truths of the Divine Word are like the revelations of the starry heavens in coming to us, and in their more and more perfect gradual discovery. By the construction, in later years, of telescopic instruments with vastly-increased skill and power, many a spot of cloudy indefinite light in the heavens, once thought to be an incomplete nebulous mass in process of development, has been resolved into clusters of bright shining worlds, clear and unmistakable. So do the truths of God, when rightly examined, break upon the soul. The *nebulæ* of the Divine Word, or what were once thought to be such, shall continually be resolved into perfect and clear-shining stars. But O the depths! Infinite on infinite, beyond the possible reach of our vision, regions of truth roll off, filled as with suns and stars, region upon region, deep beyond deep, riches unfathomable of boundless wisdom and love, that as yet no man hath seen, nor forever, perhaps, can any created understanding fully comprehend!

And let us remember that for our knowledge of the Word, in the nearness and the life thereof, we are dependent more upon the Spirit of God, than on any external advantages; dependent entirely, indeed, upon the Spirit of God. Without that, the veil is on the heart, whatever be the external facilities of knowledge; but when it shall turn to the Lord, that veil shall be taken away.

We are said to be, *known* to be, nearer to the sun in Winter than in Summer. But the increased swiftness of the earth's motion in its orbit, together with the inclination of the axis in the same, prevents the increase of heat, that otherwise would be inevitable. The surface of the earth on this account is so much less time exposed to the sun's rays, and so obliquely that the heat is diminished by the nearness. Just so, the World may be nearer to God in position, by providential advantages, opportunities, and in speculative divine knowledge nearer, and yet, farther from God's love, less affected by his mercy, less warmed and quickened by his light. So it may be with an individual heart. One man may really be farther from God in position than another, and yet have a Summer season in his soul, while the other, though nearer in point of every advantage and opportunity, may remain in the dead of Winter. The climate of the soul does not depend so much upon the nearness and abundance of the rays, if it is flying swiftly through them, and obliquely turned from them, but upon the steadiness and constancy with which they are received by a heart turned directly towards them. Looking steadily to Christ is the condition of light and life. Looking steadily to Christ, and thus only, can we see and know the Powers of the World to Come.

CONTENTS.

POWERS OF THE WORLD TO COME.

GOD.

THE REALITY.—THE IDEA.

THE Powers of the world to come! These words constitute a phrase, which, wherever it might have been met with, though in the pages of Plato or of Cicero, would have powerfully arrested the attention of a thoughtful mind. And the more such a mind should dwell upon them, the more would they grow upon the soul, and rouse the imagination.

Sometimes they seem presenting themselves as a wild rising bank of cloud in the midnight horizon, behind which and out of which the Northern lights are sending up a strange and flickering brightness, and through which the stars seem to struggle as on the verge of chaos. The sense of sin in ourselves, and the combination of certainty and uncertainty, definiteness and indefiniteness, clearness and mystery, locality and infinitude, in what is before us, adds immeasurably to the grandeur and gloom of the sway of the future. The conviction, universal and unescapable, that the guiltiness of our own character and conduct exposes us to whatever elements of terror and of retribution there may lie embosomed and awaiting us in that undisclosed world, invests even the most indistinct revelation of it with an overpowering solemnity and majesty.

What, then, *are* the powers of the world to come? What precise forms of revelation, of thought, of conception, answer to the term? Some things Nature herself teaches us, though we do not see what we *might* see, nor so far, nor so clearly, as we *ought.* We are as children in a dark room, waiting for the curtain to be lifted before some grand transparency or solemn show. It is dark here, because we have made it so by our sins; most men make this vestibule of their eternal being a dungeon; having the understanding darkened, being alienated from the life of God through the ignorance that is in them because of the blindness of their hearts.

So they know not what is before them; whether, when the curtain rises, they shall behold a world of blessedness and glory, or of terror and despair; whether the scenes that meet the amazed gaze shall be scenes welcoming the soul with songs to joy eternal, or overwhelming it with weepings and wailings, and the gnashing of teeth; whether the holy light and the ravishing forms and employments of a celestial world are to surround them, or the dreadful realities of the blackness of darkness forever. Even the quickened vision of faith sees as through a glass darkly, and to those who have the very witness of the Spirit within them that they are the sons of God, it doth not now appear what they shall be; only they know that when He who is their life shall appear, they shall appear with Him and like Him in glory.

If, now, any one of the realities in that eternal spiritual state to which we are advancing, were suddenly struck forth into visibility and brought home upon the soul, it would be experienced as a POWER, in comparison with which, nothing else could gain the least attention or influence. There are principalities and powers in heavenly places, and the smallest appreciation of their glory, the slightest vision of the array of such creatures on their thrones of light, would be a disclosure and an experience before which all earthly glories and distinctions would vanish as insignificant and worthless. *If they were seen and known;* but they are not; they may be imagined, but such things as these do not constitute men's native forms and furniture of thought—neither are they so revealed as to brood upon the soul and hold it captive. They are not the *dynamics*, but the *circumstances* of an eternal state.

Neither is it of the creature that men think, when they think of the world to come; neither is it of thrones, dominions, princedoms, or tracts of space inhabited by worlds; but they think of God. The thought that broods upon the mind, more or less distinctly, in *every* conception of the world to come, is that of meeting God. *That* is the conviction, the sense, the feeling,—*I am to meet God;* and that meeting is the decision of an eternal destiny. Everything marches towards that, everything is drawn in and absorbed as a bare attendant upon that; and therefore we are forced, first of all, to individualize and define this phrase, *the powers of the world to come*, as including whatever manifestations of the Deity we have reason to believe or to know must then be encountered, and the various overwhelming disclosures of God's attributes that shall open on the soul.

The world to come presents itself to the mind as the more immediate dwelling-place of God, where He is to be *seen*, in a sense, in which He *cannot* be seen in this world. He fills, indeed, immensity with His presence; He is here as well as there, in Divine power and glory, but in essence invisible. So that here, if men choose, they may forget God; may live, according to the indictment against them in the Scriptures, without God in the world; may keep the soul as empty, dark, and desolate of God, as the supposed vacuity and malignity of Atheism. But not so in the eternal world, where every eye shall see Him, every intelligent creature know His existence by feeling it, and find the nature of His attributes by experience as well as observation of their power. There shall be neither darkness, nor ignorance, nor insensibility. Even the blackness of darkness forever, will be no veil to hide the soul from the scrutiny and the sense of the all-seeing eye of an infinitely holy God.

There is a foreboding of all this, even in the present world. Men expect to meet God. Even the Atheist, struggling against the belief, cannot overmaster and annihilate the fear of meeting God;

cannot so abnegate the conditions of his being as not to tremble, lest what he denies may prove to be a reality; cannot pluck from his soul the twining roots of the primary law of its intelligence acknowledging a Creator. All men expect to meet God. Before all men the future world rises, as the province or scene of an introduction to the more immediate, inevitable, irresistible sight, sense, and knowledge of God.

Now in this world, even in the *idea* of God as a *belief*, or as a constitutional intuition and knowledge, which is the ground of such belief, there resides something of that power which fills the eternal world by the presence and manifestations of the personal reality. Over this fallen world the IDEA of God reigns, perverted indeed, in many cases, and deformed with monstrous superstitions and horrid miscreations of ignorance, depravity and fear, according to the process described in Romans, i. 21–25, but still a presence and a power, greater than all other powers; and both in heathendom and Christendom, it is the idea that leads on and governs all progress, all responsibility, all moral life. It is the idea that quickens and enlightens the conscience; and just in proportion as it is brought near, and the soul is made acquainted and familiar with it, it rouses the whole being. Nothing is so overwhelming to the sinful soul as a sense of God's presence; nothing is so abasing and annihilating to it as a clear sight and sense of God. The bare hieroglyphics of His power and glory in the creation are overwhelming, just in proportion as through them the soul dimly sees Him, and becomes penetrated with some faint conception of the inaccessible light, majesty, and infinitude of His attributes. All things that speak of God, and bring Him near, are full of power and glory.

But the manner in which this idea affects the soul here in this world is infinitely different, according to the character which the soul wears in the sight of God as holy or unholy, and the relation in which it stands to Him as forgiven and at peace, or at enmity against Him. The idea of God attracts and penetrates a holy soul, and absorbs it more and more, till every other thought is lost in God: being *the* power, by eminence, of the world to come, so likewise here in this world it draws and holds the soul accordingly. As a flame darts upward, so the soul of the creature, restored to its right tendency, with its sensibility purified from sin, soars upward towards God, pants to view His glorious face, longs to behold Him and to know Him.

"I beseech thee," cried Moses unto God, "show me thy glory." The great prophet had been forty days and forty nights in God's more immediate presence, and he began to have but one feeling, one desire—the longing desire to see and know more of God. The nearer he came to God, the swifter was the course of his soul, and the more burning its ardor towards Him. All thoughts and things for Moses began to be absorbed in the one thought of seeing God. He could, like Peter after him, have pitched his tent forever there, and forgotten all earthly beings and objects, all creation, all the universe indeed, in gazing upon God. Thus it is, and ever must be, that the idea of God, just in proportion as it opens on the soul, absorbs the whole being, entrances all the faculties, and fills and satisfies the holy mind and heart with bliss ineffable, inconceivable. And thus are the desires of holy souls described in God's own word, as drawn out after Him, and only after Him, everything else passing into forgetfulness and nothingness in the comparison: "Whom have I in heaven but thee? and there is none upon the earth that I desire besides thee. My flesh and my heart faileth, but God is the strength of my heart, and my portion forever!" And again: "As the hart panteth after the water-brook, so panteth my soul after thee, O God! My soul thirsteth for God; my heart and my flesh crieth out for the living God." These are expressions of holy and absorbing emotion in the vision of God begun on earth, in the heart that is drawing near to Him, and finds and feels the all-absorbing nature of His glory. God is the soul's all-sufficient good—God is the soul's entrancing happiness. Nothing is needed to make a holy soul perfectly, infinitely happy, but just for God to exist, and continue to disclose His glory, and permit that soul to gaze upon His attributes.

And so the great fact of regeneration, and of translation from the kingdom of darkness into the kingdom of God's dear son, is just the shining of God into the heart, to give the light of the knowledge of the glory of God in the face of Jesus Christ. Nothing of evil or temptation can stand against that; all things of glory and of good are comprehended in that.

And infinitely favored and happy are they to whom God thus unveils his glory, they whom God chooses and brings near to himself, revealing his Son in them, and himself in his Son, and answering for them the prayer of Christ on earth; a prayer explained only by this truth; that God is essential to the soul, and that all bliss consists in the knowledge of God, and the sight of his glory. "This is life eternal, that they might know thee, the only true God, and Jesus Christ, whom thou hast sent. Glorify thou me with the glory which I had with thee before the world was. I will that they whom thou hast given me be with me, where I am, that they may behold my glory." It is the beholding of this Divine glory that constitutes the very bliss of heaven. The Holy City has no need of the sun, neither of the moon, to shine in it, for the glory of God doth lighten it, and the Lamb is the light thereof. And the central supreme feature of the blessedness and glory of his servants is, that they shall see his face, and his name shall be in their foreheads. And thus it is that the very idea of God, whose existence is the happiness of heaven, whose glory is the light of heaven, draws all holy intelligences throughout the universe, absorbs and governs all minds, and is a Power in the world of faith, as a Power in the world of reality.

But this same idea of God, so full of glory and blessedness to all holy beings, and attractive with an all-absorbing irresistible power of gravitation, is the subject of infinite terror and aversion to every unholy soul. That which constitutes the law and power of beatific attraction to the good, is the antagonistic principle and law of abhorrence and repulsion to the evil. The very essence of repugnancy being bound up in it towards all wickedness, and in all wickedness towards it, it is the transcending terror among the powers of the world to come, producing an intractable, spontaneous aversion in the sinful soul, or rather rousing up its native, indwelling, inevitable hatred into activity. The sinful soul experiences in itself an elastic coil of repercussion against God, and springs back with a force intuitive and unconquerable, from the presentation of the true idea of God. The intensity of dread is concentrated in the thought of meeting a holy God in judgment, nay, of meeting him at all. The thought of God, brought home, distresses the soul, even now; it is a gloomy, dreadful thought; for in a sinful mind there lies beneath it, there advances along with it, the irresistible conviction of justice, holiness, power, arrayed against the soul, nay, infinite goodness, infinite love, compelled by sin to play the part of a devouring fire. God's intellectual attributes may be endured, may be admired, may be reverenced afar off, even by a sinful being; but it is impossible that his moral attributes, when their operation in regard to sin is clearly seen and known, should be regarded by the wicked with any other emotions than those of hostility and dread. And God's infinite holiness, which constitutes the eternal glory and loveliness of his character, in the sight of all good beings, is the very attribute against which the guilty soul feels itself arrayed, and that against itself, is entire and eternal opposition.

And so in the whole array of the powers of the world to come, there is the same difference to a holy and unholy soul. All the passages of Scripture, through which the light is poured down the most directly and intensely, are touchstones of the opposites of character. Take that grand and glorious passage in the Epistle to the Hebrews, "Ye are come unto Mount Zion, and to the city of the living God, the Heavenly Jerusalem, and to an innumerable company of angels, to the general assembly and church of the first born, which are written in heaven, and to God the Judge of all, and to the spirits of just men made perfect, and to Jesus the Mediator of the New Covenant, and to the blood of sprinkling that speaketh better things than that of Abel." It will be admitted that this is a glorious and radiant passage, like the flinging wide of one of the gates of Heaven, where you may stand and look in, seeing and hearing celestial sights and employ ments. But with what eyes, and with what heart, do you read and behold these records? Is there a counterpart of these heavenly images in your own soul, by the Divine Spirit drawing you towards them? Is that the blessed power which they have over you? Are they distinct and animating, or indistinct, unattractive, and by reason of the central presence, the idea of God the Judge of all, is there present likewise, with all this climacterical array of beatific scenes and persons, an element of gloom and repellency? Gloom and repellency! Is it possible to connect such impressions with the idea of God, the very centre and source of all the brightness, loveliness, and bliss of heaven? Alas! have we not seen that except there be an entire change from sin to holiness in the human heart, God, a holy God and a just God, is the transcending terror among all the powers of the world to come?

Take, then, the experience of two different men with this passage, the believer and the unbeliever, the man of God and the man of the world, the Christian and the unconverted. Take John Bunyan, and put him with David Hume, or Francis Spira, or any hardened, heedless, but dying and awakened sinner, and bring this heavenly transparency before them; turn upon them the same shafts of celestial radiance. What is Heaven to the one is Hell to the other, the character and vision of the inward individual soul being the determining rule. The powers of the world to come are there, all thronging in that wondrous figured gateway; but in one case it is the powers of a celestial world, in the other of a world of woe; in the one case it is the power of Paradise, in the other of Hell. In the one case it is all that is dearest to a renewed soul, all that a holy being loves, brought near to the heart yearning after God, Christ, holiness and heaven; in the other it is conviction of guilt, and a fearful looking for of judgment and of wrath eternal.

We see, then, that the loss and ruin of the sinner are an inevitable necessity in the nature of things, and not in any way a mere determination of the arbitrary will, but an evil which, in spite of that will, the sinner brings down on himself, by a necessity growing out of what God and holiness are, and what the sin and sinner are. Here, then, is a great touchstone of nature and of character. This first, dominant, supreme power among the powers of the world to come, the idea of God now, and the presence of God hereafter, is the preëminent and decisive test for the discovery of the habitual disposition and appropriate retributions of the soul. "I the Lord search the heart, I try the reins, even to give to every man according to his ways, and according to the fruit of his doings." For all this, it only needs the application of the attributes of a holy God. True it is, that God's own will goes with His attributes, and cannot but be, not only in harmony, but in hearty and infinite coöperation with them all. God could neither be perfect nor happy were it otherwise. But really and truly, to decide the fate of every probationer for eternity, every moral agent in the universe, it only needs that each should be made acquainted with God's attributes, and that those attributes should just play according to their nature. No other judgment, decision or sentence would be necessary. If the very inhabitants of the world of woe loved God, if the crowd of the lost angels delighted in Him, and in the operation and glory of His attributes, they would be happy in Him, even in their world of woe. But there could be no such thing as a world of woe, if there were no such thing as hatred of God and rebellion against Him. When the will is submissive to His, that change alone is enough to change hell into heaven. When the will is opposed to His, that alone would be enough to change heaven into hell.

And, therefore, this elective affinity will have its full sweep in eternity, and the elements and inhabitants of antagonistic characters and worlds will draw off by themselves, in infinite purity and separation from one another, pure unmingled holiness, and pure unmingled sin; pure and supreme love to God, absorbing all the being and entrancing it in God's own blessedness, or pure and supreme hatred against God, equally entire and predominant, and whirling the lost soul into the depths of an irremediable, unfathomable ruin. It is, therefore, plain, that for the decision of the question, to what world the soul belongs, there would nothing else be needed in the trial of all creatures, but just to stand at the gates of heaven, and see, in the turning of God's character, God's attributes, upon each soul, as it comes up into that light, what colour of answering character the soul itself assumes. If it shine with the reflection of God's holiness, if it be in sweet and blissful sympathy with that, then will it spring towards God, as flame darts upward through the firmament, to rest in his likeness and blessedness forever. If it be the darkening of sinful character that is made manifest in God's light, then will that soul draw back, and pass, silently if possible, but in gloomy abhorrence and despair, into that world of darkness, where the rule of the feeling of the inhabitants in regard to God is just this,—Farthest from Thee is best!

So then we see clearly that it is not God's will, but the sinner's, that makes hell what it is. And that world of darkness and of sin must necessarily be, in all its characteristics, the very extreme opposite of the heavenly world. This, where God is the glory, and the Lamb the light thereof, a world of light; *that*, of the blackness of darkness forever;—this, a world of holiness, *that*, of sin and wickedness;—this, a world of love, that, of hatred;—this, of serenity and peace, that, of rage, confusion, terror, remorse and despair. All things, indeed, according as God himself is the happiness or terror of the soul, will put on the same aspect, will wear the same character. "Whoso is wise, and he shall understand these things? prudent, and he shall know them? For the ways of the Lord are right, and the just shall walk in them, but the transgressors shall fall therein." The same attributes, the same ways, the same principles, will be happiness and glory to the righteous, terror and misery to the wicked. It cannot be otherwise. It would be so now, in present, instant demonstration, were it not for Christ's death. That suspends the rule, keeps in abeyance the very nature of things, and so surrounds even the soul of the sinner with an atmosphere of long-suffering and forbearance in the offer of mercy, that God is not yet felt as a consuming fire, even by the wicked; and therefore, on account of God's mercy, still waiting to be gracious for Christ's sake, men may for the present hate and disobey God, and yet not find, not in this world, from the laws of God, such a retaliation of their guilt and defiance of the Creator, such an avengement of their contempt towards Him, as would make any world in God's universe a world of retribution But by-and-bye, God will let things go. He will cast off the muzzle by which the forces of a just retribution have been restrained, to see whether the sinner would in the interval flee to Christ for mercy, and he will let those forces have their own just way; he will let the fire of sin, which the sinner would not have Him quench in this world, take its own course, and burn on unto perdition.

Away, then, with all complaints against the tremendous truth of an everlasting retribution, according to character, and complain of God, if you complain of Him at all, because He does, in such amazing mercy, for so long a time, restrain His own attributes, and the natural and just operation of things; a restraint which makes this world such a paradox to the universe, and calls forth sometimes, even out of the anguish of His own people, tortured into temporary doubt and darkness, such strains as in the 73d Psalm; and from scoffers, walking after their own lusts, such sarcasms of infidelity and contempt as those recorded by Peter, saying, Where is the vaunted promise of the coming of your Lord to judgment?

O perishing and delaying men! O presuming and abusive trespassers on God's mercy! remember ye that the Lord is not slack concerning His promise, as some men count slackness, but is long suffering to us-ward, not willing that any should perish, but that all should come to repentance. Remember what God hath distinctly declared, that it is a righteous thing with Him to recompense tribulation to the wicked, when the Lord Jesus shall be revealed from heaven, with His mighty angels, in flaming fire, taking vengeance on them that know not God, and that obey not the gospel of our Lord Jesus Christ, who shall be punished with everlasting destruction from the presence of the Lord, and from the glory of His power, when He shall come to be glorified in His saints, and to be admired in all them that believe. And remember yet once more that you have your own choice of the attributes of God, which of them you will experience; and that if you draw down His justice, instead of receiving His mercy and love in Christ Jesus, you do it against His warning, against His will, against His incessant importunity and efforts. He must be forever the same righteous God, but He would infinitely rather you would experience His righteousness in heaven, and rejoice in it, than draw down His justice in hell, and suffer under it. But as to Himself, He cannot change—He cannot abdicate His attributes; and if you do not change, if you do not flee to Jesus from the wrath to come, to be in Him made partaker of God's own holiness, then that wrath abideth on you forever.

The Denial of God.

BUT, notwithstanding all this, "The FOOL hath said (wishing, but not believing) in his heart, There is no God." He hath said it in his *heart;* but no man's *reason* ever said it, or *could* say it. There is no one word in our language capable of translating this Hebrew word, *fool.* The moral meaning is deeper than the intellectual; and how intense it is, may be gathered from the consideration, that the grander a man becomes in intellect and acquirements, and the more he has of the respect, honor, and even admiration of mankind, the more truly does this word describe his character, if the fool's heart depicted in the tenth and fourteenth Psalms be his. Those portions of God's word contain a description of the practical atheists; and there are no other atheists in the world, nor ever will be, *but* practical, although they sometimes endeavor to hide the inveterate and radical vileness of the thing beneath a veil of subtle philosophic speculation. The spring and reality of the evil is always in the heart. The fool hath said it, and none but a fool would say it, though some have said it who have thought themselves, and have been thought by others, among the wisest of mankind.

Three very striking paragraphs, descriptive of this atheistical juggling, by which the mind is subdued and blinded in the toils of a sinful heart, are presented in the tenth Psalm. First. The wicked, through the pride of his countenance, will not seek after God: God is not in all his thoughts, or in all his thoughts there is no God. Consequently, he hath said in his heart, I shall never be moved, never in adversity.

Second. He hath said in his heart, If there be a God, yet not a God caring for our affairs. He hath said in his heart, God hath forgotten; He hideth his face; he will never see it. Insensibility to God's attributes of omnipresence, omniscience, and present just providence, and thence a denial of the same.

Third. Wherefore doth the wicked contemn God? He hath said in his heart, Thou wilt not require it. Insensibility to God's *retributive* providence, and a denial of the same; and thence a denial of the truth of a future judgment; and thence a contempt of all human restraints and penalties, if by any act of power or lying they may be evaded. The whole of this Psalm is, in fact, an argument that not mere atheism, but a disbelief in future punishment, would break up all the foundations of social morality, and set men in a wild and savage freedom of "cursing and deceit and fraud." Take away the idea of a God, whose providence is personal, superintending and retributive, and you leave nothing for restraint but a present low expediency—nothing but self-interest in the present life, which, if there were no God, would be impossible to be demonstrated as on the side of virtue; for without a God, and his eternal holiness and justice, self-interest would as often lie in vice as virtue, and oftener in all forms of sustained and popular depravity.

The most aspiring form of attempted intellectual atheism is Pantheism, which is but a sublimated materialism, maintaining that all the shapes of animated nature, and man himself among them, are but organic harps diversely framed, that tremble into thought as the one intellectual breeze sweeps over them, constituting the soul of each and the God of all. All things are parts of God, and all being is to be absorbed in Him. The two things, *no God* and *all God*, might seem to be the extreme opposites and antagonisms of one another, but the truth of the existence and attributes of God is equally distant from both. The atheism and the Pantheism lead to the same fool's paradise; for as to religion, it is all one, as Howe, in his Living Temple, long ago demonstrated, whether we make nothing to be God, or everything; whether we allow of no God to worship, or leave none to worship Him. And although the attempt may be made by Pantheistic abstractions of philosophy, and delusions of poetry to cheat the world with names and with a show of piety, the system of Pantheism has been proved as directly levelled against all religion as the most avowed atheism. Indeed, inasmuch as atheism is more openly blasphemous, it is less reputable, and therefore less dangerous; while Pantheism, being too subtle and refined for a vulgar religion, and capable of assuming an appearance of most devout reverence and transcendental sentimentalism, may be really alluring, under an intellectual and poetic garb. It wears sometimes an aspect of mystic piety and wrapt devotion. It is a mist-piety, shrouding you with a kind of wet that penetrates to the very bones, if long enough continued, while a strong, drenching rain of open undisguised atheism, would have done its work only on the skin and clothes, and left a possibility of drying in the next sunshine. But this subtle system displays the semblance of absorption in God, self-renunciation, self-annihilation, union with the Infinite, and other things having some appearance of the self-denial and self-crucifixion for Christ, commanded in the Scriptures. But it is entirely inconsistent with a personal discipline of the soul under Divine grace. To lay one's being at the foot of the cross, to mortify and subject the self-will to God in Christ, is widely different from the vague, mystical absorption of the soul in a universal influence of nature. It is very quieting to the conscience, a charming anodyne for all fears of a future retribution, to believe in a vast system of necessity in which all things are parts of God, so that wicked souls themselves are but accomplishing a mission from Him, and will in the end return into Himself, as waves of His own being. Even this the fool hath said in his heart, nor indeed is there any form of madness and absurdity to which men have not resorted, in the vain endeavor to throw off a conviction of personal responsibility to a personal God of holiness and justice; a God who hates sin, and will bring men into judgment according to their character and doings, for every secret thing, good or evil.

But all this is the delusion or the speculations of a few. The great mass of mankind will ever go on believing in God speculatively, but wholly regardless of the relation of their own moral being to His attributes, and insensible as to their personal responsibility to God. Without Christ, without prayer, without hope, without God;—these are the negatives that describe the existence of most men, the habit of heart and life with ordinary sinners. A sinful man—the subject of all these negatives, may yet be, as regards society, a very moral man, so called, so considered. He may be a very moral man towards men, and a very immoral man towards God; in friendship with his fellow-men, but at enmity against God. He may be so insesible in regard to God, and voluntarily and habitually so ignorant of God's claims upon him, that he shall never have the state of his heart towards God come into notice; so that the accusation against him of being an enemy to God shall be as unmeaning, or seem as incredible, as an indictment of personal enmity towards the forty-seventh proposition of Euclid.

And yet, in all the breathings and outgoings of his being, he is opposing and violating the law of God, and the less he thinks of it, the more thoroughly and habitually is such opposition becoming the law of his nature. There is no care for God in his existence; into none of his plans does the consideration of God enter. Over none of his affections does the affectionate regard of God shed its hallowing heavenly radiance. In no province of his motives is the will of God supreme or even consulted. None of his desires are towards God; none of his meditations, if he ever meditates, dwell upon God's attributes, and not only is God never in his thoughts, but even the idea of God is never presented, or if it comes, it rises as an unwelcome intruder; it comes only to be expelled by the cares, the business, and the pleasures of life; an expulsion in many cases so absolute and successful, that the distinct impression of the Deity, or even of any one of His attributes, has no more entered the soul, or been admitted there, than the wind that breathes over the senses enters the brain, or draws a picture on the visual organs. The heart, mind, soul, whole being, have gone on for years in all their processes, with no more impressions from the nature or the providence of God to bring him definitely to the consciousness, than if the existence of God were a fable.

When we consider what a being God is, and that we are His intelligent creatures, the success and power of this insensibility in excluding God, seem astounding and incredible. For one would think that we ourselves and every other created thing in the universe would be perpetually bringing to the mind irresistible notices of God, that we never could, by any possibility, get rid of Him, that no art of blindness in the memory would enable us to forget Him, nor any veil of insensibility to exclude Him. And yet there are those who, dependent from moment to moment on the omnipresent God, have lived all their lifetime, up to the present hour, in such utter alienation from Him, that, from day to day, and from week to week, as it passed by, it may have been said at each successive interval, God is not in all their thoughts. And if one should ask you how this has been brought about, how it could have been accomplished, how such a power of expulsion in regard to the Deity could have existed in you, as might look to a being who knew nothing about sin like a stupendous miracle, what answer could be made that would explain the mystery? How has it been possible for you, the creature of God's power, so fearfully and wonderfully made by His wisdom, surrounded by His agency, pressed by the manifestations of His being, dependent every instant on His bounty; how has it been possible for you, addressed by God's word, the subject of God's warnings, invited and entreated by His own dear Son, breathing every breath you draw by God's permission; how has it been possible for you to evade the idea of God, and to keep His existence and attributes from your positive notice? By what process have you contrived to keep God out of your soul, and while surrounded and upheld by Him, to live without God in the world? What frightful power is it that you possess, what spell of destruction and darkness, what diabolical energy, that you could walk all this while in God's opened hand of mercy, and yet not see God's eye upon you, not feel His all-seeing scrutiny, not admit God to your consciousness, not have God in all your thoughts? Who has helped you to remain ignorant of your omnipresent Maker? What league are you in with the spirits of darkness, that you can shield your soul from the sense of His holiness and glory? Or who gave you this cloud of spiritual death, this garment of perdition, woven, one would think, in the deepest darkness of the bottomless pit, that you can so wrap it round your soul, that the all-pervading God himself ceases to be the object of your attention? Who helped you to get rid of God? Who tempted you to cast off the fear of God? Who supplied you with expedients, whereby you might forget God, and what could induce you to shut the eye of your own soul upon God, and plunge so deep and mad into the death of trespasses and sins? What amazement is is this in reference to God's attributes, that this body, the shell of the soul, can keep them off, as a casement of iron might keep off the flames of a conflagration! And what amazement in reference to your own indifference, that this infatuation, which must be voluntary, can be yours, and yet that such amazing guilt as it involves should make no impression on your sensibility, no alarm in your conscience.

Yes! it is an alliance with the powers of darkness, it is the mysterious permitted and tremendous agency of evil spirits, by which, in conjunction with your own will, this anomaly of guilt is preserved in the universe. There is no concealment of this fact in God's word, but a most explicit announcement of it, that in thus remaining insensible to God and his glory, and to your own interest in the propitiatory death of his Son, you are under the admitted power of Satan, you are in covenant with him, among the ranks of the lost, in whom the god of this world hath blinded the minds of those who believe not, lest the light of the glorious gospel of Christ, who is the image of God, should shine within them.

But while by this mysterious agency, in conjunction with your own will, this involution of darkness can be going on here, can be maintained now in this world, it is impossible in the world of spirits; and we have reason to believe that the devils, who cannot thus remain blind and insensible, envy the condition of souls that for a season can. The time of this possibility is rapidly passing, and you are passing from a world of faith into a world of light and experience. According to the relation in which you stand to God's attributes now, will be the operation of those attributes upon you, when you come to see and feel them. One reason why it is permitted to be possible to live in such a world as this without seeing God, is that there might be the possibility of a discipline of faith, by which we might become *like* God. The proof and manifestation of God "could not be intellectually more evident, without becoming morally less effective; without counteracting its own end by sacrificing the life of faith, to the cold mechanism of a worthless, because compulsory assent." God will have no believers on compulsion; he will leave men to their own choice; and the choice, if that of unbelief and insensibility, is that of the heart. Having the understanding darkened, being alienated from the life of God, through the ignorance that is in them because of the blindness of their heart. But the time of this ignorance is passing, and though the enmity of the heart will remain, the blindness will be gone forever, when the veiled frame of a fleshly organization and a material world shall have dropped asunder.

And what *then* will be the effect of a meeting of the soul with God? When face to face we shall behold him, when character shall be developed in the blaze of character; when the attributes of the creature shall appear in manifest conflict with the attributes of the Creator, when the moral aspect of the creature's sin shall be revealed in the lightning flame of the Creator's holiness, the hideousness of guilt in contrast with the glory of the righteousness of God and angels, will there then any longer be the anomaly of an atheistic insensibility to God, the infernal miracle of a soul indifferent to his existence and attributes? Every eye shall see him, and then, as the process here has been that of insensibility and the heedless accumulation of guilt, the process there will be that of the soul becoming all eye, all sense, all vivid sensibility to God, a quickened fiery conscience in regard to sin, a sense at once of the holiness of God and the sinfulness of man, of the glory of heaven and the terror of hell, of the brightness of light and the blackness of darkness; a sight and sense of all things as they are, and not as when the delusions of the carnal mind concealed and belied them, not as when the dust and ashes of a sensual existence were laid upon them. Is there any guilty soul that can endure the terrors of that day? Is there any soul that can pass from an insensibility in this world, maintained amidst such radiant light from the works and the revealed word of God, without change, into God's presence, without the certainty, from the very nature of things, of misery there? For without holiness no man shall see God, no guilty creature could endure the sight, for our God is a consuming fire.

If now, these paragraphs are speaking to a single soul that has hitherto lived without God and without hope in the world, let the question be asked, have you made any preparation to meet God in that condition? Are you ready to stand in his presence? Perhaps these questions may fall upon the sense of some, in regard to whom this very insensibility to God is a source and subject of astonishment, fear, and almost indignation to themselves and to others. There are those who are ready to say, O that I might see God! O that he would come out of his place of invisibility, and compel my insensible spirit to feel him, to behold his holiness and glory, and my own guilt! O that this solid world that closes me around, and hides everything but material existence from my view, might as it were open, and disclose the splendor of Jehovah in such overpowering light that I might never forget the vision! O that this curtain of creation, instead of separating between me and God, might light up indeed as a bright transparency revealing his presence in power and glory, and compelling me to fall prostrate and adore! O that I might see him as Job saw him, and be compelled to cry out, "I have heard of thee with the hearing of the ear, but now my eye seeth thee, wherefore I abhor myself, and repent in dust and ashes!"

And if this wish be sincere, then there is nothing which you would not be willing to do, to gain that purity and contrition of heart, through which alone, by faith in the Lord Jesus Christ, you can behold God in peace. Sometimes the first beginning of life in the soul towards God may be the commencing sense of this very insensibility, and the conviction of it as in itself a mighty sin, but a mightier proof and consequence of that death in trespasses and sins in which the soul has remained wholly at ease and quiet, not having God in all its thoughts. And if out of this insensibility there is an outcry after God and an effort to return to him and to find him, God will bless it. Yet there may be a great struggle and conflict. For it is a great mistake to suppose that this insensibility will be always removed the moment the soul enters on the process of return to God. In the nature of things it cannot be expected that the soul at one bound will recover from the effect of the habits of a life of sin. If a devotee of Hindostan, after holding his arm motionless in an upright position for years, finds that it has grown there unalterably, is it a strange result from the process with his physical nature? Can he expect by an act of volition to recover the use of that limb? Must it not be by a long and very gradual process, by multitudes of volitions and of efforts, each making the muscles yield perhaps a very little, and all necessary in constant repetition?

Analogous to this may be the case of religious insensibility, although God himself is the Healer, and the heart, when changed by grace, is, as to principle, wholly changed, and radically. Still, put the case in regard to your own dispositions and practices, long inured and inveterate, and it stands thus: You have, by long habit, disregarded God; your business, studies, amusements, pleasures, farms and merchandise, have absorbed you. Is the insensibility of death a strange consequence of this suffocation of spiritual life? And can you think to recover from that insensibility, except by voluntary, patient, persevering efforts? You will say, it is impossible! And yet, in another view, and the right view, it is not impossible, for it is of grace. And so we show you a better way, or rather *the* way to enter on such efforts and maintain them, with an absolute certainty of success. You are to come to Christ. Your insensibility can be moved in no other way. And besides this, besides His being the only Physician that knows your case and can heal your soul, it is only in Christ that you can see and know God. In Christ, those divine attributes, by themselves destructive of the sinful soul, and of consuming, fiery light and power, shall, with regenerating grace, subdue the soul, and renew it in their own nature, preparing it for God's holiness, by making it partaker of the same.

The Search after God.

Oh that I knew where I might find Him! The anxious heart of humanity speaks out in this sentence. Amidst all our darkness and insensibility as a fallen race, there is still a constitutional attraction in our being towards God, as well as a constitutional necessity of finding Him. Our grand attribute of intelligence and immortality is just this capacity of knowing God, and this necessity of loving Him. Our reason is a gift divine, because it enables us to see God, because the idea of God is one of its intuitions, and the heart is under a law of the reason to love God. It is only in loving Him that we can find Him and know him. "Love is of God, and every one that loveth is born of God, and knoweth God. He that loveth not, knoweth not God, for God is love."

He that loveth not, knoweth not. Let us set up that pillar of the beginning of all science, for if it be true in regard to God, it is true also in regard to all God's works. And a being constituted with the capacity of knowing God, could never be satisfied with any thing less *than* God. An imperious necessity of knowing and of loving is here. The whole circle of knowledge and of thought in the universe might be exhausted, and it would leave the soul empty and restless without God. There might come a time when, to be shut up to the whole universe without God, would be as tedious to an immortal soul, as it would now to a man with the comprehensive intellectual power of Newton, to be restricted all his lifetime to the study of the primer of his childhood. There might come a time when the universe itself would be a prison without God, and the condemnation of existence in it a burden of wearisomeness and sameness, intolerable. For the more the mind grasps, the less it can be satisfied without God; the more the soul knows, the stronger are the constitutional and eternal necessities of its being to know God; the vaster the reach of its travel in the created demonstrations of God, which are the consequences of God's existence, the more pressing and irresistible become the cravings of its immortal nature for the sight of God. For, wherever you go, whatsoever you do, whatsoever you know, rest is never in all creation, but in God; happiness is never in created things, but in God; and the universe would be but as a wheel revolving with you transfixed upon it, and maddened by its revolutions, if you know not God. Everywhere, from the depths of immortality, the unsatisfied, restless yearning rises after God. The sound of the ocean of our being, as it breaks upon the shores of eternity, is the boom and roar of a desolate tempestuous sea, if it knows not God. The depths of an infinite despair, to a being endued with intelligence and immortality, are in the condition of not finding, seeing, knowing God.

Ever, at the end of all knowledge, rises the question where is God, and the necessity of knowing Him. The more you see and know of the laws and glories of creation, the more heavily this question and necessity press upon the mind. It is the final end of all thought to think upon God; it is the ultimate object of all steps, enquiries, researches, to find God. And the more you grasp of this material universe, in your studies, your investigations, your comprehension, without God, you are but led to an open door, through which you pass into the blackness of darkness forever, if you have not found God. A created being might take the universe orb by orb, might travel from star to star, from sun to sun, from system to system, but nothing could give him rest; and everywhere, after all things were comprehended that God has made, there would only arise, with a more overwhelming pressure, the question, Where is God? The nearer you seem to get to Him, as you pass from world to world, through the trains of material glory in His infinite temple, through the folds of the veil of created systems round about Him, the stronger becomes the attraction that presses you to him, the swifter this power of gravitation, as capacity expands, and worlds are unfolded, and yet, if you see Him not, whither are you hurrying, and what can be the rest of your soul? You might meet, amidst the range of worlds, trains of angels and archangels, beings more glorious in themselves than all worlds; but the greater their magnificence and grandeur, the less the possibility of resting or remaining among them, and the greater the pressure of the question, Where is He who made them?

The more you could, by any possibility, behold and know of all things but God, the more you could find out of being and of matter, in the roll of ages, if ages were allotted for the experiment, before finding God, the more universal, absorbing, irresistible and uncontrollable, would be the necessity that carries you towards God, the necessity of seeing and of knowing Him. Amidst all these unbounded and innumerable forms and glories of being and of matter, orbs of splendor, fires of intelligence and light, but one feeling would at length absorb the soul, but one necessity would weigh upon it, the craving and necessity of knowing God. The more infinite the variety of those glories, and the more unbounded their expanse, the greater the pressure upon an immortal being, towards Him who made them all. Where, O where is God? And what in God's universe can the soul rest upon without God?

Such is what may be called the constitutional necessity of finding and of knowing God. But now there is, in addition, a still more pressing and inexorable *moral* necessity, a necessity of finding in Him a friend, the strength of our heart, and our portion forever. There is the absolute certainty of meeting God; but how do we know what will be the effect of that meeting? Rather, how can we hope, if we do *not* know Him now by *loving* Him, if we do not know Him as His dear children, how can we hope that the meeting of our souls with Him can be an event of joy? May it not prove, *must* it not prove, the most dreadful event of all our existence, and deplorably decisive for eternity?

What if, amidst all these demonstrations of God, all these manifestations of His power and glory, all these avenues of worlds leading onward to the introduction, with all this constitutional necessity of knowing God, and this absolute impossibility of rest apart from Him; what if the soul, the veil being lifted, and God's attributes seen, finds in Him an enemy! What if the state of mind and heart that has prevented God from being seen in, through, and by His works everywhere, is a state of such opposition to His holiness, His sovereign will, that when He comes to be seen and known as He is, when the veil of the universe is withdrawn, and the soul is in His immediate presence, it shall be found that He is a consuming fire! What will be the state of a mind that has groped through this present world of light in regard to God without finding God? What will be the condition of our men of assumed science and intelligence, who have read nature backwards, and the more they have seen and known of God's works, the less they have seen of Him who made them? What will he, who is now estranged from God, experience, when the attributes which he now denies, or hates, blaze upon him, no longer through the vista of a telescope of worlds, where he at present conceives himself to be at one end, and God infinitely distant at the other;

but in a revelation that brings him face to face with Jehovah, creation all behind, and none but God before him and around him? What will become of him, a sinful creature, in the presence of a God of infinite holiness, gone, against all warning, into that presence, in the midst of sin?

We do suppose that the revelation of God once made, the sight of God once seen, will command all notice, absorb all thought, leave no possibility for any created thing any longer to interpose before the soul, to gain from it a moment's attention, in distracting it from God. If the Divine attributes are the object of the soul's affectionate and confiding love, they will absorb the soul in an ecstasy of being, in adoration and praise, to us inconceivable. But if the habits and affections of the soul be opposed to the Divine attributes, then the nearer it is brought to the contemplation and sense of them, the more intolerable the condition of that soul must be. For even in this world, the thought of God to such a soul is full of terror. A sinful being can never endure the attributes of God. And yet, those attributes once revealed, nothing in the universe will be able to distract even a sinful soul from the contemplation of them; nothing will be worthy of notice in comparison with them; and indeed, both with holy and sinful beings in the spiritual world, it must be the case that nothing will, by itself, any longer confine the notice of the mind, but everything will be seen as the Divine attributes play upon it, and are illustrated in it. It is God, who will be all in all to the righteous soul, and God who will be all in all to the wicked soul. Now, God's works may be seen, and not himself; God's works may be examined with scientific pride and pretension, and yet the Author of them never be noticed; nay, His presence, His agency, if not His being, may be denied. Men may analyze the light of the sun, and boast themselves in the power of rational research and discovery, and yet never behold the light of the Sun of Righteousness. Men may examine the organization of plants and animals, and the structure of a world, and receive the worship of their fellow-men for their acuteness and sagacity, and yet, amidst all this, neither see, nor know, nor acknowledge their Creator, but live and die Atheists, in a world sustained by God's presence and filled with God's light.

But there, God himself will be seen. The veil that hides Him will be taken away; or rather, the soul being carried behind the veil, God and His attributes will fill the vision. Creatures will no more speculate about His agency, but feel it; and according as they themselves are consentaneous with it, prefigured for it, in harmony with it, or opposed to it, unfitted for it, and habituated against it, it will be the source of unmingled happiness or misery. According as they are the friends or the enemies of God, God will be to them either a fountain of love and blessedness, or a consuming fire, either the light of life, or a light revealing sin and darkness. There must come a time, when we shall meet God face to face, and that will be the revelation and the knowledge of our destiny; that will be the experience of heaven or hell. The light of these senses shall no longer hide from us the light of God; the occupations of a world shall no longer distract our absorbed sight and being from Him.

Oh, then, what shall we do to find Him? What shall we do to meet Him, not as strangers and enemies, but children and friends? And how shall we be prepared to find in Him, when we see Him behind the veil, when sense and shadows drop away from around us, and leave us in uncreated light before the splendors of His infinite holiness, to find in Him, not the terror of our souls in His avenging justice, but a reconciled friend and Father—a forgiving, loving, and beloved God? Oh the greatness, the majesty, the glory and the gloom of this mighty problem! How can men be so heedless of the meeting of their souls with God! How can immortal beings be so thoughtless of the question, What shall I be to God, and what will God be to me, when I meet Him, when I see Him, when I stand in the blaze of His attributes, in the light of His countenance—when that light, angry or glorious, destructive or life-giving, according to what I am, falls upon me? What shall I find myself to all eternity, when character is all revealed and fixed forever—when holiness discloses sin—when delusions and distractions are withdrawn—when mine inmost soul, and heart and being, penetrated with God's light, reveal their every process, habit, thought, feeling, sealed, by a contrast or similarity with God, for mine eternal destiny?

Surely this is the one absorbing question of our

being—What shall we do to find God? or, to change the question in a manner expressive of the fear, What shall we do to find in ourselves such a likeness *to* God, such a participation in His holiness, that we may be prepared for that meeting with Him, so soon to take place, when this fleshly tabernacle drops from around us? "Blessed are the pure in heart," says our Lord Jesus Christ, "for they shall see God." "But, oh!" the sinner answers, "my heart is all *impure*, and I dare not, cannot meet Him;" and so, from the depths of the condemned soul, in the anguish of a troubled conscience, the question resounds, Where shall I gain that purity? for my heart is all defiled with sin. Clouds and darkness are round about me, and in my sins I cannot see God. If I look to God through aught that I am in myself, I see him only as the righteous and revenging God of that holy law which I have violated. If I see His glorious attributes, it is but to see and feel their tremendous condemnation of my guilt. If God looks upon me, if He reveals Himself unto me, in my sin, my corruption, my ruin, I am undone; for one glance of His countenance, one ray of His infinite holiness, discloses my darkness, mine impurity of heart, my possession of all the qualities that must banish me from His holy presence, and shut me up in hell. If God stand before me, and I see Him, I must cry out with Peter, "Depart from me, for I am a sinful man, O Lord!" Till I am changed, I cannot see God; and who and what shall change me? Till I am purified, I cannot see God, for my heart is full of sin. I cannot, dare not see Him; for the very thought of His intolerable holiness, when He comes near to my soul, is more than I can bear; and my will is strong against Him, and my soul is dark to every attribute but that of His condemning and avenging righteousness. And yet I must see God. I am directed to His presence; I am hastening to His judgment-bar; His mandate is upon me; His indictment is against me; His writ is after me. I must meet the King of terrors; and after that, I must meet God. Oh, where shall I find Him? What shall I do to find Him? And where is that purity of heart, without which no man shall see God? Who has it? With whom is the fountain of it? Where shall I find it?

Oh Son of God most merciful, who didst speak those gracious words, "Blessed are the pure in heart, for they shall see God," have mercy upon me, for I am a miserable sinner! Oh Lamb of God, who takest away the sin of the world, have mercy upon me! Create in me a clean heart, oh God, and renew a right spirit within me. Oh thou compassionate and forbearing Lord God, whom I would fain see, but cannot, have mercy upon me! Oh divine Redeemer, who didst bear our sins, have mercy upon me! I look to Thee—I throw myself on Thee. To whom shall I go but unto Thee, who only hast the words of life eternal?

Yes, O yes, to Thee, O Lamb of God! It is to Jesus Christ, and to Him alone, that this sense of guilt, this fear of meeting God, this conviction of sin, and of righteousness, and of judgment to come, this sense of evil in the soul, and this outcry of the conscience after purity of heart, points the sinner, yea presses him, burdened, anguished, dying, to the cross of Christ. The first step to the character and blessing of the pure in heart is to see our own impurity; and when we see that, and feel it—when our conscience accuses us to God—when we feel that as we are, we cannot meet God, cannot endure His presence, cannot see Him and live, then, as we look about in anguish for deliverance, for some power to help, to heal, and save us, all the voices of revelation point us to Christ—to that very Being who declares to us, that the pure in heart are blessed, because they shall see God; for He it is, and He alone, that can give us that purity—that can, by the power of His own blood, wash away our sinful stains—that can, by the grace of His spirit, subdue and soften our hearts in contrition, in repentance, in faith, and prepare us to see God. He it is, who has been exalted as a Prince and a Saviour, to give repentance and the remission of sins; He it is, who can take away the hardness of our hearts, our insensibility, our indifference, our love of sinning, our pride, our self-will; He it is, who can make us meek and lowly in heart, can lead us to the mercy-seat, can teach us to plead His name and merits with the Father. Will we come to Him for this blessedness? Will we believe in His power and love? Will we make our appeal for His mercy?

Ah! perhaps we need to have God in some way come near to us in wrath, before we can be made to feel how near and how infinitely precious CHRIST is in His redeeming love, and GOD IN CHRIST! It is the sight of God that possibly we need now, in *contrast* with our guilt, in order that we may see and feel the *greatness* of that guilt. It is the light of the Divine Holiness that we need, to reveal the darkness and sinfulness of our own hearts, and the everlasting ruin that awaits us, if, with such hearts unchanged, we go into eternity. Oh that careless souls might see God in His holiness now, and feel Him in something of the terror of His wrath and justice, in order that they might be roused up from their insensibility, and driven from their indifference, and compelled by the anguish of a wounded conscience to cry out for the Divine mercy. Then might they arrive at that purity of heart without which no man shall see God—then might they be prepared by the Redeemer for their introduction to God in the eternal world.

Would to God that the corruptions of this sinful and rebellious heart might be unveiled before the sinner, that he might be taken down into the depths of them, and made to see how he is filled with them —how they expose him to the wrath of God—how they prepare him, if he enters the eternal world with such a heart unchanged, to feel the attributes of God as a consuming fire. Would to God that the hell of the sinner's own passions might beforehand be let loose upon him, that, by the experience of the conflict, the strife, the war, in deep conviction now, he might be terrified from himself to Christ, might be driven to the Saviour for refuge.

For, indeed, anything is better than the insensibility of this death of trespasses and sins. Better that men feel the burning fire of God now, in a world of probation, than feel it forever in the world of wo;—better that men see and feel the enmity of their hearts against God, and bear the stings of an angry conscience now, and hear the accusation against them in God's word as His enemies, than go on in stupid indifference, in the dream that they are His friends, only to hear His voice in an eternal judgment, "Depart from me; I never knew you!"—better that men learn their own character in season, while God gives them the opportunity of becoming new creatures in Christ Jesus, than to hear it first announced, and have it first admitted and understood, in the thunder of that dreadful sentence, "Depart from me, ye cursed, into everlasting fire, prepared for the devil and his angels!"

Eternity.

NEXT after the Idea of God, comes that of Eternity. The Reality is one of the Powers of the world to come. It may be said, perhaps, that Eternity itself *is* the world to come, but it is more proper to say that the world to come is in Eternity, while this world, and we upon it, are in Time; and the passage from Time to Eternity is by us conceived as something more than a mere going from one world into another world. Eternity! Eternity! We have indeed the *Idea* here; we meet the POWER there! The moment a soul emerges from Time, we think of it as passing from a point into an infinitude; we think of a boundlessness of which it must be conscious, an everlastingness of duration, which it knows now only in Idea, but must know then, not in imagination merely, but in self-consciousness, as a Power. The change from Time into Eternity is a change in the whole position and relations of our being, all that is partial being left behind, and a total assumed or entered on, within us and around us. Here we know in part, but there shall we know as we are known; here we see in part, but there we shall see as we are seen. The language which Paul uses in regard to eternal blessedness, will be here reversed in regard to the condition of eternal misery. In either case, the *entrance* on Eternity will be the *experience* of Eternity, a knowledge of Eternity, absolute, and not in expectation merely; the experience of an ETERNAL NOW which nevertheless will not prevent the forecasting of a still greater experience either of glory on the one hand, or of terror on the other. Our whole being is so constituted as to be perpetually now forecasting that fixedness of doom, that reality of Eternity; constitutionally we are expecting it; we are anticipating it, whether preparing and planning for it, or not. It is the great cloud before us, into which we know we are to enter; it is the great thought brooding over us, as the firmament overhangs our bodies, and we work beneath it without looking up, without thinking of it. Nevertheless, immortality in ourselves, and Eternity to be experienced by us, at the great goal of our being, when we come to the end of the present (which is but the beginning of the endless), constitute the overruling consciousness of the soul. Whether a man be wicked or good, careless or anxious, this element of his nature he can neither deny nor abdicate. He may live as a sea-monster, down in the depths of a moral medium as thick as the ocean, but yet this all-surrounding air of his accountability and immortality is above him, with its universal pressure. The change from Time into Eternity will be the fulfilment of all this mighty anticipation of our mental and moral constitution. Then, Time shall be no longer; for in this view, it is a thing only for beings on probation, and when that ends, Time ends, and Eternity begins. Time is the clock that strikes the hours of our probationary trial, and every moment is precious; but when that is passed through, we must have a clock that strikes Eternity or none at all; and doubtless, when that is passed through, our very consciousness *will* strike Eternity, as now it strikes Time. Time is nothing there, since there is no more anything depending upon it, nor any use for it, but Eternity is all in all, according as God is all in all. What is Time, to one who has entered on Eternity, whose state is fixed for Eternity? A fixedness, which makes such a change, as to leave no longer any room for either fear or hope, the eternal goal of each of these passions being reached, and an unchangeable experience begun, which is indeed to be progressive in degree, but absolute in quality, forever. Our motion on our axis may be what we please, but our orbit is in Eternity, and once launched upon it, we can do nothing but pursue it, wherever it may sweep us. Here, we have something to look forward to, of a nature that we never have experienced, but there, all is decided. Here we seem to hold our choices in our own power, as long as Time lasts; but there we lay aside our very free agency for a supreme eternal good, or a supreme eternal evil, that can never more be changed, nor our choice altered, whatever it may be. Over neither the evil nor the good shall we be any longer master, but it will be master over us, forever and ever.

This mighty responsibility of an eternal destiny

is on us all—a destiny soon to be known and sealed unchangeable, in heaven or hell. One would think this amazing truth would be supremely impressive, once announced, even if it were only probable; but being certain, we should think the pressure would be felt, as of a great mountain, upon men's hearts and consciences. How can it be otherwise? Nevertheless, how little emotion—how mighty an insensibility! And though the Judge standeth at the door, yet, because judgment against an evil work is not executed speedily, therefore the heart of the sons of men is fully set in them to do evil. Absorbed in the trifles of time, men give themselves no leisure to look beyond the present moment, and accustom themselves to anxieties only about the present life. The power of habit in this consequent insensibility is tremendous, and most disastrously successful. The merest, maddest vanities and dreams of time shall thus outweigh the interests of eternity. The miserable pursuits of the present moment are held so close to the eye of the soul, and its affections are so fixed upon them, that nothing else can be seen or thought of. We may hold a shilling before the eye so near, that it shall shut out heaven from the vision; we may, with a mote between the glasses of the telescope, cover the orb of day. So men shut out the things of God, Christ, eternity, heaven, hell, wholly from their view, even by the barest consideration what they shall eat, drink, and with what their bodies shall be clothed; and so the god of this world, even by things of this world, blinds the minds of those who believe not, keeping off the thoughts of eternity, and absorbing the heart with other things, instead of the interests of an immortal soul. This power of the world to come, in such a case, is veiled, is hidden; it is as if it did not exist, or only as an unmeaning abstraction. But yet it does exist; and whenever and in whatever way the idea of eternity gets hold upon the soul, and gains the mastery there, it turns out every other idea; it shows its power by its despotism; it blasts the fairest visionary castles of the mind; it turns the pleasures of the world into ashes. And God can, any time, bring this idea sweeping on the soul, like an army with banners.

We have heard of such things—heard of men seized, as by an invisible power, at the sight and hearing of the ticking of a clock in a crowded court-room, and carried forth into the open world, and pursued through all the lanes of life and din of business, unable to escape, till pressed to God's foot-stool in secret, and compelled to pour out, as a dying sinner, the prayer for God's salvation, wrung from the soul by the pressure of sin and the thoughts of eternity, and the question, In what world shall I dwell, when this world passes away, and I pass from it forever? You have heard of the flood-gates of such thought, thrown open by the bare utterance of that one word, eternity, and, as if the fountains of the great deep were broken up, a cataract and storm of angry, gloomy, prophetic wailing and despair rushing through the soul. Under such a sense of guilt and eternity, no man can bear up; but if re-tribution unchangeable have not already commenced, or a judicial desolation and petrifaction of the soul, must cry out, God save me! I am a lost creature! God have mercy upon me, a sinner! Lamb of God, who takest away the sin of the world, have mercy upon me!

Now, as it is in the power of the Spirit of God at any time to bring in this idea of eternity upon the soul with an exceeding and eternal weight, whether of glory or of gloom, we need not wonder at the instances on record of persons awakened by the mere hearing of the word eternity, or merely seeing it printed on a page. I think it is Hannah More, to whom we owe the authentic account of a lady of social distinction and gaiety in England, who returned one night from a party or a ball of great splendor, and found her maid waiting for her, employed in reading a religious book. As she glanced at it, she exclaimed, "How can you contrive to amuse yourself with poring over the pages of such a melancholy work!" But her own eye had been an unsuspected inlet to the mind for one of the powers of the world to come, that it might enter, sweeping with all its solemn train the visions of her worldliness quite away. She retired to rest, but lay tossing in anxious thought, and when her maid the next day inquired the cause of her pale and gloomy mood and appearance, she confessed that it was wholly that one word Eternity, beheld in the pages of that book, which had startled a world of convictions, anxieties, fears, remorse, forebodings, that at length completely overwhelmed her, and no peace could be found till it was gained in Christ Jesus, till in

Him she had gained that preparation for eternity, of which the word had roused her to feel her need as an immortal being. And at any time that one word eternity may be the power of the Holy Spirit in the soul, to break up the fountains of the great deep of thought in regard to our everlasting responsibility and destiny.

And truly, a right impression of eternity is sufficient to make everything here, everything transitory, however splendid, however coveted, seem insignificant and worthless. A constant impression of eternity would make a man superior to all life's changes, shows, temptations and delusions. It has much the same effect with that of severe and overwhelming affliction, though in a different way; for whereas overwhelming sorrow may bury a man as in a sepulchre, making him dead to the world, because he cannot enjoy anything,—the deep and vast impression of eternity raises him quite above it, to a place of serene and commanding observation, where he sees its vanity and madness. "I greatly deceive myself," said the great Edmund Burke, when prostrated by the death of a son, as an oak by a hurricane, "I greatly deceive myself, if in this hard season of life I would give a peck of refuse wheat for all that is called fame and honor in the world." But the deep sense of eternity will make a man feel that all the riches and honors of the material universe are are not worth a peck of refuse wheat, even with the greatest zest and spirit for their enjoyment, except the soul is prepared to meet God, prepared for its abode in eternity. A strong sense of eternity, in its power of reducing the bubbles and shows of this world to their intrinsic vanity, and paralysing its grasp upon us, is like the near approach of death, and for the same reason. Indeed, death itself borrows nearly all its power over us from eternity, all its power to move us. The brutes have no fear of death, because they have no life after death, nor the possibility of conceiving of it.

In like manner, the mighty idea of probation borrows all its solemnity from the idea of eternity. We are on trial in this world, not for any limited duration of destiny in the next, but for an existence that shall never end, an existence determined by causes which here in this world we set in operation, and habits which here in this world we form or begin. Everything bears upon eternity, and takes its dignity and importance thence, nor can we live, in whatever way, without living *for* eternity. All moral influences and causes run into eternity, and in human action and thought they are so innumerable and incalculable, that the whole of what is sown here not only determines the whole of what is reaped there, but it may take immeasurable ages to develop particular fruits from particular seeds here deposited. In that respect the mind of man may be like the universe of God, in which there are worlds whose light may have been travelling towards us ever since the dawn of the creation, and never yet have reached us. But it must come, it never can perish; it may be millions and millions of years upon its way, but still it wings its wondrous flight, and will produce, somewhere, if there remain an eye to meet it, the image of its object. So it is with men's actions, characters, lives. As the planets are coming up in space, so may things transacted here come up in their reality, in their power, in their knowledge, millions of ages in the bosom of eternity.

And therefore the idea and reality of time, which as to its moral character is very much the same with the idea of probation, borrows, in like manner, all its solemnity from the reality of eternity, the reality of an endless existence, the character of which time determines; determines it indeed, not by itself, but by our use of it. What we make of time, time makes of our eternity. Time is the weaver of the garment of our existence there, and unrolls in an everlasting web, whatever elements of character, whatever threads of action, we put into his loom, we fasten to his shuttle, here. Time is the season of sowing, eternity of reaping, and the rule is, whatsoever a man soweth, that shall he also reap. This being the case, as time governs eternity, eternity gives to every moment of time an infinite preciousness and solemnity. To-day has all the importance of eternity attached to it, concentrated upon it.

Oh Eternity, Eternity! By what way can careless men be waked, be roused, to a sense of eternity? How shall that idea be stirred within them? The moment its power is felt, how do all the vastest interests of time dwindle and fade into insignificance! What are the proudest reputations, what the highest degrees of honor, what the most successful gains of ambition, or of boundless wealth, or of personal gratification, whether sensual or intellectual? Extended to the largest measures of time, what are they, when the end comes, and eternity is before the soul? Oh for a permanent impression of Eternity! Oh to have the mind and heart kept under that mighty guardianship, beneath the full weight and pressure of that power of the world to come! How shall this be accomplished? It cannot be done without prayer. It cannot be done without coming to Christ. It cannot be done without a living faith in him, as the way, the truth, the life. Apart from him, all truth is frozen, desolate, ineffectual. The idea of eternity must be inspired with the life of love, or it has no power as an abstraction. It may waken the soul, but Christ only can make it a permanent element of living, loving duty. But earnest prayer, by a soul coming to Christ, can do everything. In prayer, eternity is brought near, is realized.

In prayer the soul is baptized by the Holy Spirit with power, and is transported from time into eternity, from shadows to realities, from dreams to the energies of life. When the soul wrestles in prayer, God causes the powers of the world to come to wrestle with the soul, and they enter into it and possess it mightily. The very insensibility of the soul is a thing which must be brought to God in prayer, and men must groan and agonize before God to have it taken away, and it will be conquered. It cannot be done without God's word; but prayer causes the word of God to live within the soul, to burn in it as a fire, and to carry it away as on the wings of a whirlwind. Habitual intimacy with God's word draws all the realities of the eternal world around the soul, and touches its forms of interminable and dreadful glory into life and power within it:—the clouds of heaven, the great white throne, the thronging angels, the books of judgment, the lake of fire, the holy city, the jasper walls, the golden streets, the crystal river; principalities and powers of thought endowed as regal fixtures, as burning mountains in a vast horizon, as an atmosphere or firmament brilliant with sparkling stars. When the soul is much conversant with the word of God in prayer, then the Spirit of God brings out its infinite treasures, kindles its fires, lights up its propositions, till they shine as suns, and carries the soul down into the abyss, or up into the third heaven, till all the powers of the world to come pass into a foretasted experience. For the Divine Spirit acts by the word, and reveals it within the soul as an irresistible agency, so that it is quick and powerful and sharper than any two-edged sword.

Then there are other forms of truth which the same Divine Spirit makes efficacious, if a man will wait upon them. Let a man, for example, take Baxter's Call to the Unconverted, or Doddridge's Rise and Progress, with John Foster's Essay prefixed, and set himself to its prayerful perusal, and it will be strange indeed if the Powers of the World to come do not reveal themselves, and take hold upon his inmost being. Then, too, let a man watch the providences of God. Oftentimes they are greatly effectual in unsealing the prisons of the soul, and calling dead entombed convictions into life, and removing the grave-clothes of custom, insensibility, unbelief, that swathe divine truth itself from the sight and feeling of the conscience. It is astonishing to see how suddenly a whole embattled squadron of thought and argument, that had been dead and buried out of sight beneath the insensibility and blindness of the heart, shall be roused into action. A patriarchal preacher in the northern part of our country, after a vain attempt to convince a couple of deniers of the truth of an eternal retribution, passed away in almost hopeless sorrow. But the word only waited the providence which was ready to give it pungency and power. One of those men, not long after, was cutting down a tree in the forest, and when it fell, and lay motionless where it fell, the text in God's word, *As the tree falleth, so it lieth*, came to the mind of the wood-cutter with a force that carried away all his unbelief, let in the flood of the Divine Argument upon the soul, and brought him at length, in humble repentance and faith, at the feet of the Redeemer. Sometimes God's Word, Providence and Grace are thus united in so remarkable a manner, in subduing the heart of the sinner, that every step in the process can be distinctly traced, nor is there anything more interesting and instructive than the record of such cases.

But let us remember that no impression of eternal things can be lasting, unless it brings the soul to Christ, unless, coming to Him, we secure His presence, power, life and guidance. There are no means of grace, however promising in their first efficacy, but will become lifeless, will wear out, and leave the soul more insensible than ever, unless it truly comes to Christ. All the awakening books and providences in the world will fail to reach its state, will fail at length to move it, unless it obeys their voice, and does that for which they are granted, for which all the interpositions of God are thrown in, unless it is brought to Christ, unless it gives up all to Christ.

Probation.

We have seen that from the Idea of Eternity that of Probation derives all its infinite solemnity. A trial for Eternity! What a weight of importance, immeasurable, indescribable, in that phrase! Yet, Probation is not so much the trial of character, as it is of the truths of God's word *upon* character. Character is already a setttled thing; the problem presented in a world of probation respects the possibility of change for the world to come. For this purpose, through interposition of the Son of God, keeping in abeyance the operation of retributive justice, the powers of the world to come are revealed as truths and ideas, and are not known as yet experimentally as powers. For in order that a knowledge of the powers of the world to come may prove effectual in producing a preparation for that world, our state in this must be an arrangement by which experience is deferred, while information, instruction, warning and persuasion are employed upon us. Such is God's arrangement for us by the power of the Cross; God's goodness vouchsafes to us in that cross, a wondrous demonstration previous to our experience.

The great difference between this world and that which is to come, or the thing which necessarily makes the two worlds so different, is that this is a world of preparation for that. But in order that it may be such, we must be forewarned here of what we are to meet there; we must know here in idea, what we are to meet there in reality. When we meet the powers of the world to come, our manner of meeting them, and the character in which we meet them, will determine our destiny. We cannot change that destiny, after so meeting them. We may wish, too late, that we could. We may have disbelieved in those powers here, or taken up wrong ideas in regard to them, and we may find that on being translated among them, they destroy us; a thing which perhaps the Apostle himself refers to in the expression, *if so be that being clothed we shall not be found naked;* but it will then be too late to make another choice, or to undertake to meet them in a different manner. We must prepare for such a meeting *now.* This is God's very argument; because I will do thus and thus unto thee, therefore prepare to meet thy God, O Israel!

Now, as God's attributes are veiled, even when revealed, and some of them veiled, even in order that they may *be* revealed, we must, of necessity, exercise faith in regard to them. If we will not believe, and act accordingly, they will destroy us. There are some of them, which to know in this world any other way than in idea, would be our perdition. If a man will not believe this, and will not prepare to meet God, he must take the consequences. If you should travel to the brink of a volcano with a man who had never seen volcanic fire, nor known anything about it, and if he should not believe you on your telling him that it would burn like any other fire, but should throw himself into it, he would be destroyed instantly. Now, in regard to sin, and the unbelieving unrepenting sinner, we are distinctly told that our God is a consuming fire. If a man will not believe that, but marches on as he is, to meet God in his sinfulness, then the fire of God's holiness and justice must consume him. In this world, God's justice is an attribute quite hidden from us by His mercy; we know His mercy in *reality*, know it in ten thousand ways; but we know His justice only in His word. His long-suffering we experience; His justice we do not experience; and therefore He seems to be slack concerning His promise, just because we are permitted to experience His long suffering, in the hope that we may be induced to escape the infliction of His justice before the time comes, when the blow can no longer be suspended.

It is the wonder of the universe that it can be suspended at all; for God's justice is just as dear to Him as His love; indeed, it is but part of His love—an essential element of love. There could be no such thing as love without justice, and no such thing as justice without love. But as ours is a world in rebellion against God, it would be unjust in Him not to execute His justice, unless there were some plain reason for such forbearance; for He has given a demonstration of His justice in all that He has done upon the angels that kept not their first estate; and what justification can there be why the same measure of justice should not be meted out to us as to them? Do not the same compulsions of justice and reasons of state call for our punishment as theirs? What is the reason for this apparent capriciousness? How can God be just, and not punish sin now, if He could not be just, and not punish sin then? Just this, and this only, is the reason—because of the interposition of His beloved Son, who did interpose, not for the fallen angels, but for lost man.

Now, to secure the benefits of this interposition, our world must be the scene of a second probation. It was at first a world of probation for the good, to see if they would sustain their trial, and persevere in holiness against temptation to sin. That experiment failed, and now, and ever since, our world is a world of probation, to see if the wicked will become good—to see if they will accept God's offered mercy in Christ. And to this end, as a matter of necessity, the penalty of God's law is warded off, is kept at a distance, in abeyance; the avenging fires of justice are kept down; the mouth of the bottomless pit is covered; the energies of retributive justice are muzzled; God's hand is twisted in the mane of the lion, and his bridle and bit are in the jaws of Leviathan. And thus the world stands, 'twixt upper, nether, and surrounding fires, which yet do not burn upon us, because a form like unto the Son of God is seen walking with us. He, by the power of His cross, His sufferings, His death, keeps off these flames; He stands beneath this firmament, and holds it closed, that else would spout cataracts of fire upon us; He gathers the thunderbolts of Divine justice into His own bosom, yea, His own soul, (for Thou, oh God, didst make His soul an offering for sin); and so, as to us, they fall harmless, while the long-suffering of God, thus enabled righteously to wait upon us, spares us, and works with us, to bring us to repentance. He holds back these impending mountains of retribution that quake over us on every side, and the arrows of those angry eyes of Nemesis that glare upon us, and would blast us, and the fierce flames that would consume us in eternal despair; and, instead of letting them execute their mission of justice, He turns them into mercy. He makes the very law that destroys us our schoolmaster, to bring us to Christ; He sheathes the lightning, and lets it play for our warning merely. We hear the roar of the thunder; but it is God's voice, calling us to repentance, and to a quick, sure flight from the wrath to come. We see the angry eyes; but there is a mournful tenderness in the light they shoot upon us. God's lightnings and judgments flash and play across this world, just enough to waken the conscience, and convince the soul of sin, of righteousness, and of judgment to come, but not enough to blast with angry fire unto perdition irremediable. God makes this a *disciplinary* world; He is enabled to do it, because Christ has died;—a disciplinary world in so wondrous a degree, that He will make men's very sins to chastise them, and save them from perpetuity in sin. God afflicts, overturns, disappoints, casts down, uses all the whips and thorns in the storehouse of His providence, for the discipline of a probationary state. Sometimes He shuts up a sinful mind in such terror and anguish, that it seems as if the world of God's inflicted justice could have no greater horrors, but in the addition of despair; and yet He does all this that the soul may be taught wisdom—may be brought to a timely repentance—may be kept back from madly pressing on to the experience of eternal justice, in the endurance of the penalty of God's violated law.

Often, indeed, God's representations and providences alike fail; and sometimes both men and nations come so near to these walls of restraint, with such savage madness of sin, as almost to break through them, even in this world—break through into hell violently out of a world of probation. This was the case with Sodom and Gomorrah; this is the case sometimes with individuals, who, instead of walking humbly, or enduring God's restraint, dash themselves, as it were, with headlong sins, against the thick bosses of Jehovah's buckler, and impale themselves upon the flaming spikes of justice. You may often see men thus grasping God's sword by the blade, and indefatigably gathering the lightning-rods of retribution into their own hearts; you may see men rushing into the mouths of lions, that otherwise would merely have roared afar off against them, for their warning and repentance. But in general the scene runs on, as a scene of wondrous forbearance on the part of God, perfectly unaccountable, whether to good men or angels, except on the ground of the interposition of a dying Christ, that He is with us; that this is His world, where He suffered for us, loved us, died that we might live, and lives Himself now to save us by His life, as He hath reconciled us to God by His death. He hath reconciled God also to the possibility of enduring, with much long-suffering, a freedom for his enemies from retribution, even in sin, if haply they may, by Christ's dying love, be subdued to the power of mercy, and come to repentance. He has made it consistent with God's universal justice and love to let there be, in the sight of the whole universe, such a spectacle of apparently successful rebellion; of creatures in rebellion, and yet not punished; of miserable, vile worms in this external Tophet, wriggling themselves in contempt and sneers at God's very forbearance, and crying out to one another and to God's prophets in scorn, Where is the promise of His coming? Do not the wicked flourish like a green bay-tree? Who is the Lord, that we should regard Him? There is no God who will ever trouble Himself to regard us.

These things, says Jehovah, hast thou done, and I kept silence. Thou thoughtest that I was altogether such an one as thyself. And the quiet of Jehovah, or rather of Jehovah's thunderbolts, in such a world as this, is indeed wonderful. But farther even than this, God's restraining hand not only grasps the reins, to hold back the fiery coursers of his own justice, but is laid also on the very passions of his rebellious creatures, which otherwise would create a hell even this side the judgment.

God is here, in Christ Jesus, waiting to be gracious, and therefore he not only confines, keeps down, and keeps back, these fires and quaking crags of an eternal retribution, waiting to be just, but these inward fires of depravity also, in sinful souls, that otherwise would burst forth, defying all restraint, the fountains of a great deep of internal all-devouring passion broken up, and rolling in fiery billows. God keeps off this catastrophe, that otherwise would be the very realization of hell beforehand. He reins up even the very nature of things, and the necessity of moral causes, thereby for a season almost falsifying what he himself hath taught us, and what we know is true, namely, that wickedness in its very self, and by an immutable necessity, burneth as the very fire. He checks all this, and allows not these native energies to put forth half their strength, but arches over men's own tempestuous sea of wickedness in the very heart thereof, and makes a channel as it were, in which there is air to breathe and a space to move, and a practicable way laid down, on which they may pass from sin to holiness. By the very nature of this vast probationary discipline, by mutual checkings and restraints in this vale of a selfish humanity, which otherwise would be nothing better than a broad valley of the shadow of death, he makes possible a transit into life. Yea, even by setting passion as sentinel over passion, and making men's own sins grim watch-wolves against one another, he keeps them in comparative quiet. The pressure of men's own selfishness compels them to restraint, and self-denial. The wind sometimes sweeps over the ocean in such a broad condensed typhoon, sweeps down upon it with such exceeding weight of fury, that the waves which otherwise would rise as mountains, are pressed down as with a colossal flat-iron, are concentrated in upon themselves, and cannot even break in angry foam, because of the immense pressure. And so it is with men's passions under the discipline of God in this world of restraint and probation. It is not because the Lord is slack concerning his promise, as some men count slackness, but because he is long-suffering to us-ward, not willing that any should perish, but that all should come to repentance.

And now just consider for a moment the astounding effect, which through the incredible deceitfulness and desperate wickedness of men's hearts, this very forbearance of God in so many cases produces. Instead of escaping with all haste to the mountain refuge of salvation, while God's angels, under the commission of the Crucified, stand behind sinful men, warding off a tempest of fire worse than that of Sodom and Gomorrah, they turn this interval of peace, and hope, and proffered mercy, into an interval of delusion and indulgence in their sins, and not yet seeing and feeling the fire, will not believe it. And because sentence against an evil work is not executed speedily, therefore the heart of the sons of men is fully set in them to do evil. And there they are, on the way between Sodom and Zoar, sporting themselves with their own deceivings. Because the crags of fire are kept from falling, and the firmament over us does not tremble in flakes and cinders, God's guilty creatures here mock at the promise of his coming, and turn the very possibility of repentance, which, at the expense of Christ's sufferings and death, he has provided, into a most diabolical distorted argument to make men believe that he will never execute his justice. Was the like ever heard or known, even in hell itself? Nay, for there, not the ideas, but POWERS of the world to come they grapple with, and the devils themselves believe and tremble. They cannot doubt or deny God's faithfulness.

But on earth the delusion and denial run yet further, and inasmuch as by this probationary discipline men's own sins are kept down from raging, and they have leisure and peace to be amused and gratified, and God himself indulges them with his goodness, on very purpose to persuade them to repentance, they cajole themselves into the persuasion that they are very amiable creatures, and that sin is a very venial thing, and that God will surely pardon them even without repentance. Because they are occupied and mollified with earthly enjoyments, and seek and find honor one of another, and the passions of their souls, not thwarted and disappointed at every step, do not break out into open, angry malignity against God, they distort this quiet also, this apparent absence of a furious hostility, into an argument against their own depravity, and a persuasion that they do not need such a mighty change as the gospel proclaims necessary for them, and a delusive hope, nay, a lying assurance, that they are nothing, and have done nothing, so vile, as to expose them to God's wrath, which therefore they need not be afraid of. Thus they turn God's very cup of mercy into poison for their own souls. His costly, precious medicine of salvation, and the gentleness, compassion and forbearing patience, whereby he renders it possible for them to be healed, they use as an anodyne in their sins. Truly, what a climax of iniquity is this! If there be judgment for nothing else, surely such wickedness as this demands it.

From such a view of the nature of our probation, we learn something of the strength of the argument within and without, that demonstrates eternal misery to those who die in their sins. To die in one's sins is just to begin to live in them in all the terror of the second death. If here on earth men would not part with them under a system by which the Eternal World itself could be brought into this world, to bear upon men's consciences, without consuming their souls, what will they do in that world where all things will be left to work out their own nature and power to the utmost. Here, it is retraint; there, it will be perfect freedom. Habits concealed and partially confined here will break out there into an uncounteracted despotism. All evil passions will have perfect sway.

We see, therefore, the necessity of the change from sin to holiness *in this world*, and clearly, in this world, or never. Here only, the nature of sin can be known, with a purpose and possibility of acting on that knowledge, where Christ Jesus himself keeps it from devouring us, that we may, under experience and discovery of our disease, come to Him to be healed. We must have conviction of sin, with faith in the consequences of sin, in a world where, as yet, those consequences are kept off. We must believe in the consequences, and be prepared against them, before they come. It will be too late afterwards. And as to the examination of the argument from the nature of sin, and the investigation of the state of our own hearts, if we do not examine these things now, it will be too late to do so when we experience them, when all that was restrained is let loose upon us. For this examination, we must have a laboratory in which we can breathe. We could not analyze gunpowder in a room where the air was flame. We could not try the properties of arsenic if we were compelled to breathe the fumes of it. Here is Christ's open laboratory, both for experiment and change. Here is the place of the Divine Mercy. Here is the theatre of the sufferings and the death of Christ, here the trial of the virtue of His blood. Here, and here only, the law of the spirit of life in Christ Jesus can set us free from the law of sin and of death. Here is the scene and season of the application of all the influences of a Saviour's Cross, and all the motives of the gospel, all the hopes of heaven, and all the terrors of hell, all the powers of the world to come, and all the amazing experience of the goodness of God. When this scene is closed, when the shop is shut up, there can be no more such chemical experiments and changes. Now, the goodness of God leadeth thee to repentance, but when all these influences cease, when all these merciful agencies are withdrawn, and God lets things go into operation according to their essence, then there will arise another demonstration, essential to the glory of God, and the good of the universe, the demonstration of God's justice. Then they who mocked at His warnings, and despised His long-suffering here, cannot do otherwise than experience His justice there. Surely He will laugh at their calamity, He will mock when their fear cometh.

We learn, too, from such a survey, what is the nature of the experiment we must make in regard to salvation, and how to make it, and to whom we must come, that in us the purposes of God's long-suffering may be accomplished. There is no being but Christ Jesus, from whom, for us, there is any hope. This world is Christ's world, given Him by the Father, that He should give eternal life to as many as will come to Him, as many as will believe in Him. He is our peace, our hope, our refuge; He and He only, neither is there salvation in any other. We owe all possibility of our salvation to Christ, and it is both for His sake, and by Him, that this great and wondrous system of Divine forbearance and offered mercy to the chief of sinners is kept up, with all the wondrous remedial agencies of providence and grace applied. Our building is in flames, and it is just falling upon us; but Christ Jesus stands beneath the burning rafters and holds them; stands beneath the great arch of the gateway, and bears up the pillars, and cries to all to escape

Once to Die.

It is appointed unto men once to die, but after this, the judgment. How impressive, how solemn, even to sadness, is this little word *once.* Sometimes it is the most solemn word in our language. In many of its connections, a world of meaning, yea, an eternity of thought and feeling, is thrown upon it. It stands in such a connection, and bears such a boundless weight, in that exceeding solemn passage from the lips of our blessed Lord, When *once* the Master of the house is risen up, and hath shut to the door. That once determines the eternity of millions.

It is appointed unto men once to die. There are a great many things that we can do *only* once. There are opportunities that we can *enjoy* only once. There are forms of trial that we can pass through only once. There are precious peculiarities of blessing that can light upon us only once. If in such cases the object fails, if their design is lost, if the one opportunity is wasted, it can never be recovered. There is probably one decisive trial in every man's life, one point where all the currents of his probation pass into their eternal course. When

Once to Die.

It is appointed unto men once to die, but after this, the judgment. How impressive, how solemn, even to sadness, is this little word *once.* Sometimes it is the most solemn word in our language. In many of its connections, a world of meaning, yea, an eternity of thought and feeling, is thrown upon it. It stands in such a connection, and bears such a boundless weight, in that exceeding solemn passage from the lips of our blessed Lord, When *once* the Master of the house is risen up, and hath shut to the door. That once determines the eternity of millions.

It is appointed unto men once to die. There are a great many things that we can do *only* once. There are opportunities that we can *enjoy* only once. There are forms of trial that we can pass through only once. There are precious peculiarities of blessing that can light upon us only once. If in such cases the object fails, if their design is lost, if the one opportunity is wasted, it can never be recovered. There is probably one decisive trial in every man's life, one point where all the currents of his probation pass into their eternal course. When it comes to that, then everything is suspended on this once. A man may have many sicknesses, many warnings of death, but he can die only once, and when that time comes, not all the urgencies of the universe can put it by.

On this word *once* hangs all the solemnity of every important crisis of our life; for the moment you say *twice*, the solemnity and responsibility are not indeed divided, but carried forward from the first to the second, and then it becomes again *once*, and everything of importance is thrown finally and forever upon that once. It is only when the last opportunity has come, that men really feel the power of this solemnity, the weight of this responsibility. Given: a hundred days more of life: how many of them will the man of prayerless, irreligious habits be likely still to spend without God and without hope in the world, without any preparation for death and the judgment? Or, given: a hundred days more, not all certain, but within which *some* day will be the man's *last* day—that is, he may not live out even the hundred, but certainly, some day within that number, he will die,—how long, in *that* case, would he be likely to go on without repentance? We say, without hesitation, that ordinarily, a man whose habit of procrastination has gone with him, or has carried him through many years unaffected by the consideration of death and the judgment, unmoved by what he owes to himself as an immortal being, and to God his Creator and Judge, will not likely be much moved by the announcement, that he has only a hundred days remaining, and possibly not even a hundred. There is scarcely a doubt that, for the present, he would pursue the same course as heretofôre. As he drew near towards the close of the allotted period, he might begin to be anxious; but, even in the very last day but one, he would be very likely to say, There is one more opportunity, one more day remaining: I can close up all to-morrow, and make my peace with God Or, it may be that, under the influence of long habits of insensibility, united with a gloomy sense of the impossibility or hopelessness of change, he might say, It is too late; I must take my chance, come what may. In either case, not till the very last day would he fully realize the greatness and solemnity of the crisis. Something like this course of combined insensibility, anxiety and procrastination, does really take place in almost every case of fatal sickness; and, doubtless under the dread power of the soul's great adversary, a sullen despair often enters and takes possession before there is reason for it, and the victim of sin is struck down by those words, *too late*, before it really *is* too late.

It is only when the last opportunity has really come that men begin to feel the power of that one word, *once,* and the solemnity of such a crisis. Only once more! When it comes to that, the solemnity deepens indeed. The last performance of any duty, any action, any detail in the routine of life, to which we have been long accustomed, even though it be trivial, possesses something of this solemnity. Even to a prisoner confined for years, and now at length to be liberated, the last time that he should walk his cell would have something of this solemnity; and the last remnant of any very precious thing is solemn indeed. Your last sight of the sun, or the moon, or the stars, or the ocean, if you knew it was the last, would partake of deep solemnity. The exile's last look at his home, his native land; the last look of the mourner at the face of the dead; the last farewell word or kiss of the dying,—what unutterable solemnity may be concentrated in such occasions! Paul's last interview with the dear church at Ephesus, when they fell on Paul's neck, and wept sore, and kissed him, sorrowing most of all for the words which he spake, that they should see his face no more; it was just *that* that made the interview so solemn—the sight of the face of that beloved apostle for the last time. One may remember an account of a bank note found in the pocket of a despairing, wretched young man, who had destroyed himself, on which was written something like this: My last bill; the last remnant of a fortune miserably squandered, and I lost! Or we may remember an account of a man in a great emergency, when life for himself and some others depended on the instant successful kindling of a fire, finding that there was but just one match left, their last possibility. What a concentration of interest and solemnity on that sole possibility!

But time,—when it comes to that—one more day—your last day—your last remnant of a thing so infinitely precious as that! Oh, who shall convey any adequate sense of the solemnity of the last draft of time upon eternity! What if that draft were an unavailing effort of terror and despair, and on the back of it were written those tremendous words, *Too late!* How inexpressibly mournful is the lamentation, The harvest is passed, the summer is ended, and we are not saved! How heart-breaking the wail, even of the weeping Saviour, over that beautiful and beloved city, once the Zion of the Holy One of Israel, and indulged with so many warnings, so many waitings, so much mercy, so much patience, so much long-suffering and forbearance, so many seasons of such gracious and gentle visitation, so many and such precious opportunities, precious and available, even to the last, and the last infinitely the most precious of them all! "Oh that thou hadst known, even thou, at least in this thy day, the things that belong to thy peace! But now they are hid from thine eyes. How often would I have gathered thy children, even as a hen gathereth her chickens under her wings, and ye would not! Behold, your house is left unto you desolate."

In this there is a most impressive and admonitory appeal to every individual soul. For such is the dread experience of multitudes of men, trifling with Time, and permitting all precious opportunities, one after another, to pass unregarded, unimproved, till the last comes, and all are hidden forever! Hidden forever as mercies, but only to reappear in another guise; hidden from sight and from all possibility of recovery, now, but only to come up in the judgment. And with what tremendous power of retribution will such despised occasions of Christ's merciful visitation come armed there! Not more terrible the gory apparition of murdered John the Baptist to the startled soul of Herod, than the avenging horror with which such murdered mercies will pass before the conscience of the careless sinner. Of all transactions in that Coming Day, perhaps none will occasion a more intense bitterness of remorse, and unavailing regret, or an angrier, keener anguish of despair, than the review of slighted, wasted opportunities of eternal mercy.

Indeed, we take it to be this that is especially referred to in that incomparably solemn passage of God's word, "Because I have called, and ye refused; I have stretched out my hand, and no man regarded; but ye have set at naught all my counsel, and would none of my reproof; I also will laugh at your calamity, I will mock when your fear cometh: when your fear cometh as desolation, and your destruction as a whirlwind; when distress and anguish cometh upon you. Then shall they call upon me, but I will not answer; they shall seek me early, but they shall not find me; for that they hated knowledge, and did not choose the fear of the Lord. They would none of my counsel, they despised all my reproofs, therefore shall they eat of the fruits of their own way, and be filled with their own devices. For the turning away of the simple shall slay them, and the prosperity of fools shall destroy them."

In this profoundly-instructive and warning passage, it is the turning away, the mere turning away of the soul, from invitations, admonitions, opportunities of salvation, that shall accomplish the destruction, otherwise *not* accomplished, and shall be the very heart and seal of desolation to the lost soul, otherwise saved. Every gracious opportunity is God's merciful call, every day of time, and of light from the cross, is a new emphatic gesture of God's outstretched hand; and when all these oft-repeated and compassionate efforts of Divine love disregarded come up for review, with the cost at which every one of them was exercised, and the manner in which they were all treated, then will the sight and sense of these things alone, were there nothing else of judgment, be a calamity like a whirlwind, taking away the soul.

But how can men persist in such madness? What indescribable folly, what desperate fool hardiness, so to deal with time, in reference to eternity! What madness to defer, we will not say to a *convenient* season, but, as generally happens in such a case, to the *last* season, the soul's efforts for eternity! Think of the madness of throwing all your fortunes, like an insane dicer, on the last throw. If you were merely at a distance from home, and it were necessary for you to return by a set day, you would feel it important for you to take an early train, and not throw the whole possibility of a seasonable return upon the last train. And so with regard to any and every very important interest.

Now the whole amazing weight of all these considerations comes down upon this one word ONCE, in reference to death and the judgment that 's to follow. This very word, in the great and solemn text in Hebrews, is chosen, and the whole thought is arranged, with all this solemnity that we have described, and more than all that we can conceive, investing it. It is appointed unto men once to die, and *only* once, and then they are forced across the tremendous verge, for ETERNITY. You cannot die, and make the experiment of what is to come after death, and then, if you do not like it, return to have one chance over again, or to make a new choice in your mode of life, and your manner of entering the eternal world. You cannot die but once, and that once settles your life or death for eternity. It is the last train. And yet, from the neglect of all men to prepare for death, an unknowing beholder would say, There must be other trains; this cannot be the final passage. For how can men busy themselves with the trifles of time, in such amazing unconcern as to the great object and end of time,—ETERNITY!

Is there anything that can give any adequate idea of such madness? Let us suppose that Sodom and Gomorrah had been cities in the sea, like Venice, and that the only mode of access and departure had been by a steam-vessel, and that the last evening before the destruction of those cities, it had been distinctly made known that a steamer would leave for the opposite coast precisely at the hour of nine, the only steamer, and the last voyage ever to be made, the last opportunity of escape from the impending ruin. It has been distinctly announced that on the instant departure of that steamer, the storm of fire and brimstone would burst over the whole city in avenging flames, and there are some professed believers in that overhanging perdition, who have resolved to set sail in that very steamer. But instead of being on the pier at the appointed hour, watching and praying, they were waiting to pack up their jewels, or to enjoy one more social festival, one more masquerading ball in Sodom's theatre, one more ballet dance in Gomorrah's scenic opera, or to finish one more speculation in their city lots, in case the ground itself might not be swallowed up, and they could return and build again upon their property. Yet, after all this, they hurried in their carriage to the pier, but only to arrive there just as the steamer had cast off her moorings, and was darting on her way. They had but half believed that she would go; but now they see her for the last time, and it is too late. They had not half believed that the storm of fire would come; but now the pitchy lurid cloud of fire and smoke has rolled over the whole city, and the roaring of the thunder is so near, incessant and terrible, that their souls are paralyzed with despair, and the flakes of fire are already dropping upon them, and there is no escape. It is manifestly too late; conviction has come too late; decision too late; there is no remedy.

But would the terror of such despair be any adequate measure of the calamity upon the soul of being too late for an eternal salvation? Alas! nothing can measure that. And yet, the *madness* of such infatuation in Sodom, such procrastination in Gomorrah, *would* be some faint image of the folly of a soul, dancing on in sin, and dreaming on from speculation to speculation, always counting upon time, and neglecting, till too late, all preparation for death and Eternity. It is possible to be prepared; to be prepared to-day, in case you should be called to-morrow. Yea, by going to Christ to-day, it is possible to be so prepared, that if to-night thy soul should be required of thee, to-night thou shouldst be with Jesus in Paradise. What infinite madness therefore to delay! If you could not *be* prepared till some future period, then were there some excuse for some little procrastination; but where grace is at your disposal *now*, if you will accept of it, what madness to neglect it! If you were sure of another opportunity, you cannot be sure that then it will be available.

The other day, just as a railroad train had started, a man was seen at the top of his speed to overtake the cars, and he barely succeeded in laying hold of the handle to throw himself upon the steps, when his foot missed, and he was thrown by the very violence of his motion under the wheels of the cars, and died instantly. He was too late, and the very effort to recover his last and lost opportunity, destroyed him.

Again, the other day, just as a steamer was starting from the ferry, a man was seen to rush in reckless haste to the edge of the floating pier, and thence with all the impetus of his motion, leaped for the deck of the steamer, but even while he was leaping, the distance had enlarged, and he sunk beneath the boiling billows. He was too late; and the very recklessness of despair hurried him to his ruin. So it is with multitudes who have put off a passage in the Ark of Salvation to the last opportunity, and the last is too late.

Not long since in England, a grave, respectable man, perhaps sixty years of age, stood by the cars just as they were starting, undecided whether to go or not. There were friends within the carriage, urging him to step on board, but he kept saying, "No, not this time," and yet kept hold upon the very handle of the door, half inclined to go, and balancing between going and staying, when the motion of the cars threw him from his balance, and before they could be stopped, he was crushed to death between the cars and the platform. He was undecided up to the last moment, till it was too late, and his very indecision was the cause of his destruction. So it is in multitudes of cases, with those who mean to go, but are never quite ready, not just now, not just this opportunity, till already it is the last opportunity, and the unhappy victim of indecision and procrastination knows it not.

With great power of solemnity the *once* employed in scripture, on the subject of death and the judgment, teaches us the hazard of the habit of delay. It is the habit that all men have formed, who have not fled to Jesus Christ from the storm of fire that is coming. Every day it grows stronger and stronger. Every day there is greater power of self-delusion, persuading you that to-morrow shall be as this day, and much more abundant, while every day there is greater certainty that to-morrow will *not* be as this day, and greater probability that to-morrow *may* be the day when you shall meet the decisive *once* of the text, that is to settle your whole eternal destiny. Are you prepared to die? If not, every hour of your life is madness, and every action of your life is a new mortgage of Satan upon you. Are you prepared to die? Thus only are you the master of your own life, but otherwise, it is completely in the power of Satan, and may remain so to the last moment. Are you thinking to be prepared? Ten thousand thousand have been thinking in the same way, and while thinking, have died. Are you yet undecided? Then you are leaving death itself to decide the matter for you, and if death decides for you, he decides against you. Then, too, every time you think of being prepared, of coming to Christ, and do not come, you deliberately decide against *him*. It is not merely saying, by and by, but positively declaring, *not now*. After every such negative, your likelihood of dying unprepared is greatly increased. Your habit of deciding wrong is strengthened, your habit of indecision as to the right is strengthened also. The case is mightily against you, if you do not break from this habit, this very day. If you leave the decision to sickness to startle and impel you, the probability is, nay, the almost certainty, that you leave it to death. Take your health, and not your sickness, take your hour of life, and not of death, for going to Christ. Take to-day, for that is the direction of the Holy Ghost, and only when you obey God to the letter are you sure of salvation.

The Judgment.

THE doctrine of a day of judgment, and the details respecting it, are matters of pure revelation. Our natural theology, through the human conscience, and by the convictions of mankind, in view of the inequalities and imperfections of the present state as the system of a moral Governor, does indeed demonstrate a future reckoning and righting of all things in regard to the righteous and the wicked—demonstrates a future state of retribution. But of a day of judgment, and of the appointments and arrangements of God in regard to it, there is nothing taught outside the Book of Revelation. All pretended new revelations in regard to these things, so far as there is any truth in them, are but fire stolen from God's word, and palmed upon the world as new, original discoveries; and this is a species of plagiarism of which none but a being who could say, Evil, be thou my good! would dare be at the foundation. Accordingly, it is found to be a characteristic of all such pretended discoveries, that they diminish the sanctions of God's word. Their object is, not to give us higher truth, but to narrow, degrade and falsify, or neutralize the truth already in our keeping. Whatever they teach is lower than that which is already taught, and diminishes its sanctions. If there were many such progressive revelations, all positive truth would at length be annihilated. There are two passages in regard to all such pretended revelators, that stand as fiery cherubim, with drawn swords, at the gates of the sacred word, before which one would think the most daring soul would tremble. "There be some," says Paul, "that would trouble you, perverting the gospel of Christ. But though we, or an angel from heaven, preach any other gospel than that which we have preached, let him be accursed." The other passage is that at the close of John's Revelation: "If any man shall add unto these things, God shall add unto him the plagues that are written in this book. And if any man shall take away from the words of the book of this prophecy, God shall take away his part out of the Book of Life."

The revelations which God has given to us in regard to the day of judgment for mankind, are remarkably connected with information concerning two other grand subjects—namely, the judgment of the fallen angels, and the change or destruction of the material universe. The passages that teach these things are sublime and explicit; they are like sudden bursts of thunder from heaven; and being uttered, there they are left, and not a word is added; —an example of solemn silence, full of awe. "If God spared not the angels that sinned," says Peter, "but cast them down to hell, and delivered them into chains of darkness, to be reserved unto judgment, the Lord knoweth how to deliver the godly out of temptation, and to reserve the unjust unto the day of judgment, to be punished." "The angels which kept not their first estate," says Jude, "but left their own habitation, He hath reserved in everlasting chains, under darkness, to the judgment of the great day."

"Of old," says David, in the 102d Psalm, "hast Thou laid the foundation of the earth, and the heavens are the work of Thy hands. They shall perish, but Thou shalt endure; yea, all of them shall wax old like a garment. As a vesture shalt Thou change them, and they shall be changed. But Thou art the same, and Thy years shall have no end." Now, in reference to those who denied or disbelieved such a coming change in the material universe, in connection with a general last judgment, Peter says that they are wilfully ignorant; that the same heavens and earth which by the word of God were created, are by the same word kept in store, reserved unto fire, against the day of judgment, and perdition of ungodly men.

Now, these things are such accompaniments or forerunners of the judgment, that of their infinite awfulness and sublimity we can have no possible adequate conception. By these heavens the psalmist meant all that the eye could reach, all that the human mind could know, of the expanse of rolling worlds.

All this universe is to be burned up. "Lift up your eyes to the heavens, and look upon the earth beneath," exclaims Isaiah, in reference to this destruction. Go forth of a starry evening, gaze upon the countless glittering orbs above, beneath, around your own small globe, and think of Jehovah as folding them all up together like a worn-out garment, and whelming them in a universal sheet of fire! It is a great triumph of faith to bring these things as realities within the scope, not only of our conception, but confident belief. The sacred writers seem to have had no more doubt upon these subjects than they had in regard to the simplest practical truths of the gospel; indeed, they appeal to these tremendous revelations for reproof, for correction, for instruction in righteousness, just as they do to the plainest disclosures of man's responsibility. We can go no farther than the sacred writers; but as far as they go, we are bound reverentially and solemnly to follow.

On one of the most memorable and explicitly recorded occasions of Paul's preaching (that is, before Felix), it is said that he reasoned of righteousness, temperance, and judgment to come. The main body of his discourse seems to be here described; and it is added, after mention of the judgment to come, that at that point in the sermon, *Felix trembled.* This was indeed one of those terrors of the Lord, with which the preachers of the gospel were instructed by the Holy Spirit to knock at the door of men's hearts. "For we must all stand before the judgment-seat of Christ. Knowing, therefore, the terrors of the Lord, we persuade men." This recorded sermon of Paul, or the brief note which we have of it, is a single illustration of the impressive style in which he and his fellow ministers of Christ labored for the awakening and salvation of an immortal soul. It had been given to Paul, according to the Redeemer's promise, to know both what and how he ought to speak; and under the guidance of that Divine inspiration, every thought and sentence of his discourse was conducted. He was to preach concerning the faith in Christ; and, first of all, in the chariot of the terrors of the Lord, he drove directly at the conscience of Felix. No other mode of dealing would have been suitable for such an audience, even if it had not been Paul's habit, under the teaching of the Holy Spirit, thus to make the law a schoolmaster, to bring the soul to Christ. But Felix was a very bad man, and if fragrance and flowers would not win even a common sinner, or bring him to his senses, much more would it have been lost upon this Romano-Jewish Judge. He was a villain in state-robes and ermines; and yet, the word of God, under Paul's management, did get hold upon him, and we doubt not, mainly by that power of the judgment to come. With what majesty and glory would Paul have demonstrated the claims of the Divine Law, and the nature of that holiness, without which no man shall see God. With what pungency to a guilty conscience would he have portrayed the self-denial and habitual purity of heart and life required by the Supreme Jehovah! But if he had stopped there, probably the iron would not have entered into Felix's soul, although Felix knew in his inmost heart that he was himself a person of a manner of life right contrary to all that Paul had been insisting on. Yet men can very quietly listen to essays on the nature and the obligations of virtue and holiness, and the baseness of vice, and say amen to the whole of such a preachment, if you stop short of retribution and the vengeance of eternal fire. The beauty of holiness and the ugliness of sin even the most sinful men admit.

But Paul did *not* stop there, but drove on with his burning eloquence, and carried Felix pale and trembling into the eternal world, beneath the terrors of the Lord God of an eternal judgment. He reasoned not only of righteousness and temperance, but of the judgment to come, where every transgression of God's holy law, should meet a just recompense of reward. That tremendous judgment to come! It is the first and only note we have, in the divine record, of any of Paul's sermons on that subject. What would not the whole intellectual and Christian world give to have heard that sermon. Yet we can tell, pretty nearly, from Paul's own compositions, in what style of argument and imagery he would have thundered with God's artillery upon the conscience. We need only to connect a few sentences from his own Epistles to show what must have been the tenor of his appeal on this solemn subject. "For the wrath of God is revealed from heaven against all unrighteousness and ungodliness of men. And we are sure, Oh Felix, that the judgment of God is according to truth against those who commit such things. And thinkest thou this, Oh man, who judgest them that do such things, and doest the same, that thou shall escape the judgment of God? or despisest thou the riches of his goodness and forbearance, and long suffering; not knowing that the goodness of God leadeth thee to repentance? But after thy hardness and impenitent heart treasurest up unto thyself wrath against the day of wrath, and revelation of the righteous judgment of God. For he will render to every man according to his deeds; to those who by patient continuance in well doing, seek for glory and honor and immortality, eternal life; but to those that obey not the truth, but obey unrighteousness, indignation and wrath, tribulation and anguish, upon every soul of man that doeth evil. For is God unrighteous that taketh vengeance? God forbid! For then how shall God judge the world? Yea, and he will judge it with the righteous judgment of God, when the Lord Jesus shall be revealed from heaven with his mighty angels in flaming fire, taking vengeance on them that know not God, and that obey not the gospel of our Lord Jesus Christ, who shall be punished with everlasting destruction from the presence of the Lord, and from the glory of his power, when he shall come to that devouring judgment."

But all this reasoning of righteousness, temperance and judgment to come, was only preparatory, on Paul's part, at the door of Felix's conscience, for the introduction of the claims of the Saviour and the cross. He did not indeed begin with the cross, but grappled the law first upon the conscience of his hearer, preparatory to bringing the man to Christ Jesus. He seems to have thought that it would be but a waste of words to tell a heedless hardened hypocrite like the corrupt judge before him, of the character and claims of a Redeemer, unless he could convince the man of his own sin, and then he intended to have displayed the whole scheme and glory of the gospel, and the mercy of the Lord Jesus to the chief of sinners. And he would doubtless have gone on preaching Christ to Felix, had not Felix's impatience and procrastination stopped him. When Felix began to tremble, the man certainly was not far from the kingdom of heaven. If he had cried out, Oh man of God, what shall I do to be saved, or if in silent anguish of soul at the view of his unveiled guilt and condemnation before God's law, he had humbly waited to hear of a crucified and forgiving Saviour, then might the result have been the triumphant conversion of the Jewish Judge, and his translation into the kingdom of heaven. But at the very first pangs of conviction, he broke up the whole audience; he would stay to hear no longer, but concealing his sense of guilt and his terrors of conscience, he cried out, go thy way for this time; when I have a convenient season I will call for thee. It was not so much procrastination, for it is doubtful if he had the least design of recurring again to the subject; but it was the sense of guilt, and the terror of conscience, under this sudden and unexpected revelation of the judgment which he could not and would not endure. It is appointed unto men once to die, and after that the judgment; and that judgment was a power of the world to come, appalling and intolerable to the guilty soul.

It always is. Next to the reality of eternity, rises that form of truth and justice on the soul, which stands in the gate of eternity—that reckoning with God—that discovery, decision, and judgment of character for an eternal destiny—that day of doom —that last decisive day! Once death; and after that, the judgment! Death is a power of this world; eternity and judgment are powers of the world to come. The idea of that day of doom receives its grandeur and its horror from the stupendous reality of that eternity to which it is the introduction; and the idea of eternity itself, on the other hand, owes its solemnity and power over the conscience to the certainty of judgment, and an endless destiny in heaven or hell. Considering the interminable array of all that has passed in the guilty experience and history of the whole human race; that it is all to be recovered, in all its personal relations, and to sweep again before the mind, beneath God's eye, in that day of doom; and considering the certainty and infinitude of what is to follow, the idea of judgment, next after that of God and eternity, is the mightiest, the most comprehensive, the most solemn and weighty, of all human ideas. All other conceptions of the mind are transitory and insignificant in the comparison. It is a power of the world to come, which, when it once takes hold upon the sinful mind, fills it with an overmastering terror, that nothing but the hope of Christ's mercy can allay. Under the conviction and dread of its nearness, the souls of men have often been stirred, in great masses, with agitation, horror and dismay. Sometimes, whole cities have poured forth their inhabitants weeping, wailing, fainting, dying, at the very thought that the day of judgment was nigh; sometimes, an earthquake, or the sun's eclipse, or any great portent of dissolving nature, such as we might suppose will usher in that day, has thrown a whole community into such prevailing and despotic fear, that all business has been suspended, all thoughts of earth and energies of mind have been paralysed, and men have stood shivering and pale in expectation. There have been seasons when men have anticipated daily the thunder of the trumpet that shall wake the dead.

These mighty agitations show that this power of the world to come, this idea of the day of judgment, is as a ground-wave in men's convictions, and, when moved by the wind from eternity, sweeps everything before it. It is because we are a guilty race, and have a guilty, accusing conscience, and a sense of responsibility to God, and a foreboding of Divine justice; it is because that day of judgment is believed and known to be the day of doom, eternal, unalterable, according to the declaration of God, that we must all appear before the judgment-seat of Christ, that every one may receive the things done in his body, according to that he hath done, whether good or bad. Even where the light of Divine revelation has not reached, there has been this brooding sense of the judgment to come—sometimes more definite, sometimes less so, but always active and powerful, according to the activity of men's consciences. Yet men keep it at bay, as they do the devouring fire of conscience itself, which they ward off by an insensibility, sustained by their all-engrossing devotion to the things seen and temporal. The things unseen and eternal are thus hidden, and kept out of view; so that it is wonderful to see how near men dwell upon the verge of them, and yet how distant they live from them—how far off they hold them—how dim and faint their thought and vision of them. And for this very neglect and strangeness, so much the more overwhelming is the terror with which these realities take hold upon the soul, when they suddenly advance upon it, and stand forth to the quickened imagination as just bursting on the world. The actual belief of the judgment, in its nearness, is a thing against which the soul cannot stand. It drops everything else, as a man engaged in a midnight robbery drops his spoil and flies, when the officers of justice break upon him. Confronted with the terrors of the Lord, it cannot endure them.

If this day of doom were announced throughout the crowded city, as to break upon the world to-morrow, or next week, and men really believed it, who can describe the mighty change that would be effected; the dropping of men's schemes of business and pleasure; the relinquishment of their unrighteous and ill-gotten gains; the abandonment of commerce; the solemnity and loneliness of 'change; the astonishment, anxiety and terror, that would sway the streets; how men's hearts would fail them, and all faces would gather blackness, and many would go insane, and many would die, from the mere excess of sudden fright and conviction! Yet now they are wholly at ease and quiet; they dream on in their fancied security, dancing on the verge of doom, and this power of the world to come has as yet no grasp upon them. When Felix trembles, the god of this world is at hand to shield him from the truth; he betakes himself to his merchandise, or rushes into the next night's ball, or draws around him the scenic shows of an opera, or busies himself deeper than ever in his successful worldly speculations. For thus, and with a mighty despotism of worldliness, the things seen and temporal intercept before the vision of the eternal. The fires are burning there, waiting there, the revelations and the fires of judgment; and the midnight horizon of the soul sometimes glows ruddy and wild with their light; and the brooding, dreaming, restless, anxious thoughts reflect it, just as the low clouds gleam through the darkness in the fire of a distant conflagration. But still, because sentence against an evil work is not executed speedily, therefore the heart of the sons of men is fully set in them to do evil.

Now in perfect correspondence with these mysterious depths of man's nature, in which God seems to have set, as in the bottom fountain of a well, the deep reflection of some of heaven's profoundest truths, and from which we sometimes hear rolling up, as from subterranean gongs, the vast reverberation of voices from the powers of the world to come; in perfect correspondence with these buried, muttered thunderings of conscience, God has concentrated, in the terms of His own revelation of this day of doom, some of the most solemn and mightiest images of grandeur and glory. In correspondence with the regency, the kingly power in the soul, of this terrible consciousness of accountability to God, and of an advancing day of reckoning and retribution, God has invested its announcement with a dread array of images, of tempestuous magnificence and sublimity. It reminds us of many passages in Habbakuk and the Prophets, and the Psalms: Clouds and darkness, trembling and burning mountains, the cleaving cataract-sound of many waters, the channels of the great deep upturned, lightnings and thunderings, hail-stones and coals of fire! Before him went the pestilence, and burning coals were under his feet. And he rode upon a cherub, and did fly; yea, he did fly upon the wings of the wind. The wreathing smoke, the bickering flames, the arrowy darting fires, the bowing heavens, the pavilion of dark waters, the blast of the breath of his nostrils, the elements themselves on fire, and melting with fervent heat, the heavens dissolved, and worlds fleeing with a great noise from the face of God; these are some of the draperies let fall before the breaking of that Day. "I beheld in the night visions till the thrones were cast down, and the Ancient of Days did sit, whose garment was white as snow, and the hair of his head like the pure wool: his throne was like the fiery flame, and his wheels as burning fire. A fiery stream issued and came forth from before him; the judgment was set, and the books were opened." "I saw a great white throne, and him that sat on it, from whose face the earth and the heaven fled away, and there was found no place for them. And I saw the dead, small and great, stand before God, and the books were opened, and the dead were judged out of those things which were written in the books, according to their works. And the sea gave up the dead which were in it, and death and hell delivered up the dead which were in them, and they were judged every man, according to their works." "And Enoch also, the seventh from Adam, prophesied, Behold the Lord cometh with ten thousand of his saints, to execute judgment upon all, and to convince all that are ungodly among them of all their ungodly deeds, which they have ungodly committed, and of all their hard speeches, which ungodly sinners have spoken against him." "Behold he cometh with clouds, and every eye shall see him, and they also that pierced him, and all kindreds of the earth shall wail because of him."

But of all the solemn references to that great Day, and descriptions of it, the one by our Blessed Lord, in the 25th chapter of Matthew, with its grave and awful minuteness and yet vastness of detail, is the most overwhelming. "When the Son of Man shall come in his glory, and all the holy angels with him, then shall he sit upon the throne of his glory, and before him shall be gathered all nations; and he shall separate them one from another, as a shepherd divideth his sheep from the goats. And he shall set the sheep on his right hand, but the goats on the left. Then shall the King say to them on his right hand, Come, ye blessed of my Father, inherit the kingdom prepared for you from the foundation of the world. Then shall he say also unto them on the left hand, Depart from me, ye cursed, into everlasting fire, prepared for the devil and his angels. And these shall go away into everlasting punishment, but the righteous into life eternal."

And these things are near us, pressing, crowding upon us. Only death keeps them off; once death, then the judgment. How strange it is that we can, with so little effort, put these realities so far from us, that in effect, if there were an Eternity between them and us, we could hardly be less excited by them! The things present and temporal are set by us as a screen before the things unseen and eternal. Oh that God would mercifully, by his grace, break up this blinding habit, remove our insensibility, and inspire within us that daily and perpetual faith, which shall be in us "the victory that overcometh the world!"

In the admirable writings of Jane Taylor there is a poem entitled, "The World in the Heart." It is a beautiful and searching chapter in the christian conflict, and in some of its lines the nearness of the things eternal is presented with a solemn and startling impressiveness; and the sense of that nearness is truly described as an experience, of which the most careless minds are not always destitute, though alas, in most cases, it is transitory and ineffectual, the soul being careful and troubled about many other things. The world in the heart is a dreadfully successful barricade against the powers of the world to come.

And yet, amid the hurry, toil, and strife,
The claims, the urgencies, the whirl of life,—

The soul—perhaps in silence of the night—
Has flashes, transient intervals of light;
When things to come, without a shade of doubt,
In terrible reality stand out.
Those lucid moments suddenly present
A glance of truth, as though the heavens were rent;
And through that chasm of pure celestial light
The future breaks upon the startled sight.
Life's vain pursuits, and Time's advancing pace,
Appear, with death-bed clearness, face to face,
And Immortality's expanse sublime,
In just proportion to the speck of Time;
While Death, uprising from the silent shades,
Shows his dark outline ere the vision fades.
In strong relief against the blazing sky
Appears the shadow, as it passes by;
And though o'erwhelming to the dazzled brain,
Those are the moments when the mind is sane.
For then, a hope of Heaven,—the Saviour's cross,
Seem what they are, and all things else but loss.
Oh, to be ready! ready for that day!
Would we not give earth's fairest toys away?
Alas! how soon its interests cloud the view,
Rush in, and plunge us in the world anew!

Affirmations of Conscience in reference to the Judgment.

There is a sense of the future judgment in the heart. Every sinful being is conscious of it. There is no sin ever committed, but it carries with it a monition, a prediction,—I shall meet that sin again. The mind travels forward, with the speed of thought, to the time when all things shall pass in review. The consideration of that review may not always be distinct in the consciousness; nay, there may be, there almost always is, a shrinking back from the idea of the future judgment, an attempt to avoid its acknowledgment. Men avoid looking in the face the thought which nevertheless springs up in the soul, For all these things God will bring thee into judgment. If this declaration of God's word, echoed as it is in the depths of men's being, were listened to seriously, it would prevent a great many sins. A man is engaged in some sinful indulgence, pursuing some unholy train of thought, prosecuting some wrong enterprise, committing some unlawful action, perhaps simply making some malicious or ill-natured remarks. Meantime there is a murmur, sometimes distinct, sometimes indistinct, going on in his conscience. If now he would stop and listen, and while he listens, think what conscience is speaking and meaning, it would often arrest the evil; if he would say, when conscience murmurs, Speak louder! What were you saying? There is often this threatful muttering in a man's being, this suppressed rebellion of his moral sense, when he does not notice it, or rather, he is so accustomed to disregard it, to give it, as we say, the "go by," that he lets it sound on, and it makes no abiding impression. Just so, externally, persons become accustomed to the noise of a factory, though the whirring of the machinery, when it is heard for the first time, is quite stunning. So persons on the sea-shore become accustomed to the roar of ocean, and it ceases to excite notice, whilst persons from the inland are filled by it with the most sublime impressions.

But we easily become more accustomed and insensible to the motions of our inward being, than our external senses do to external sounds. Amidst sin, or sinful indulgence, we do not like to listen to the voice of conscience, and would rather she would speak in indistinct murmurings, than in clear tones. But if men would attend to what is going on within them, a great deal of sin and misery might often be saved. It requires a great deal of hardihood and obduracy to look conscience distinctly in the face, and with her eye, like that of God, upon you, proceed to the very sin against which she warns you. Let a man's attention in such a case be wholly given to his conscience, and it will stay his sin. But the attention in such a case is so occupied with the sin, that the face of conscience is hidden, and the voice of conscience, though it sounds on, is like a whisper in the presence of a cataract. But when the noise of passion has subsided, then the sound of conscience for a season is awfully clear; when the crime is committed, the soul is at leisure to attend to itself; then at once it hears the judgment now past, and remembers the warning before given.

Now if men would beforehand attend to conscience as they do afterwards, it would make a great difference in their conduct. If every man, in pursuing a course which he doubts or suspects is wrong, if every man, in entering into temptation, would let conscience speak out, would attend to her uneasy moanings, and would say, What is it? Speak, for I will listen; then, that indistinct feeling of condemnation, indistinct in the presence of passion, but awfully distinct in the remembrance, would become clear, loud, alarming. The indistinct idea of sin, of God, and of the judgment, would become as if an angel had stood in your way, and had said, This is wrong, God sees you, for this there will be judgment.

The voice of conscience always speaks with reference to the judgment. The voice of conscience is not merely condemnatory, but prophetic. It is not merely by the present sense of sin that conscience acts so powerfully, but by the sense of a coming condemnation. Conscience is a prophetic miniature of the judgment, in that inward court which she holds in the soul. God will bring thee into judgment, God will bring thee into judgment; this is what she is evermore repeating; this constitutes her sanction, the foundation of her power. This is the essence of all those forebodings, those gloomy presentiments, that sometimes fill the souls of wicked men, and which they vainly strive to dissipate. There is sometimes a state in the sinner's soul like that chill rawness in the atmosphere, which precedes a wintry storm; there is a gloomy shivering, when there are, as yet, no clouds; the guilty mind may hear the distant moaning of the storm, when as yet it has not darkened the horizon. It is a striking expression in the scriptures in regard to the wicked, that a dreadful sound is in their ears. It is there, whether they attend to it or not, just as the roar of ocean is still there, though men living by the sea-side cease to notice it.

Wicked men so accustom themselves to live upon the borders of the ocean of eternity, and to dance and trifle on its shores, listening only to the music of their own sins, that the sounds that come across it are scarcely ever attended to. And yet, there it is before them, the ocean of eternity, and a sense of it is always brooding over the mind, and there is sometimes a consciousness of it. Sometimes the sense of it is like a night-mare upon the soul, for which men know not how to account. Sometimes their indistinct sense of what is buried in the future pursues them into the midst of their busiest occupations, their most absorbing pleasures, and the worm of conscience is gnawing away in secret, when there is the consuming care of gain, or the flush of wine, or the excitement of the dance upon the countenance. Many men have these seasons, who never tell of them; hear this dreadful sound, who never mention it to others. I doubt not that sometimes professed infidels have written their works beneath this brooding sense of indistinct avenging evil in Eternity. There was something in the very bosoms of Hume and Voltaire, that was always giving the lie to their own pages.

Sometimes, when such men come near to death, the cloud is all lifted, a lurid light strikes through it, the inward eye sees far out over the ocean of eternity, the inward ear is rendered keenly and painfully sensitive to the tempest sounds that come booming and wailing across it. Sometimes even great and hardened sinners enter into the shades of avenging retribution before they die. We have seen a man of great powers of mind, great experience in guilty pleasure, great contempt for religion, great wit and richness of intellect in conversation, beneath a gloom so deep under the hand of disease, that we could scarcely doubt that the images of the despised future were busy with him; the spirits with which his evil life had peopled the eternal world were beginning to return upon him, to peer in through the darkness of his infidelity, to show their dreadful faces, and to wake up the snakes in his own heart, coiled in his conscience. We shall never forget the expression of that man's countenance, as we once saw him gazing into the pale face of a dead man, a former companion of his pleasures, carried beneath the window in a coffin. How often, when we little think it, are the wicked like the troubled sea, whose waters cast up mire and dirt!

A very graphic writer describes an interview with an imprisoned murderer, who, at the close of the conversation, "folded his arms, leaned back against the wall, and appeared to sink gradually into one of his reveries. I looked him in the face, and spoke to him, but he did not seem either to hear or see me. His mind was perhaps wandering in that dreadful valley of the shadow of death, into which the children of earth, while living, occasionally find their way; that dreadful region where there is no water, where hope dwelleth not, where nothing lives but the undying worm. This valley is the fac-simile of hell, and he who has entered it, has experienced here on earth, for a time, what the spirits of the condemned are doomed to suffer through ages without end."

It is a fearful thing to see a man passing through that valley, beset by the fiends in it, his sins having found him out and fastened upon him. But if it is dreadful to see another in it, how much more dreadful to experience it! And yet, perhaps insensibility is worse. It has sometimes been witnessed. A notice of the death of Hume, by a thoughtful and masterly observer sets the fearfulness of such insensibility in great solemnity before us. "We behold him," says John Foster, "appointed soon to appear before that Judge, to whom he had never alluded but with malice or contempt; yet preserving to appearance an entire self-complacency, idly jesting about his approaching dissolution, and mingling with the insane sport his references to the fall of superstition, a term of which the meaning is hardly ever dubious, when expressed by such men. We behold him at last carried off, and we seem to hear, the following moment, from the darkness in which he vanishes, the shriek of surprise and terror, and the overpowering accents of the messenger of vengeance. On the whole globe there probably was not acting, at the time, so mournful a tragedy, as that of which the friends of Hume were the spectators, without being aware that it was any tragedy at all."

How dreadful to face death with conscience for an enemy! In such a position, how powerfully does conscience act with reference to the judgment! What instruction may be gathered from the keen desire of restitution for fraud and injustice, sometimes evinced on a dying bed, and often also in a season of health, beneath powerful conviction of sin! It seems as if the soul could not die beneath a sense of injustice to others, unconfessed and unatoned for. The soul often seeks atonement in restitution. But who shall make restitution to God for a life of injustice, ingratitude, injury towards him? And if fraud and wrong towards a fellow-creature can so afflict and torture the soul, when it comes to be remembered and felt even in this world, what will be the misery produced by a sight and sense of sin in eternity as committed against God?

The doctrine of the atonement once revealed, it does not seem possible that any man who believes in a future judgment, and has ever looked into his own heart, can have the hardihood to reject so divine a truth. Accordingly we find that with its denial, men have coupled the disbelief of the judgment, and the denial of a future endless retribution. Perhaps we ought to say, the *attempt* at such disbelief, for every man's own moral constitution makes him a believer, however unwilling. And when a man looks over his own life, and into his own heart, and begins to realise in some measure the nature of that revelation, which is to take place in eternity, What can he do? There is no reparation that he can make, no restitution that he can offer to God. But with infinite power of consolation to a wounded conscience the divine reality of the atonement rises on the soul. Behold the Lamb of God, who taketh away the sin of the world!

Disclosures of the Judgment.

In one of the sea-side sermons by our blessed Lord, beneath the unclouded sky and sweet, open air of Judea, He told the people (and the Omniscience of God, the meanwhile, seemed brooding upon them, in the all-surrounding transparency of cloudless light) that "there was nothing hid that should not be manifested, neither anything kept secret, but that it should come abroad."

Two propositions are contained in this disclosure. The first is, that there is nothing hid which shall not be manifested; the second, that the purpose for which anything, for a time, is kept secret—the reason why such temporary secresy is permitted, is, that it shall come abroad. We could not have known either of these propositions, had not He who knoweth all things revealed them to us. They embrace a great universe of truth; the nature of our probation and accountability; the certainty of a future judgment; the justification of God's present government, under which so many crimes seem to go concealed and unpunished; and the fact, that these things are permitted now, only to be revealed and set right hereafter. Had not God taught us this truth, and made us thus to look into futurity, we should have supposed that many things might forever remain unknown, except to the beings who transacted them; or, at any rate, that thoughts, purposes and feelings, inscrutable by mortal sight, might remain eternally hidden from mortal knowledge. But God tells us that there is *nothing* hid which shall not be manifested; and this proposition extends to the thoughts and intents of the heart, and leaves nothing, either of event or motive, out of its circle. All things shall be manifested, shall be *made* manifest, shall come abroad, shall be introduced to others' knowledge. All things *are* known to God, and cannot be otherwise; but they shall also be *made* known to others. There is no place of concealment, and no such thing as concealment, in the universe.

In the first place, there is a sense in which there is nothing, even in the counsels and works of God, which shall not be manifested by Him, for His glory. All things were planned and made for the display of His perfections; and even as it pleases, and when it pleases, the great and glorious Sovereign of the universe, the veil shall be taken from them, and they shall be known. The strength and acuteness of reason in God's intelligent creatures shall be employed in searching out His works and ways forever; a blessed employment, which, by reason of the infinitude and incomprehensibility of God's perfections, must be eternal. And God will forever make such manifestations of Himself to all holy beings as will forever increase *their* glory and blessedness.

But, in the second place, and in a more absolute,

unlimited sense, there is nothing *out* of God, nothing in His creatures, now hidden, which shall not be manifested; there is nothing in the counsels and works of man, nothing thought, nothing spoken, nothing acted, in secresy, in darkness, which shall not be made known. No length of time, nor depth of loneliness, is any security of concealment. No oblivion can cover a single transaction, either inward or external; no interval of forgetfulness can banish one circumstance, or dim or wear away one past reality, or diminish its brightness. And thoughts are realities more eternal than things. Thoughts lead to things, give birth to them, and dwell forever with them; and neither thought nor thing can be annihilated, or its trace perish. Ages on ages might roll on, and no remembrance occur, no association bring it up, no indication take place, by which the existence of such a fact might be dreamed or suspected; but having once been, it is eternal; and when it is renewed in the mind, the present and the past consciousness shall be brought together, and made as distinctly and clearly one, as if no interval of time had elapsed. It shall be as if a vacuum between two objects were removed—as if two leaves of a book, that had been torn asunder, and removed to distant and different quarters of the globe, had been brought together, there being no interruption of the sense by that removal. There is no more separation of the mind's identity and consciousness from any thought or event in its past existence, whatever interval of time may have elapsed, or different experience ensued, though it were whole ages, than there would be between the sense of these words, on the bottom of a page in John's gospel, "*The hour is coming, in the which all;*" and those words that begin the next page, "*That are in the graves shall hear His voice,*"—than there would be between these two propositions, if you were to tear these words asunder, and carry the last without the first into Asia Minor. Whenever these words are brought again together, the whole sense again is as perfect as if they never were separated; and so it is with the mind's identity and consciousness.

The past can no more be separated from the present, than the present from the future. A thing may for the present be forgotten, but it cannot be lost, being an eternal possession of the mind, a transaction of its stewardship, for which account must be given. It may be buried in utter forgetfulness, nearly the whole span of a man's life; but the smallest, most trivial association may reproduce it. Sometimes the mind suddenly and unaccountably goes back and lives over again in perfect freshness a scene of its past being, not remembered for years. A mote in the sunbeam, an odor wafted on the wind, a tone in the voice, a strain of music, a falling leaf, the shape of a cloud, the title of a book, the glance of an eye, the song of a bird, a color in the sky, may bring it all up at once, without an effort of the will, or a thought that seemed leading to it. There may have been *that* in the scene, which the soul would fervently wish could be annihilated; there may have been *that*, which is of such a nature, that the soul itself would rather now be itself annihilated, than dwell with the remembrance of it. But involuntarily, unsought for, in spite of will, wishes, fears, up it comes. A man can trace no magic circle for his being, within which the past shall not intrude; within which he can stand in safety, and stretch his wand of power, and say to the pale ghosts of his sins flocking towards him from the darkness, Keep off! They will not mind him, and sometimes they seem to come crowding and shoaling towards him all at once, struggling for the mastery. He can separate himself from no past frame or experience, habit or action, thought or result, of his being. Neither the evil nor the good can be forgotten. In this sense also the words of Ecclesiastes are true, The thing that hath been, it is that which shall be; unto the place from whence the rivers come, thither they return again.

More than three thousand years ago a handful of grain was deposited in an Egyptian tomb. More than three thousand years passed away, and the buried grain was discovered. It had all the germinating properties of life hidden within it, and when, after this long interval, it was planted in a garden in London, it sprang up, and produced its appropriate harvest. So it is with buried, hidden, forgotten thoughts and things. They never die, never can die. They may be entombed *with* the dead, but they never lose their vitality. They may pass out of the consciousness, and be forgotten; but they are to be sown again, and to bring forth their fruit for weal or woe, in the mind, in eternity.

This is the security, from the nature of the human

mind, fearfully and wonderfully made, for the fulfilment of this assurance, that there is nothing concealed which shall not be manifested. A man's being is a chain of experiences coiled up, and coiling on, every link indissolubly connected with the preceding, so that it cannot, in any part, be severed, and so that, if you have one link in hand, you are sure of all. And a man's own self is to go back step by step and uncoil this chain, and examine every link of it, and hold it up to the light, and it is to be seen how it was forged, from what furnace in the mind, by what process of the will, with what moral and mortal tempering and hardening.

But there is a higher security of manifestation than this, and that is, the purpose and word of the living God. Neither was anything kept secret, *but that it should come abroad.* It is kept secret, only *in order to* come abroad. Nothing would be kept secret, suffered to be hidden, were not *that* God's design. There is this inscription on every hidden thing, *To be manifested.* Therefore it is safe, it cannot be lost. The very fact that it is hidden makes it sure to come abroad. There is a particular insurance from God upon it, that makes it more safe from forgetfulness and loss, than if it had been transacted in open day, and were among the known things of a past eternity. There is a superior certainty, over the chaos of things that have been known, connected with those that are unknown, of being brought out into the light; for that is the particular design with which God put them by, as it were, and suffered them to pass into oblivion.

Whatever remains concealed, God's purpose is connected with such concealment, and that is as if every such concealed thing or thought were labelled, and written in a book, catalogued, numbered, with place, time, circumstance, to be brought up at the great appointed day. There is such a book; the fires of the last day cannot consume the record. "For God shall bring every work into judgment, with every secret thing, whether it be good, or whether it be evil."

And now as to the purpose of God in permitting such secresy for a season, some things are plain. Many things are kept secret, in order that they may be completed, the purpose of the agent fully revealed, and so far as God permits it, accomplished. If there were not this possibility of present secresy, men could hardly be said to be free agents. Doubtless, then, it is partly for the development of character, that God permits evil to be concealed, and the wicked to go unpunished. A man who will sin, though he knows the eye of God is on him, merely because his fellow-beings do not see him, is essentially wicked. A man who will sin against his own conscience and knowledge of truth and righteousness, though neither God nor man should see him, or because he alone sees himself, is essentially wicked. A man who would refrain from sin, because men see him, while he would not, if God only saw him, is essentially wicked. God will let men therefore for the present, play the hypocrite; he will let men's inward wickedness develop itself, while they say, no eye seeth me. He will try what men are. He will see what a man is, alone; he will let him think he is alone; he will let him forget God, and act out his evil nature, that the universe also may see what he is, *alone.* So things are kept secret, in order to be revealed. A daguerreotype is formed, and can only be formed, in the darkness; that is, the plate must be shut from the surrounding light, and receive only the light transmitted from the person to be taken, in order that when it is produced, it may bear, without blur or dimness, the lineaments of the face it has reflected. If the light were let in upon it, the process would be stopped; there would be no picture. So it is in some respects with men's characters in their development.

Secresy is often essential to the commission of crime, and essential to the production of evidence in regard to men's character. How many a villainy would have been stopped, how many a sin crushed in the bud, how many a fraud or murder arrested, if there had been a single eye known to be in the room, on the face, on the hand, on the paper. If the first concoction of evil plans were seen in their commencement, in their originating steps, there are comparatively few that would be finished. Some persons indeed, in great power and boldness, sweep on in their career of evil, regardless with what transparency the world may see their motives. But in general men cannot accomplish their schemes of selfishness, without concealment. And in this world many a crime goes unpunished for want of evidence. There will be evidence enough in the eternal world. Every murderer, who thinks he has removed every witness of his crime, has only sent the witnesses out of this world into the next, out of the porch or ante-room into the judgment hall itself. He has only sent forward the evidence, by which he is to be tried. Every man who has secretly injured or defrauded another, has had the fraud or the injury inscribed and catalogued for eternity. Every man who has neglected prayer, neglected the word of God, neglected his own soul, has had the neglect, every instance of it, not only written down in the book of his own conscience and memory, but checked as it were, in the record of things to be manifested in eternity. Every man, every day, is filling up his character. God keeps a book of character. Every thought, every act, goes into it; every attitude of the moral being. The book is filled up, in order that its great leaves may be unfolded and read for the knowledge of the universe; that all may see what man is, what God is; that every mouth may be stopped, and all the world plead guilty before God; that man may be seen in the greatness, wilfulness, and inexcusableness of his depravity, God in the holiness and justice of his punishment. The more secrecy, hypocrisy, and successful wickeness there is here, the more clearly will the justice of the condemnation of the wicked appear hereafter.

It may be that secresy in sin is often permitted in mercy. God does not keep secret His own expostulating and restraining words and influences; He sends them abroad, pours them upon sinful minds and consciences, hedges up the path of the sinner with them, to turn him from destruction to repentance. But he often permits men's sins to remain secret, so that they may come to a hearty repentance before God, and not be shut out from society, or from paths of usefulness, by the wide-spread knowledge of guilt. God conceals every man's heart from every man; for the heart is deceitful above all things and desperately wicked, so that none but God can know it. Hence the apostle says, Some men's sins are open beforehand, going before to judgment, and some they follow after. Likewise also the good works of some are manifest beforehand, and they that are otherwise cannot be hid. Some sins are so plain, so glaring, that they carry the thoughts at once to the bar of God, and spectators are led irresistibly to speak of the fearful account that must be rendered; and such sins are as swift reporting messengers sent onward to the judgment. Other sins are not fully completed, till after the author of them has gone to his grave; the results of them are not developed, the purposes of them not accomplished; but as fast as they are, so fast the witnesses of them travel on after the author, to overtake him in the eternal world.

The witnesses against some men, we have reason to believe, will thus be crowding into the eternal world to the end of time, the indictment against them not being filled up till the last result of their iniquity is developed. A man, for example, who writes an immoral, but immortal book, may be tracked into eternity by a procession of lost souls from every generation, every one of them to be a witness against him at the judgment, to show to him and to the universe the immeasurable dreadfulfulness of his iniquity. A man whose teachings or whose influence remain behind him for evil, does in a solemn sense remain sinning in this world, long after his soul has gone forward into the land of spirits. And it must be an awful reception which such a man gives to the witnesses of his guilt, as they come into his company, covered with the mantle of his sins, filled with the element of perdition ministered by his soul to theirs. It may have been the dread of that, that made the rich man in his torments beseech father Abraham to send Lazarus to testify unto his five brethren, lest they also should come into that place of torment.

But the good works of good men are as immortal as the bad works of evil men. They, too, are swift messengers, but bright celestial ones, before the throne of God in judgment. They, too, come trooping into the eternal world as witnesses, long after the authors of them have entered on their reward. And who can tell the blessedness of such men as Baxter, Bunyan, Doddridge, Flavel and others, when they see, generation after generation, the results and marks of their own earthly labors, in souls that follow after them to glory. No good that they have done can ever be hid. Not a cup of cold water given to a disciple, nor a widow's mite put into Christ's treasury, nor a penitent tear, nor a fervent, faithful prayer, nor any thought or deed of self-denying love, but is recorded in the book of life, and sends on its witness for the great day. "Blessed are the dead who die in the Lord! Yea saith Spirit, for they rest from their labors, and their works do follow them."

The pursuit of this subject teaches us most impressively what a solemn world we live in. We seem to walk by ourselves, we are often alone with ourselves, and there is no window in our bosoms, through which men can look into the recesses of our hearts and see what is going on there. But there is no such thing as absolute concealment. Our deeds are all done, our characters all formed, in open light. There is no such thing as darkness. What appears darkness to us is light to God, and every thought and every thing, every feeling, every action, is thrown from us into the light. How solemn, how beautiful, are the declarations in the scriptures: "Thou hast set our iniquities before thee, our secret sins in the light of thy countenance. If I say surely the darkness shall cover me, even the night shall be light about me. For the darkness hideth not from thee, but the light shineth as the day. The darkness and the light are both alike to thee. Can any hide himself in secret places, that I shall not see him, saith the Lord? There is no darkness nor shadow of death where the workers of iniquity may hide themselves. Mine eyes are upon all their ways, neither is their iniquity hid from mine eyes."

And if it is hid now, for a season, from the universe, it is only because it shall be revealed when God pleases. So with every thing, whether good or evil, the one just as indestructible, indelible, unconcealable as the other. If we ever think or act in the darkness, it is for the light. As rockets are shot into the sky, to explode and blaze there, so our thoughts, words, deeds, shoot into the eternal world, to have their development there, but not like the transitoriness of a meteor in the evening sky. The good thoughts, the good deeds, the good words of good men will shine in the firmament of their own consciousness and remembrance, and in the light of a Saviour's love, forever. The evil thoughts, evil deeds, evil words of the wicked will be as baleful, everlasting fires, darting from every quarter their corrosive influence. So the good man shall be satisfied from himself, and the wicked shall be filled with his own mischief. In the light of eternity, under the disclosures there, every being need only be left to the unrestrained development of the character with which he went out of this world into that, and this would be enough to constitute everlasting happiness or misery. The seeds are sown, the elements established in this world. Say ye to the righteous that it shall be well with him, for they shall eat the fruit of their doings. Woe to the wicked, it shall be ill with him, for the reward of his hands shall be given him.

And here let the solemnity of these principles be noted, as to our sins of omission, and let any man, the most careless, the most hardened, ask himself if he is prepared to meet the revelation of them. Our negative life, or what we call such, is as determined in its moral character as our most positive; and in the light of that great declaration of God, To him that knoweth to do good, and doeth it not, to him it is sin, our negative life may sometimes be the guiltiest of all our existence. When the universal stewardship is reckoned, for which God is to hold every man to his account, it is not perhaps the question, What have you *done* with your talents, your wealth, your opportunities? that will prove the severest trial to the soul, but, What have you *neglected* to do, failed to do, refused to do, or left *undone*, that you had the time and occasion given you to accomplish? It is this last question that in most cases will work the greatest revelation of guiltiness, and the greatest remorse and woe.

Alas! too often it is the emptiest hours, the most unmarked, that most upbraid us. Where are the many days, almost a blank in our existence, that might have been filled, or marked at least, with memories of prayer, with thoughts of God, and aspirations deep and earnest after heaven, with efforts to do good, however baffled, and voices of supplicating sorrow, even amidst defeat? Alas! they have gone sinfully vacant to the judgment, even as the case from which the jewel has been stolen is reserved to prove the theft. Of many of our days, we can tender to God, as of a wasted talent, only the folded napkin. Each day is as a vase, a precious crystal vase, bestowed of God to be filled with grace from His own fountain, with living water from His own throne, with some precious treasures of words and deeds of love, and sweet opportunities, not utterly neglected but usefully employed. Each day should bring something to God, the precious vase, with some little offering, though it were but a cup of cold water, or a publican's prayer. God gives it whole; but every day, in the careless, prayerless, godless man's life, returns it empty, broken. But for every empty and every wasted day, thou must give account to Him.

We are taught the prayer of the psalmist, that God would make us sensible of our hidden sins; but from ourselves a great many things are concealed, not by the darkness, but the glare of light. A great master of thought and style in our English tongue once likened the realities of our moral being not revealed as yet, to the stars, invisible by day, but which are only waiting for the obscuring daylight to be withdrawn. He employed that phrase in reference to the repressed and hidden thoughts, memories, and possessions of the mind, brought suddenly into view in an hour of darkness and of judgment, like the dying moments of a drowning man. Then, all the past of life rises from its obscurity into clear and awful light. Now, the distractions, the gaieties, the business and brightness, of our daily worldly existence, hide us from ourselves, and make most men more ignorant of their very selves, their own real character in the sight of God, than they are of the most abstruse of the sciences. In such ignorance there may be a sullen peace at present, there may be calmness and stupidity of conscience, but only while this ignorance lasts. But when the distracting and obscuring shows of this world die from the vision; when the light from things seen and temporal, that now veils and obscures the unseen and eternal, shall be drawn away, then will all that we are not, in comparison with God's standard of all that we ought to be, and all that we are, in comparison with God's standard of all that we ought not to be, become insufferably clear. How dreadful must be that inevitable revelation of sin in all the life, and of guilt within the soul, to the man of gaiety and pleasure, who never in this world would admit the indictment of God's word against him; to the fools that danced through life, making a mock at sin; and to all those who never here, amidst their round of amusement and pursuit, would look either at God's word or their own hearts long enough to see and feel their real character in God's sight!

And who, when that revelation takes place, can meet God without a Saviour? What, even now, can the dying sinner do, when it pleases God to draw aside the obscuring veil, to set his sins in array before him, and to give him some insight into the deep and dread reality of the character he has formed, while living without God and without prayer in the world? He can do nothing but despair, were it not that, just at this place and condition of utter guilt and irremediable ruin, Christ Jesus interposes. And here, to the Cross of Christ, this subject brings us all; for, apart from Him, what can we do, when God makes us known to ourselves, as He himself knows us? He has set our iniquities before Him, our secret sins in the light of His countenance; and what refuge can there be, when they are so set before us, so illustrated by the holy eye of God, if Jesus Christ have been rejected by us? It is the partial illustration that God now gives, and the partial conviction of sin which follows, in minds not utterly hardened, that reveals, and was intended to reveal, both the solemnity and terror of the judgment, and the necessity of the cross.

And while this power of the world to come shows the need of just such a Saviour, and just such a salvation from sin, as are brought to us in the gospel, it also shows the blessedness even of the most painful conviction of guilt, and the merciful and compassionate intent of God in producing such conviction. Truly, the greater the severity of God, the greater is His goodness. How frivolous, how unreflecting, how perfectly groundless and inconsistent, is the objection brought by some men against the system of the gospel, that it is a harsh and gloomy system! To be sure, it is gloomy to determined sinners, to impenitent men, who wish to sin on, undisturbed by conscience and the fear of coming wrath; and if it were not gloomy to such, it could not be from God, and never a single dying sinner could be saved. But it is gloomy to such, just to drive such to the cross, just to bring them to the Saviour; and then and there it is all brightness, and a brightness the greater and more glorious for the gloom.

Knowing therefore the terror of the Lord, we persuade men. We persuade them from the sin to the Saviour, from the law to the gospel, from the gloom to glory, from conviction to pardon, from death to life. Let the conviction of sin come, and let it press our guilty burdened souls in anguish to our Saviour, for that is our only hope. Let no man shrink back from the revelation of his sins now; now while pardon may be found, it is mercy unspeakable to have your sins set in array before you, to have some leaves in the Book of Judgment illuminated for you beforehand. Draw not away your vision; let the soul, though affrighted, gaze; it may do you good, it may save you. Draw not away your shrinking heart from the sword of the spirit, from the hand and probe of the merciful heavenly physician, searching and revealing your guilt. Yea rather pray God so to manifest your sins now, beforehand, and to make you so painfully and despairingly sensible of the guilt and the burden of them, that you shall be compelled to cry out, Lord save me, I perish! God be merciful to me a sinner!

The Person of the Judge, and the Evidence.

WHEN our blessed Lord stood upon the earth as the Saviour and the light of the world, He said, "If any man hear my words, and believe not, I judge him not; for I come not to judge the world, but to save the world. He that rejecteth me, and receiveth not my words, hath one that judgeth him; the word that I have spoken, the same shall judge him in the last day."

There is in this passage a striking testimony as to the independence, self-evidence, and self-existence of the Word of God. It is not man that can judge the word, but the word itself is the judge of man, and the judge more particularly for the sin of unbelief in rejecting the Saviour. Not to receive Christ's words is to reject both him and them; and Christ's words are God's words, both in the Old Testament and the New, as is plain, not only from the oneness of Christ with God as God, but from direct palpable passages, such as that in 1st Peter, i. 10, 11, where the old prophets are represented as searching what or what manner of time the Spirit of Christ which was in them did signify, when it testified beforehand the sufferings of Christ and the glory that should follow. Now Christ, in the character of the faithful Witness of God, declares that at present if any man hear his words and believeth not, he judges him not. Nothing else will be needed, even at the last day, for his judgment and condemnation, but just to hear the word which he has rejected. And so nothing else will be needed for the condemnation of those who have resisted the light, but just to see the light.

This is the condemnation, that light is come into the world, and men loved darkness rather than light, because their deeds were evil. When men neglect God's word and reject it, they are neglecting and rejecting that, which not only carries its own irresistible Divine evidence in itself, irresistible to a good and humble heart, but they are also investing it, in that very rejecting, with the ermine of their Judge; they are arming it as the instrument and power of their condemnation. The fact that its evidence is in itself and irresistible, takes away all excuse for not attending to it, such as the criminal might plead if there were a long array of external evidence, which he must consult and decide upon before coming to the word. And considering the nature of the light, its neglect as well as its rejection condemns him; its neglect *is* its rejection. How shall we escape, if we *neglect* so great salvation? This heedlessness as to God's voice is both consequence and proof of depravity.

But in this passage the word judge must not be taken as meaning the person, or supplying the place of the person, who shall sit in judgment at the last day. It is rather to be taken as intimating the nature and strength of the evidence, which will judge and condemn. Thus we say, if a man is brought in before an earthly tribunal accused of murder, and in the course of the investigation a letter addressed to him from a distant party is found in the Post Office demanding money as payment for concealing that very murder, we say of such a letter that it judges the man at once, it condemns him; or if a man steals his neighbor's goods, and yet denies that he knew they were his neighbor's, and a writing is produced in court found in the possession of the man, showing beyond all possibility of doubt that he knew whose the goods were, and had the intention to steal them, we say of such a writing that it judges and condemns him. In this sense it is, that the WORD is said to judge and condemn the sinner.

Let us enquire, more directly, first, as to the judge in person in the last day; second as to the accuser; third as to the evidence against the criminal at the bar.

A man advancing to trial for some great crime, of which he is accused, will be anxious to know who is to be the judge, the day when his particular case comes to be tried. Perhaps among the judges on that circuit there is one, with whom the prisoner has in past time held transactions that go far to establish, if known, the proof of his guilt. Perhaps this judge holds a claim against him, which he has resisted and denied, and in addition to that, may have foreseen the very crime for which the man is to be tried, and may have forewarned him against the temptation and the danger. If this be the case, then, the moment that judge's name is named to the prisoner, his soul will sink within him; he will say to himself, Then it is all over with me, for he knows my guilt, and must condemn me. Whoever might be the jury, the prisoner would come to trial before such a judge with the hopelessness of despair. The very name of the judge destroys all possibility of deliverance. Considering the uprightness of his character, the evidence that will come before him, and the amount of his own knowledge, there is no hope.

Now, how stands the case with guilty man, arraigned for his sin against God, in the judgment at the last day? Has he no anxiety, advancing swiftly to trial, and perfectly conscious of his guilt? Is there any question as to the person of his judge? If that person were a being who had but one unsatisfied claim against him, and that claim iniquitously denied and resisted, or who had been cognizant of but one of the transgressions for which he is arraigned before God, having met him in time past, and forewarned him against it, and forbidden him the course which was leading to it, even then he would despair of acquittal, he must be perfectly sure of condemnation. But if the judge be a person knowing not one merely, but all his crimes, if he have had an eye, the eye of Omniscience, upon all his steps through life, if he have seen his iniquities in their very first thought in his soul, their earliest indeterminate and shadowy but not resisted beginning, if he have known the growth of them from motive into act, and from act into habit, and all the while against all light, check, and warning; what then? And if he be a person not merely knowing all these things, and irradiating them with light, as the sun irradiates and marks the leaves it shines upon, but also, the very Being against whom all these things have been committed; if he be the Law-giver, upon whose authority the criminal in the reckless violation of his laws, every step of his way through life has dared to trample; if he be also the kind and gracious expostulator, admonisher and prophet, who has met him every step of his ways, as a friend, to bid him beware; and not only so, if he be also, in mysterious love, one who, to make an escape for him from the perdition of his ways possible, has died for him, and yet whose death he has despised as foolishness, or denied as an unreal, unmeaning parable; if he be the Being, to whom he owes his existence, protection, support, and every blessing; if, in fine, he be the God, Creator, Preserver, Redeemer of the sinner, and if all these attributes, claims, authorities, and retributive demands and necessities, meet in the person of his Judge; can human language state strong enough the certainty, or depict the terribleness of the prospect before him?

Under such a prospect, with such a cloud of vengeance lowering, has he any being with whom he can entrust his case, any lawyer in the chancery of Heaven, any Advocate with the Father, who dare or will undertake the hopeless cause, or plead a suit for the criminal at God's bar? Is there any created being who *can* do it, man or angel? If there were, is there any creature who dare or will do it; any creature in heaven or on earth, who would have the heart, the disposition, even if it were permissible under God's government, to stand up in behalf of a criminal, whose guilt is not only undoubted, unquestionable, and to the bottom known, but has not one redeeming quality, and is attended with every possible exasperation under heaven? If there be none among good beings in all God's universe who can, or whose unmingled purity and goodness and delight in God's justice and holiness would let them, even if they could, stand up to plead for the exemption of such unmingled guilt from deserved punishment, is there one among *evil* beings, one of the demons below, under whose guidance the criminal at the bar has rushed on to such excesses and uninterrupted continuance of sin, who would speak for him? Alas! *they* will stand, if opportunity be given, as his fierce, malignant accusers. The tempter is the enemy and accuser of mankind. There is no lawyer either in heaven, earth or hell, who can or will undertake his cause. He must stand alone. His guilt isolates him, as to his personal accountability, conflict, and desert and endurance of the penalty, from all the universe, while it connects him as to its aggravation, its consequence, and its evidence, *with* all the universe. It isolates him as to friends, it gives him over to enemies.

There *was* an Advocate, a friend, a Redeemer, to

whom the criminal *might* have committed his cause, no matter for its utter blackness and desperateness, whatever may have been the depth, enormousness or malignancy of his guilt. There was an Advocate appointed of God for this very purpose, and with a title which no other being in the universe dare take, the Friend of Sinners; a title and an office without parallel under God's government; a Being appointed by the injured law-giver himself, as a Counsellor of Mercy, to save the guilty from deserved punishment. His name shall be called Wonderful, Counsellor. But this wonderful Being, this Advocate with God, must be applied to by the sinner himself, and in this world; and if such application be refused, or neglected, then the case goes forward on its own merits, to the judgment, and there the criminal stands alone, surrounded by the evidences of his guilt, but isolated in it from the whole universe of God, with none to befriend or deliver him. The judgment being set, the witnesses summoned, the assizes opened, he has had his choice, his voluntary disposition of all things, and there can be no change; and the very fact of no Advocate appearing in his behalf, were there no other positive evidence against him except the accusation, would be sufficient for his condemnation. He must stand alone, with innumerable participators in his guilt, indeed, and accessories to it, and accusers of it, but not one defender; alone, without an advocate, in utter despair. Alone, cut off from God, overwhelmed with the conviction of sin, and unable to open his lips except to cry out guilty before God!

And the Judge in this case! Who is he? How shall we describe his appearance, his attributes? We have supposed a case, and it is the reality; but we can take the description only from God's word. "And I saw heaven opened, and behold a white horse; and He that sat upon him was called Faithful and True, and in righteousness He doth judge and make war. His eyes were as a flame of fire, and on His head were many crowns; and He had a name written that no man knew but Himself. And He was clothed with a vesture dipped in blood; and His name is called the Word of God. And out of His mouth goeth a sharp sword, and He treadeth the wine-press of the fierceness and wrath of Almighty God. And He hath on His vesture and on His thigh a name written, King of kings and Lord of lords."

Can we recognize the Person of this description? Have we ever seen or imagined this King of wrath and glory, or has He ever been revealed to us in any other character? Have we seen Him, have we fled to Him, as our Advocate and Intercessor with the Father, our Redeemer and not our Judge alone? "Behold He cometh in the clouds, and every eye shall see Him, and they also which pierced Him; and then shall all the kindreds of the earth wail because of Him." Look back once more to the most sublime of all the visions of the Prophets, whose subject is the judgment of the last day, and compare the burning imagery of the Old Testament with the answering flames of the New. "I beheld till the flames were cast down, and the Ancient of Days did sit, whose garment was white as snow, and the hair of His head like the pure wool; His throne was like the fiery flame, and His wheels as burning fire. A fiery stream issued and came forth from before Him: thousand thousands ministered unto Him, and ten thousand times ten thousand stood before Him: the judgment was set, and the books were opened." "When the Son of Man shall come in His glory, and all the holy angels with Him, then shall He sit upon the throne of His glory, and before Him shall be gathered all nations. And He shall separate them one from another, as a shepherd divideth his sheep from the goats; and He shall set the sheep on His right hand, but the goats on His left. And He shall say to them upon His right hand, Come, ye blessed, but to them upon His left hand, Depart, ye cursed. And these shall go away into everlasting punishment, but the righteous into life eternal."

Thus far God himself has guided and rendered both possible and lawful the excursions of the human imagination in regard to the Judge at the last day, and the unparalleled scenes of the judgment. Farther no eye can pierce, no mind can follow, till that day when the Lord Jesus shall be revealed from heaven with His mighty angels, in flaming fire, taking vengeance on them that know not God, and that obey not the gospel of our Lord Jesus Christ. Till then, He stands in the midst of the seven golden candlesticks, for the redemption of mankind. But even in that position of forgiving mercy, how august, how glorious, and to be feared with holy fear by those who love Him. "His head and His hairs white like wool, as white as snow, and His eyes as a flame of fire, and His feet like unto fine brass, as if they burned in a furnace, and His countenance as the sun shining on His strength, and His voice as the sound of many waters."

From the Judge we turn, under the guidance of God's word, in the midst of this awful and glorious scene, to the accuser. This is none other than the Divine Law itself, in all its majesty. It has a two-fold office of indictment and conviction; that of the guilt of man for breaking the great moral law of God revealed on Sinai, and that of his guilt in the rejection of Christ and His words in the gospel. "Do not think," said Christ to the Jews who did not believe on Him, "that I will accuse you to the Father. There is one that accuseth you, even Moses, in whom ye trust. For had ye believed Moses, ye would have believed me, for he wrote of me." Even so the law, in its original charge against us, and conviction, and penalty of death upon us, is our schoolmaster, to bring us to Christ. But if it fail of that—if we reject Christ, whether trusting in the law that we have broken, and in a miserable, patched-up morality of pretended obedience to it, or, in utter insensibility and heedlessness both of the law and the gospel, disregarding Christ, and so rejecting Him,—then the law also accuses the soul in regard to such rejection. God's law, both in the Old and New Testament, one and the same, the law of precepts and the law of love, makes the accusation. It comes down upon the soul; and by it is the knowledge of sin, and every mouth is stopped, and all the world becomes guilty before God. And the greater the knowledge of sin by the glory and clear-shining holiness of the law, the greater the guilt of the soul, and the showing of that guilt, in the rejection of the Saviour. If it were iniquity to break God's law, what incomparably greater guilt, when the law itself pointed to a Saviour provided of God for redemption from the guilt and the consequences of such violation!—what incomparably greater guilt to set at nought that salvation, to trample on the claims of the Divine Redeemer as well as the Divine Law—nay, as God's word sets the guilt of such rejection forth, to trample under foot the Son of God! If they who despised Moses' law died without mercy, under two or three witnesses, of how much sorer punishment, suppose ye, shall he be thought worthy who hath trodden under foot the Son of God, and counted the blood of the covenant an unholy thing, and done despite unto the Spirit of grace? And this is the guilt of every rejection of Christ Jesus, under whatever circumstances. Call it what you please, disguise or mask or flatter it as you will, it comes to this; it is the climax of human guilt; it is the last, preponderating, overwhelming act and proof of man's depravity against the love, as well as the majesty and holiness of God.

And now, do we want confirmation of all this? Is proof needed at the judgment? The criminal himself is stricken with despair, guilty before God. The law only need appear against him, and it condemns and silences him. Its bare accusation is awful, irresistible proof; he is struck down by it.

But is there a *manifestation* needed, a judge and a judgment of his guilt, in the very showing of the law under which and against which he acted, such as will fill all minds with a conviction as deep and abiding as eternity, as outshining and glorious as the holiness of God? We suppose there is; we suppose, indeed, that this is one great object of a day of judgment, to vindicate, in the sight of all the universe, the ways of God to man. We suppose that its processes will be conducted with reference to this very purpose. Accordingly, the original evidence shall be called up. Against *what* has the criminal sinned? What was the light that shone upon him? What the manifestation of the Divine glory that stood in his way? And as to the last completion and seal of his iniquity, its highest possible development in this world, and its seal of unchangeableness and perpetuity in the eternal world, in the rejection of the only and infinitely merciful remedy offered from heaven, what is the demonstration of that? "He that rejecteth me," says Christ, "and receiveth not my words, hath one that judgeth him. The WORD that I have spoken, the same shall judge him in the last day."

Let, then, the universe hear that. Let its glory be seen by bright intelligences. Let Him speak again, who spake as never man spake. Let the beauty and the power of his teachings, and the loveliness and compassion of his example, and the tenderness of his invitations and promises, be spread before the universe of souls. Let him be heard saying, "Come unto me all ye that labor and are heavy laden, and

I will give you rest." Let the law appear in the glory of its transcript of God's holiness and goodness, and the gospel in its thrilling manifestation of the wonders of God's forgiving love. Then shall it be seen that against all that light, love, and mercy, against all that tide of tenderness and expostulation, and the current of providence and grace, the sinful man pursued his way down to ruin. It shall be seen that though the blood of the Lamb of God stood before him, he trampled over it; that though the merciful and gentle Spirit of God warned him, and strove with him, he heeded it not; that when the sword of the Spirit was flashing the terrors of God's law upon his soul, it was of no avail, nor of any avail all his experience of the goodness of God's leading him to repentance. It shall be seen to be his condemnation, that light came into the world, and into his soul, but that he loved darkness. It shall be seen that by that light the things into which the angels in heaven desire to look, and by the wonderful glory of which they are ravished, were shown to him, but he cared not for *them.* That though the attributes of God in the cross of Christ were demonstrated to him, as intense, eternal, and unalterable against sin, he cared not for *that;* that though the transcendent spectacle of a dying Saviour, the incarnate Son of God, lifted up for *him*, was shown him, he cared not for *that;* that when a thousand times it was shown him that on his acceptance of this Redeemer hung his last and only hope of forgiving mercy from his God, and that his contempt and rejection of this divine effort would seal him up to inevitable and eternal guilt and misery, still he received Him not.

All these warnings, restrainings, converting influences, were in the word, and all this demonstration of guilt arises out of it; the conviction of ingratitude, of selfishness, of unbelief, of ambition, of the pride of evil, and the fear of man, and the shame and disregard of good men and of God, and the treasuring up of wrath against the day of wrath, and revelation of God's righteous judgments. And it will be found that in the midst of all his darkness the Word of God followed him; that in misery it got hold upon him; that in the visions of the night it terrified him; that in a thousand forms it was laid before him; that good men and good books, and the prayers of saints, and the providence of God, brought it home to him; that it lodged in his conscience, and was an element there, of which he endeavored in vain to rid himself, but never could exclude it from his being; that it was ever pressing him to God, while he himself was pressing farther from Him; that it set him on fire round about but he knew it not; that it drew him to the light, but he would not follow. The demonstration of his guilt from the word of God will be as clear as God's own holiness, and as definite as the actions of his life.

Oh guilty, dying sinner! Thou must have an Advocate with God, or thou art lost forever! What canst thou do, in the day when He shall reckon with thee? Thou art advancing to thy trial; hast thou retained thy counsel? There is one appointed Advocate, whom thou mayest have without retaining fee, and mayest put thy whole cause securely in His hands, and He (Oh wondrous mystery of grace!) will justify thee! yea, JUSTIFY thee before God, thou guilty, dying sinner! Wilt thou trust thyself with Him? Wilt thou tell Him all the secrets of thine heart? Wilt thou let Him intercede for thee?

Friend of sinners! Wonderful, Counsellor, Advocate, both of the government and the criminal! Yea, appointed of God to be a Prince and a Saviour, to give repentance and the remission of sins! Oh that every heart would hide in Him, would trust Him, would love Him, would receive His glad salvation!

The things Written in the Books.

In the last revealed exposition of the judgment we see the dead, small and great, stand before God; and the books are opened, "And another book was opened which is the book of life. And the dead were judged out of those things which were written in the books, according to their works."

It may be that this is not figurative language. It is commonly so regarded, at least that part of it which speaks of books. But we know nothing which should prevent us from interpreting even that with a degree of literal simplicity. Not that any man would dream of there being books at the judgment made out of perishable matter, and bound with parchment, any more than a sane mind would expect to find palaces or streets of solid gold in the New Jerusalem. But there may be a literal record, in form and space, of the life of every creature, answering to our idea of the reality of a book, which shall truly be opened at the judgment, and be there used in determining the eternal sentence of every individual.

It may be said that the Divine Omniscience is of itself such a book; but in the passages which speak of this matter, there is manifestly a special record by that Omniscience referred to, which special record is to be opened in form. And who can tell but that every attitude of his moral being, every movement of his heart, his will, his affections, as well as every word of his lips, and every action of his life, goes down, by some mysterious arrangement, spontaneously into such a record? There may be a series of moral and spiritual daguerreotypes thus perpetually drawn from every intelligent creature, by as fixed a spiritual necessity as the physical arrangement by which the sun inevitably draws the picture of the face upon the plate prepared for it. And as that picture is drawn without any disguise or mistake, exactly as the face is, in whatever position it happens to be, or with whatever expression it happens to wear, so with the series of pictures or reproductions of our moral selves, our elements of character, our habits of action, our attitudes of thought, feeling, expression, which go into God's book for the judgment, out of which, when it is filled up, can be read at a glance the whole character and destiny of the individual.

Let us, then, look for a moment, first at the contents of this book of God as a book of character; also at the certainty with which, supposing it were opened beforehand, even in this world, the end could be predicted from its tenor; and again at the only cause or agency by which its condemning tenor can be changed into mercy. Our life, then, under the operation of the Divine Omniscience, becomes a solemn book, on the leaves of which are written, though invisibly to mortals, the processes of our real existence, the goings on of our inward, hidden being, the movements of real, undissembled, absolute character and motive. Our appearance in the eyes of men, our actions with the world, our life which the world notices, occupies but little of the writing in this book. By far the greater part is taken up with the processes of a life which men do not and cannot see, which God only sees fully and clearly, and of which we ourselves seldom read more than one page at a time. For though no part of the writing in this book goes into it without our consciousness, yet the moment it is there, the moment it is recorded as a development that has actually taken place in and of our nature, we forget it, and pass on to the next. Every fact, every development in it is indestructible, is eternal. Every event, every thought, every feeling of our existence, every passion, every wish, every impulse, is a part of ourselves, a part of our character, a part of our actual life, a part of the evidence by which we are to be judged, a part of the realities with which the book is filled, for us or against us. A thought once conceived, a feeling once indulged or experienced, a word once spoken, a movement or event once acted, goes down into the record, cannot be withdrawn from it, cannot be obliterated; may now be invisible, but it is perpetual, is laid up for the judgment. It may be invisible now to every eye but God's, and yet it is visible now, whenever our own consciousness, the notice from ourselves, which was present when it was acted, when it first went into being, is again fixed upon it. And that may be at any time, and in a manner the most unexpected. The consciousness is sometimes carried back to a single word or feeling in the pages of this book even after the lapse of years, and there it pauses, bringing out the letters as in fire, reading them as clearly as if the hand had this moment traced them, and remembering the very atmosphere of character connected with them.

Every letter in this book is preserved, every letter is important. The minutest processes of thought, the evanescent shades of feeling, the succession of uttered words, that seem almost as swift, as idle, as without law, and as countless, as the trembling and whispering of the leaves, when the wind breathes over a vast forest, must all be put down, all go to make up the whole meaning, all are parts of that mysterious, sacred, immutable, awful, eternal reality, called character. I write immutable, because, when the book is filled, there shall be no change forever. The very last entry or record made in it *in this world* may change the whole for eternity; *may* possibly, by the grace of Christ, do this, as in the case even of the thief upon the cross, when that last development, the last dying breath of the wind of life over the forest,—Lord remember me when thou comest into thy kingdom,—changed the character of the whole book of the existence of that immortal being for the judgment. But when the last stir, the last whisper, upon the leaves has passed, the book is finished, and character is immutable, eternal. And ordinarily, nay, almost always, the last entry made in the book, the last recorded syllable, is just as was the preceding, just follows in the train of habit and of life written down in all the previous pages.

And again, because immutable, I have written awful. Yes! the reality of character, fixed for eternal duration, is a most solemn and awful contemplation. There is no idea in the whole compass of our conceptions more solemn than that of character. What you are now, what you have been thus far through life, in all likelihood you will be through eternity. We say in all likelihood, because, if you are now an unconverted soul, then, judging from all human experience, and from your own habitual neglect thus far, of the opportunities of change, the probability is that you will not change before you die. And what you are when you die, you will be, not in all likelihood, but in all certainty, through eternity. There is, therefore, nothing more solemn than the contemplation of character, nothing more intensely interesting than to watch its development.

We have said that every letter in the book is preserved. There may be actions, there may be words, there may be thoughts and feelings, so seemingly idle, so shadowy, so evanescent as the summer lightning, in a man's existence, as by themselves to seem of no importance; but they all go to spell some words, and the words go to make up sentences, and the sentences complete the book, and make up the final sentence at the judgment. There may be interjections and glancings and points of thought and language, almost as meaningless and characterless by themselves, as the fount of type distributed in the printer's cases; but when they come to be set up together, and copied in the book, even a comma gives meaning. And therefore it is said by our blessed Lord that for every idle word that men shall speak, they shall give account thereof in the Day of Judgment. Letters form syllables, syllables form words, and words are connected by points so minute, that a hundred of them together might not form a single syllable; but their position fills them with meaning. It is not their greatness in themselves, but the place in which you see them in the book, that gives them interest, makes them of consequence. And so it is with the almost invisible, imperceptible tenor of men's words and fancies, the current of men's unmarked, unnoticed life. Even a comma gives meaning, and a word that seems idle now, may be found, when you read the impression it makes in its own place, set in connection, to be very far from idle, nay, to have some deep and solemn meaning, or to throw an important light upon some other train of meaning. Sometimes things that seem as evanescent as the flashes of heat lightning in a summer's night, reveal a whole horizon of character in an instant; just as in a single flash from amidst the darkness you may see revealed, with almost the distinctness of day, trees, buildings, mountains, and the whole line where earth separates from heaven.

The materials of character lie in our being and habits, distributed apparently without law or order, as a superficial observer might suppose, just as the type in a printing office seems scattered without meaning. But there is a law of character, a law of development, by which they are set up; the evolutions of our being put them daily, hourly into shape, into publication, and then comes their record in the Book; then they are indestructible, eternal, and full of meaning. That record is as clear and correct as the eye of Omniscience. No mistake is ever possible. The sun does not strike upon the plate of a daguerreotype a reflection of the image set against it with half the unerring precision, with which our thoughts, words, feelings, our whole elements of being, character themselves, register them selves, engrave themselves, in that Book for eternity. The clear white paper does not receive the impression from the type forced upon it, with half the exactness or power, with which the Book of character receives and preserves, in unmistakable, indelible identity, the whole image, or reproduction, of the minutest processes of our being.

No syllable nor idle word can be lost. But even if it could, even if there were not this infinite, and to a wicked mind, intolerable exactitude of a reproduction; even if there were no greater accuracy than that with which the human mind can turn off its own creations, calculations and processes of thought, and numberings of event, by mere material machinery, with the perishable visible qualities of ink and type; even then there could be no material mistake. Though a word be lost, and even whole sentences, you may almost invariably determine their purport unerringly by the context. Even manuscripts almost illegible, may be clearly decyphered by the skill of man, and lost inscriptions may be restored, in a manner that leaves no doubt whatever in any mind in regard to their meaning. And so in the context of a man's life, when it has flowed on for a few pages, you could not only guess, but might read unerringly the meaning not only of words, but even of sentences here and there lost or illegible.

And if God should open to you the Book of Judgment, that invisible record of which we have been speaking, and make its pages visible to you only for a little distance; if he should show you what is already written down in the record of any man's life up to the present moment, you could predict yourself, with unerring certainty, from that part alone, what the tenor of the next page will be, except for only one cause, one possible change that may be effected. One cause put out of view, you could tell as unerringly that the next page of existence will be of the same moral tenor as the past, as if you stood in futurity on the eternal side of the page, and read it as already past. One cause only excepted, and there runs through the record of a man's existence an inalienable despotism and identity of impression and law of character from beginning to end, from time into eternity. It is the law of sin and of death in our corrupt nature, which you are as sure will come out and be reproduced in every successive page of existence, and rule the whole, except for one cause, as you are that you have already seen its development in any one page or sentence. The beginning is declarative of the way, and the way of every man is declarative of the end of that man. You may not only predict with dread certainty that the next page of life turned over, and noted down, will be the same with all the past, but you can predict and read the end, as certainly as if you stood at the end; as certainly as if God placed you by the dying sinner's bed, with your ear so close to his departing spirit, that not even a breath of impulse or feeling in his soul could stir unknown.

Except for one cause you know that the soul of the man whose life, as it is written for the judgment, God has opened before you thus far, showing you that it has run on hitherto without God, without prayer, without an element of life indicated in it, will enter on the eternal world and pass to the eternal judgment, and be engulphed in the eternal destiny, just as hopeless and prayerless and lifeless as it has lived, with just the same elements of character and none different, with just the same ceaseless and determined absence and rejection of all the life of heaven, and just the same adherence and immutable despotism of the death of sin.

And now, what is this one cause? What is that solitary interposition, the possibility of which throws a bare single uncertainty into a calculation otherwise unerring, a prediction otherwise as sure as if the Eternal himself had uttered it? What is that principle, or mighty agent, that can or may possibly interfere, and change the tenor of that book of character and judgment, which you have thus far read with the most perfect conviction that this man's life is flowing on to inevitable perdition? Perhaps there may have been not even an indication of any such agency, not a solitary trace of the effort or operation or existence of any such principle, in all the almost countless variety of impulses, thoughts, feelings, plans, desires, expectations, efforts, attainments, disappointments, developments of character, which you have been perusing. Perhaps, amidst all that variety of selfish, sinful development, and all the succession of events and changes, and trials of God's providence upon the soul, there may have been one unvaried continuity of hardness of heart, and insensibility and carelessness of mind, in regard to all considerations drawn from the eternal world; an abandonment and destitution of all feeling, all alarm, all anxiety on the only subject on which the soul of man ought to be anxious, while on every other subject it is full of interest. And if so; if this insensibility has become the habit of the soul, of which you are reading the development thus far, to judge of its character and end for the future; and if you can trace no presence or effect of a higher power, life and effort, than that of the law of sin and of death in this fast ripening nature, then you have double reason to conclude that there never will be a change, but that this nature will go on developing as before, and is only fulfilling and ripening for endless ruin.

But it is scarcely possible to find such a case; it is scarcely possible but that there must be, in some part of the record of this individual life, this development of character, and of influences for its formation, some trace of the presence of that agency, some proof of the working of that principle, which alone is to change, if it ever be changed, the tenor of this record for the judgment. And indeed, if you look carefully, you will see in ten thousand instances in the chain of events, circumstances, providences, causes, trials and blessings, prosperous and adverse discipline traced through the book, the undoubted presence and effort of a heavenly agency, the indications of a cause working to turn the current of the man's being, if possible, towards heaven.

You will find seasons of warning, of visitation, of solemnity—you will find the record of innumerable interpositions, both of Providence and grace—you will find the history of seasons, in which seed was sown that had almost taken root and sprung up in the man's character, to bear fruit to life everlasting. You will find, above all, the solemn record of the man's Sabbaths of mercy, and of the course of his feelings and experiences beneath them, and of the manner in which he turned aside from them unchanged, and withdrew his soul away from their merciful influences; and as you see how, year after year, he came up to them, passed through them all, and entered again into the world a prayerless, unchanged man, you will feel with a deeper and deeper solemnity that the man's prospect of ever being changed is smaller and smaller, and the certainty of his going on to the end of his career as he has thus far pursued it, greater and greater. You begin to see that that agency which alone could defeat the certainty of your prediction as to the end of that man, has manifestly been at work already, and been successfully resisted. You will perhaps meet with the record even of precious revivals of religion, set down in the book of this man's character for the judgment, and all the experiences of his soul in the midst of them—experiences of God's warning and gracious providences, and offers of the most inestimable kind.

And if you meet with *one* such season, where the converting influences of God's Spirit have been descending on the souls of others around this man, but have had no effect upon him, leaving him, to say the least, just as hardened and careless as before, you will think that the possibility of an interposition *now* in his case, to change the whole tenor of his character, and make a new record for the judgment, even the record of faith in Christ, of a holy sorrow for sin, of heartfelt repentance, of forgiveness and eternal life, is indeed faint. You will feel that the way of this man is declarative of the end of this man; and that, in all probability, the next page of the journal for eternity which you have been perusing will be of the same hopeless tenor as the last; and that just thus the record will go on, till the last day of life, with its mercies, is wasted, and the last leaf of character filled up, unchanged, for the eternal world.

But it is time to change the argument from supposition to reality, and to turn the glass through which we have been gazing at the book of another's destiny in upon ourselves. May there not possibly be readers of these very pages, whose individual consciousness recognizes and claims the portrait as their own? Are there not those, whose consciences say distinctly and undeniably, Thou art the man, and this is the prediction of thy destiny. If you have not yourself fled to the Redeemer of your soul to have *your* name entered as a penitent in his book of Life, whose character have you been reading thus far in God's book of Judgment? Is it not your own, in forgetfulness of God, in procrastination, in neglect of your eternal interests, in resistance against the Holy Ghost, in the waste of innumerable opportunities, in presumptuous sins against the Divine mercy, in hardness, insensibility and unbelief?

And what now is the prediction of your own destiny, and what think you in your own case of the principle that the character and way of a man is declarative of the end of that man? Is it not as certain as that the sun shines, that you will continue, unless you cry out for God's mercy, unless you seek the arresting and renewing power of God's grace, that you will continue just in this dreadful neglect of all opportunities of grace, till the book of your character is filled up entirely for the judgment, till the last moment of your life comes, without one element which is not an element against you, without one, which is not an element of sin and death? Oh then, if you entertain the least thought of salvation, have mercy on your own soul! Let it not pass on any longer in life beneath such a prophesy of death, beneath such a tremendous weight of evidence for your destruction. Rest not, till you get some element besides your sin and condemnation in the book of Judgment. If there be not the element of love to Christ, of faith in Christ, of reliance on Christ, of sorrow for sin, if there be not the element of repentance and prayer, there is nothing there, which is not utter desperation, which will not banish you forever from heaven, which will not whelm you in inevitable ruin.

Now, in more than a dream, as you look over your past life, God opens to you the book of Judgment; but thus far, if you have not repented of your sins, it is for you the book of guilt and ruin, the book of exclusion from Heaven, and the title-deed of your soul to the world of woe! But praised be God, it is not yet filled up, there are pages in it yet unwritten. What shall be the tenor of the next page, even if one day's leaf still remains for your will, your character, to turn over? To think of its being at your own disposal, to fill up, as you will, for Eternity! If now you will but write CHRIST'S name there, and write your own name beneath it, though yours is the name of a poor, guilty, lost sinner, a worthless name, yet if you put it there as your own humble believing signature, God will put it with Christ's own name in his book of Life. And then the whole nature of this book of Judgment shall be changed for you from a book of only sin and misery to a book of grace and glory! Let it be written on this page in your history, that there was weeping and prayer on earth, and joy in heaven over one sinner that repenteth!

The Resurrection of the Just.

IN the affirmation of things revealed to faith, and received on the ground solely of the word of God, the sacred writers always assume them as absolute knowledge. There is no shadow of doubt admitted or intimated. So with the disclosure of the resurrection of the just. The link by which the argument of Divine truth is fastened to its practical conclusion of duty is just this—*forasmuch as ye know.* The encouragement, the animation, the impulse to duty, is not hope merely, but knowledge. The apostle speaks, at the close of the great resurrection-chapter, given to him for the church, in a firm, unhesitating manner, as of a thing demonstrated, and not to be questioned.

Then, again, the point or period where this assurance of reward for all the labor of the righteous in Christ Jesus has its termination, its fulfillment, is to be considered; the vista, through which the mind of the writer runs on to far distant ages, stopping nowhere short of the final coming of the Lord in glory and for judgment. Ye KNOW that your labor is not in vain in the Lord. But it was not from any present victory or success, not from anything in the saints' then present experience, or even earnest, of the inheritance of glory; for they were then passing through great trial, and were regarded as the off-scouring of creation; and it was not by any appeal to sight, or proof from sense, that the conclusion was established, but wholly by faith, founded on God's word, God's promises, through the cross, death, and resurrection of the Saviour, bringing future eternal glories near, as known, undoubted realities.

BECAUSE CHRIST HAS DIED AND RISEN AGAIN. This is the whole and sole foundation laid by the apostle; and this stupendous fact once admitted, that He, who was in the beginning with God, and who was God, and who is God over all blessed forever, became man, God manifest in the flesh, suffering, dying, rising, we KNOW that the purposes of God in this amazing transaction cannot fail. Whatever object God had in view in the incarnation, death, and resurrection of the Lord of life and glory, must be accomplished. There is no more possibility of a failure, than there is that Jehovah should abdicate the throne of the universe. The blindest faith may find light here, and the deepest despondency may be encouraged here, in this one fact, undiscoverable, unimaginable, but by Divine revelation, that Christ, the incarnate Son of God, has died. It is the central fact of all our knowing; it is as a sun shot into the chaos of human speculation, and a radiance spreads from it through infinitude, and a power is in it vivifying all knowledge. The discovery of the law of gravitation was not so simplifying and explanatory in the theory of the physical universe, as the knowledge of the death of Christ, by Divine revelation, in the moral universe. If we believe this fact as God has revealed it, then we know that all God's promises, made with respect to this fact, and on the ground of it, are sure; they are all yea and amen in Christ Jesus. They all hang and hinge upon this fact, cluster and revolve around it, and derive their life and activity from it. Whatever else *might* fail, nothing that is attached to the cross of Christ *can* fail.

Now, as to the nature of the resurrection, as a demonstration grounded on this transaction, we may find it briefly summed up in a passage in the Epistle of Paul to the Thessalonians: "For if we believe that Jesus died and rose again, even so them also which sleep in Jesus will God bring with Him." This constitutes the whole argument in the fifteenth chapter of the First Epistle of Paul to the Corinthians, the dying and rising again of Jesus. By Him is the resurrection of the dead. For this purpose He both died and rose again, that believers in Him, having died to sin and risen in holiness, might rise also from the dead unto life everlasting. The resurrection of the dead is to be the great revelation of the Divine glory; it will be the scene in which all the processes of grace and of God's providential wisdom, that have been drawing on silently and in concealment, will come to their most glorious outbreaking development before the whole universe. Till that day everything lies hidden, or in germs, or like the processes of a living vegetation under ground. Before that day, the very providences of

God are as seed sown, and preparing, out of sight, to rise into light and glory. There can be no conception, beforehand, of the greatness of that glory.

If a man that had never seen in its blossoming perfection that plant that blooms but once in a hundred years, were to look upon the rough stem, or uncouth leaves of the tree, could he form the least conception of the consummate loveliness of the flower, when it shall appear, the exquisite beauty and grace to be developed? If any man had lived all his days in a twilight prison, or subterranean cave, and had never beheld the sunrise, could he have the least imagination of the glory of that scene? But far less can it come within the scope of a human intellect to behold in the seed-corn of God's operations the infinite glory of the future, or to conceive the nature of that scene, when the Lord Jesus shall be revealed from heaven with his mighty angels, to be glorified in his saints, and to be admired in all who believe. The resurrection itself is a transaction of inconceivable, incomprehensible power and glory. The time when it takes place is the time of the Redeemer's second coming. Hence "the coming of the Lord," and "the appearing of the Lord," being connected, in the minds of the disciples, with such glorious expectations, came to be the signal phrases, by which they described the consummation of all things in God's scheme of redemption. When the Saviour cometh in the clouds of heaven, and all the holy angels with Him, he cometh to raise the dead, and to judge all nations. When Paul says that those also who sleep in Jesus will God bring with Him, he means that the dead in Christ shall be raised, and carried into heaven to be forever with the Lord. In nearly all his epistles he presents the same great fact, as the great ground of encouragement and joy, and sometimes in a logical strain not unlike the one in the great resurrection chapter to the Corinthians.

This also is in fact the grand heart of that triumphant chapter, the eighth of the epistle to the Romans. If the Spirit of Him that raised up Jesus from the dead dwell in you, He that raised up Christ from the dead shall also quicken your mortal bodies by his Spirit that dwelleth in you. And the triumphant strain in the second epistle to the Corinthians has the same key-note, the same theme, the same conclusion. "We, having the same spirit of faith, according as it is written, I believed, and therefore have I spoken, we also believe, and therefore speak; knowing that He which raised up the Lord Jesus, shall raise up us also by Jesus, and shall present us with you. For all things are for your sakes, that the abundant grace might through the thanksgiving of many redound to the glory of God. For which cause we faint not, knowing that our light affliction worketh for us a far more exceeding and eternal weight of glory, and that when the earthly house of this tabernacle is dissolved, we have a building of God, a house not made with hands, eternal in the heavens."

To the same purport is the great passage in the epistle to the Philippians. "For our conversation is in heaven, from whence also we look for the Saviour, the Lord Jesus Christ, who shall change our vile bodies, that they may be fashioned like unto his glorious body, according to the working whereby he is able to subdue all things unto himself." These different passages are like the ground waves in a vast deep sea, or like the tidal movement of the whole body of waters under a heavenly orb. The tide of emotion, in faith, hope, joy, love, rolls up in one and the same mighty argument, addressed to different minds, at different times, yet always for the whole church of Christ, and with the same conclusion. In the fifteenth chapter of the first epistle to the Corinthians the argument is drawn out into greater detail than anywhere else, not only as to the raising of the dead, but as to the kind of body with which the dead are to be invested. It is sown in corruption, it is raised in incorruption; it is sown in dishonor, it is raised in glory; it is sown in weakness, it is raised in power; it is sown a material body, it is raised a spiritual body. Its model is the Lord from heaven; for as is the heavenly, such are they also that are heavenly; and as we have borne the image of the earthly, we shall also bear the image of the heavenly. For this corruptible must put on incorruption, and this mortal must put on immortality. So when this corruptible shall have put on incorruption, and this mortal shall have put on immortality, then shall be brought to pass the saying that is written, Death is swallowed up in victory! O Death where is thy sting, O grave where is thy victory!

Now we are to remark that all this is not the mere resurrection, but the resurrection into the image and likeness of Jesus Christ. The two things are widely different, although the one is not to be conceived apart from the other, and both are merged in one and the same mighty event of Christ's coming. The bare raising of the dead is not the thing which is so much insisted on in the New Testament, as perhaps the mightiest to us conceivable exercise of God's power; but the raising of the dead in the glory of Christ Jesus; that is, the righteous dead, those who sleep in Jesus, to the possession, in body as well as spirit, of a sonship of God that shall make them joint heirs with Christ, to be glorified together with Him. The earnest expectation of the creature waiteth for *that* manifestation of the Son of God. And we ourselves also, says the Apostle, who have the first fruits of the Spirit, even we ourselves groan within ourselves, waiting for the adoption, to wit, the redemption of our body. It is not the *resurrection* of our body, but the redemption, which certainly includes the great reality and consummation of glory in the possessed and perpetual likeness of Christ. All before that is but the earnest of an inheritance *until* the redemption of the purchased possession unto the praise of His glory. The bare raising of the dead is not a thing so difficult or impossible to conceive, nor does it seem to us the most amazing exercise of Divine power conceivable; but the investment of our immortal being, and change of our mortal, with this spiritual and glorified body like unto Christ's is referred to as an exercise of Divine power, so entirely beyond the possibility of conception by the human mind natively, that the Apostle prays for an inspiration, baptism and illumination from above, "that ye may know what is the hope of his calling, and what the riches of the glory of his inheritance in the saints, and what the exceeding greatness of his power to usward who believe, according to the working of His mighty power which He wrought in Christ, when He raised Him from the dead, and set Him at His own right hand in the heavenly places, far above all principality and power and might and dominion, and every name that is named, not only in this world, but also in that which is to come; and hath put all things under His feet, and gave Him to be the head over all things to the church, which is His body, the fulness of Him that filleth all in all."

Now, sitting down before this last passage, if we endeavor to analyze the elements, and sound its depths of meaning, we speedily find that there are involved in it ideas and processes not only sweeping the whole universe of God, but rising to the ineffable and incommunicable perfections of Jehovah, in that light inaccessible and full of glory, to which no creature can approach nor hath seen, nor can see. And yet this infinite glory of God in Christ Jesus, and this exercise of infinite Divine power in His resurrection and ascension at the right hand of the Father, is presented as the type by which, and according to which, to measure the glory of the redemption of our body. We must consider, therefore, that there is here a transference from the grave of mortal flesh to the throne of eternity, a transference of a human being, not indeed ever at any moment separate from the Divine, but the transference still of the Man Christ Jesus, raised from the dead, past all orders of intelligences, angels, archangels, principalities, powers, thrones, dominions, almost infinite on infinite, past them all, to the very throne of God, for it is the throne of God and of the Lamb, to which He is exalted; the transference, or transfiguration *and* transference, of a body that lay in the tomb, quickened, glorified, beyond, *far beyond*, all forms of glory and of power, and all possible conception of such forms, that had ever been created, up to a glory and a lordship, such as the Eternal Word had with the Father before the world was. Considering this, we perceive the need of a baptism of the soul by the spirit of wisdom and revelation in the knowledge of Christ, before we can begin to understand the greatness of such a transaction. And considering this, we begin to comprehend how unsearchable, how incomprehensible is the exercise and manifestation of the same Divine power in us, according to the working of that mighty power in the resurrection and enthroning of Christ with the majesty of Supreme Deity, the same Divine power in us, according to that pattern; even the investiture of all the redeemed in Christ, with the same likeness and life out of the embrace of death, enthroned in glory everlasting!

If now we wish for a still more direct confirmation of this theory, a more explicit proof of this being the definite sense to be put upon this passage, we have but to turn to that wondrous promise in the third chapter of the Revelation of John, where our

Saviour says, To him that overcometh will I grant to sit with me in my throne, even as I also overcame, and am set down with my Father in His throne. What is here meant no man can tell this side the grave, any more than John could tell what the being a joint heir with Christ meant, when he said, It doth not yet appear what we shall be, but we know that when He shall appear, we shall be like Him, for we shall see Him as He is. But *that* is meant, whatever it be, which the Apostle prays, in such strong and fervent language for grace to understand, that which is shadowed forth in the description of the mighty power of God, when Christ Jesus himself was raised from the dead, and seated on the throne of eternity. His prayer is, that the God of our Lord Jesus Christ, the Father of Glory, may give unto you the spirit of wisdom and revelation in the knowledge of Him, the eyes of your understanding being enlightened, that ye may know what is the hope of His calling, and what the riches of the glory of His inheritance in the saints, and what the exceeding greatness of His power to usward who believe, according to the greatness of His mighty power which He wrought in Christ, when he raised Him from the dead, and set Him at His own right hand, in the heavenly places. The illumination, divine, supernatural, by the Holy Spirit, is here prayed for, that we may know something of this glory here and now, even in this mortal state, that it may not be to us as a succession of unknown hieroglyphics, but revealed to our hearts at least, by the Spirit; but to know it absolutely and perfectly here, is impossible, and therefore there is here just such a hyperbole of thought, logic, expression, as in that other wondrous prayer, that we might comprehend with all saints what is the length and depth and breadth and height, and know the love of Christ, *which passeth knowledge*, and be filled with all the fullness of God. In either case, in both cases, it passes knowledge indeed; and what definitely is meant, we cannot know, till we ourselves, and Christ in us, and we in Christ, are revealed in eternity. A meaning in any sense answering to those amazing words of God and promises of Christ, a meaning in any sense corresponding to that astonishing declaration, that Christ Jesus, who is now seated on the throne of the universe, will give to the overcoming believer to sit down with Him on His throne, as He is seated with the Father on *His* throne, must surpass the possibility of our present faculties and state to know, and must shadow forth a glory utterly beyond our conception. And we are reminded by such expressions of the declaration of the inspired Apostle concerning even himself and his fellow Christians, that now we know only in part, and that here we see only as through a glass darkly. It is not *dimly* that we see, but in fact, in comparison with that which is to be seen, in comparison with the excess of glory and of light soon to be revealed, we see *darkly!* What then will it be, when we know even as we are known!

Awakening in God's Likeness.

In the fifteenth verse of the seventeenth Psalm, David exclaims, "I shall be satisfied, when I awake, with thy likeness. I will behold thy face in righteousness." In the 15th verse of the 49th Psalm David says, speaking of the universal death of mankind, "But God will redeem my soul from the power of the grave, *for he shall receive me.*" This is precisely similar to the language of the 73d Psalm, "Thou shalt guide me with thy counsel, and afterwards receive me to glory.' Before this reception into glory there comes the sleep of death. The repose of the grave is before the resurrection, and the resurrection is not from death merely, but from the grave. Death, and the lying down in the grave, are as a sleep, from which the resurrection is an awakening. This was Job's and David's conception of it; this was Paul's exhibition of it. Paul loved to present death as a quiet, peaceful slumber in the Lord. "I would not have you to be ignorant, brethren, concerning them which are asleep, that ye sorrow not, even as others which have no hope. For if we believe that Jesus died and rose again, even so, them also which sleep in

Jesus will God bring with him. He that raised up Christ from the dead shall also quicken your mortal bodies by his spirit that dwelleth in you." They that sleep in Jesus are to be raised by virtue of his resurrection, as they have been forgiven and justified by virtue of his death, and sanctified by the grace of his spirit. Christ is risen from the dead, and become the first fruits of them that slept. He is the first born from the dead, the beginning; that in all things he might have the preeminence; Christ the first fruits, afterwards they that are Christ's at his coming. All will not sleep, nor be raised. There will be those living in the body, when Christ cometh to judgment, who will not go down to the grave. There will be a world of people, as living, as active, perhaps as careless, as the world at this day, when the peal of the last trumpet breaks upon the universe. There will be believers, perhaps a multitude, who shall never see death. But all will be changed; and what the resurrection is to those who sleep in the grave, the change will be to those who are living when the graves are opened. But the dead in Christ, they that sleep in Jesus, will be raised first of all, in an incorruptible, glorious, celestial body, and then all living believers will be changed into the same body, so that the effect will be the same with them, as the awakening from the sleep of the grave with those who slumber there. This corruptible must put on incorruption, and this mortal must put on immortality. Whatever be the process going on, while the sleep of death continues, it is a sleep in Jesus, from which the awakening will be the positive entrance of the soul into everlasting life, in an immortal, incorruptible, spiritual, glorified body.

Now, the glory of that awakening passes all conception, this side the grave. It is clear that it is of the nature of an awakening; that is the word best fitted for it. There must be something like a dream, a sleep: the language of inspiration clearly intimates as much. There are no processes of nature that meet the case, except by faint analogy, such as the grain of wheat falling into the ground and dying, and then awakening into the light of day, and the green, fresh life of sunny nature; or such as the chrysalis, the grub, the worm, awakening from darkness and deformity, from a confinement to earth, into illimitable freedom, in exquisite beauty of form and color, on bright, glittering wings, in the pure liquid air. But these wondrous transformations and resurrections are of things material and corruptible, with all their loveliness, and can by no means shadow forth the yet incomprehensible glory of a change from the material to the spiritual, from the corruptible to the incorruptible, from the sleep of the grave to the glories of eternity. Whatever be the nature of that sleep, whatever the state of the soul while the body is in the grave, the awakening from it will be a surprise of infinite and overwhelming glory. The grand surpassing thought in it is that of the likeness of God; and who can arrive in this world at any adequate conception of that glory? For a sinful creature to find itself suddenly and entirely perfect in God's likeness, would itself be a surprise and a blissfulness overwhelming, even here. For a creature to lie down in death, in this body of sin, with all the consciousness of sinfulness, which accompanies most vividly the most holy in this world; for a sinful creature thus to lie down in the cradle of the dying body, rocked there to sleep, as by the Saviour's love, and then, out of that sleep, to awake in God's perfect likeness! All the images and analogies that we could summon to our aid would fail to convey any appropriate imagination or description of it. If a man were translated from the deepest dungeons into the light of noon, that would be nothing—if a man were snatched from the central deserts of Arabia, and transported into the fresh, cool verdure of gardens like the Paradise of Eden, that would be nothing—if, out of the dark, unfathomed caves of ocean, a prisoner should rise to the bright air of day, and the open life of creation, that would be nothing. For, oh! there is nothing to compare with the change from the sinfulness of a fallen race into the holiness of God—from the gloom and corruption of a body of sin and death, into the spirituality, the light, the glory, the dazzling radiance, the infinite purity, of the glorified body of the incarnate Son of God!

Take Job, as a child of God, and suppose him dying, amidst his extreme affliction and suffering. Take David, with all his attainments, in advanced old age. Think of his decrepid frame, stiffening and helpless, health and warmth deserting it, with his mind perhaps verging towards second childhood; and can any imagination conceive the change from such bondage, imprisonment and weakness, into the perfect likeness of God? Take Lazarus, full of sores—take Latimer, burning at the stake—take Baxter or Flavel—and look at the form and state of their mortality, and see if you can command any imagination of the overwhelming surprise of glory comprehended, of necessity, in a translation and transfiguration into God's own likeness. We may take the experience of the dying Payson, one of the nearest approximations of heaven to earth, and of earth to heaven, ever known; but even there, great as was the tide of ineffable happiness God was pouring through his soul, yet there is nothing that can convey to us an adequate image of the astonishment of wonder and of rapture with which such a being must find himself awakened, in immortal life, in God's own perfect likeness.

The consideration of this subject brings together and illustrates a great number of passages both in the Old and New Testament, but especially in Paul's epistles, all shedding a grand and glorious light on one another. Of this nature is that expression of Paul in the epistle to the Philippians, *That I may know him, and the power of his resurrection*, in connection with that great prayer for illumination, by the spirit, in the epistle to the Ephesians, on which we have already dwelt. These passages are illustrated with great glory, when we bring David's wonderful expressions in the 16th and 17th psalms in connection with them, showing the dependence of the church in body and soul upon, and its connection with Christ's resurrection. The power of his resurrection is not only that power by which he himself was raised, but that efficacy of his resurrection, by which (as he is the head, and believers are his body) the body, and every member of it, will experience the same glorious resurrection with the head. For our conversation, says Paul in another passage to Philippians, is in heaven, from whence also we look for the Saviour, the Lord Jesus Christ, who shall change our vile body, that it may be fashioned like unto his glorious body, according to the working whereby he is able even to subdue all things unto himself. And again, he is the Saviour of the body, and we are members of his body, of his flesh, and of his bones. With this stands connected that expression, Christ in you the hope of glory, and also, in the same first chapter of Colossians, the mention of Christ's death and resurrection, according to the pleasure of the Father, having made peace through the blood of his cross, by him, in the body of his flesh through death, to present the saints, holy, and unblamable, and unreprovable in his sight, without spot, or wrinkle, or any such thing, without fault before the throne of God in his likeness.

Also here are illustrated those passages in the eighth chapter of Romans, in connection with the 5th chapter of the 2d Corinthians, and the 4th and 5th of the 1st Thessalonians with the first chapter of the second epistle to the same; all, parts of one and the same magnificent and mighty anthem, looking for, hastening unto, and yearning after the coming of the day of Christ, and the glory to be revealed when he shall come to be admired in his saints, to shine out in them, and they in him, according to that expression, "When he, who is our life shall appear, then shall ye also appear with him in glory." Then shall be that manifestation of the sons of God, for which the earnest expectation of the creature waiteth, and that redemption of the body, for which the soul, even in the enjoyment of the first-fruits of the spirit, yearneth and groaneth. And here are illustrated all those fervent and almost impatient desires after Christ's appearing, expressed so frequently in the New Testament, and which became so habitual and peculiar a characteristic of the saints, that they were described as those who long for his appearing. For then only would they appear with him in glory, then only be delivered from this body of sin and death, and through their transformation into the likeness of Christ's glorified body, obtain a full introduction in that body of light, into the knowledge and enjoyment of all the glories of the celestial world. And hence, too, the anathemas pronounced against those pernicious infidels, who denied that Christ had come in the flesh, as well as those who denied his resurrection. And hence the frequent repetition by our blessed Lord, in his sermon on this subject in the sixth of John, of that cheering passage of promise to the believer, And I will raise him up at the last day; a thing impossible except by the coming, dying, rising, and supreme glorification and enthronement of Christ in his mediatorial kingdom.

We have cause to believe that one of the reasons inducing the assumption by our blessed Lord of a human body for accomplishing the work of redemption was the utter impossibility, except by such incarnation, and our transfiguration into, and possession of, its image and glory, in a body like Christ's, that we could ever see God. For he dwelleth in light inaccessible, whom no man hath seen, nor can see; and this impossibility of seeing God in that inaccessible light, of beholding God's face in righteousness, and of awakening in his likeness, could be taken away only by God in Christ becoming man, God manifest in the flesh, assuming a mortal body, which itself, by the power of the divinity in Christ's own death and resurrection, should be changed, glorified, and formed a type, according to which, and according to that alone, and by transfiguration like it, it would be possible to be admitted amidst the glories of heaven, with the possibility of communing with them and understanding them. Our utter incapacity now to form any definite conceptions of the glories of the heavenly world may be the want of that very medium, through which alone the heavenly world can be definitely seen and conversed with, that body which is the image and likeness of Christ's body. When clothed upon with that house which is from heaven, then the soul will see and understand, and then it will be satisfied. It will be as familiar with the scenes of heaven as the angels are, and those scenes will be as familiar and as suited to the souls of the redeemed in Christ's image in their glorified spiritual body, as to the souls of angels. But it may be absolutely impossible, without that spiritual organization, to come into such communion with the spiritual world, as that after which David was longing, that to which all the redeemed are advancing, that which all the angels, and the spirits of the just made perfect, forever enjoy.

The Resurrection of Damnation.

The Sabbath of this announcement was one of the most marked in the ministry of our Saviour. It was that in which, after a great and merciful miracle of healing, he justified to the Jews his own working on the Sabbath day by the example of God himself, the Creator and providential governor of the universe. And when the Jews interpreted that as making himself equal with God, our blessed Lord, instead of disavowing any intention of claiming such equality, went on to declare and explain it still more distinctly.

He revealed to the Jews the great fact that all works whatsoever which the Father doeth, the same doeth the Son likewise, and that even as the Father raiseth up the dead, and quickeneth them, even so the Son quickeneth whom he will. Moreover he told them that all judgment was committed to the Son, in order that all should honor the Son as they honor the Father. He told them that the hour was coming, and even then was, when the dead in trespasses and sins should hear the voice of the Son of God, and they that heard should live. For that, as the Father had life in himself, so had he given to the Son to have life in himself, and authority to execute judgment also, because he was not only the Son of God but the Son of man. He told them that they need not marvel at that announcement, for the hour was coming in which all that were in the graves should hear his voice, and should come forth; they that have done good unto the resurrection of life, and they that have done evil unto the resurrection of damnation. A series of disclosures was here made to the people, in regard to the character and glory of Christ, of amazing magnitude and importance, but with the plainest simplicity and distinctness. Announcement followed announcement, with the grandeur of great thunder-bursts of truth from heaven, yet in serene calmness and majesty, and with a plainness that could neither be questioned nor misunderstood. It was God manifest in the flesh, revealing himself in that form, as possessing divine authority and attributes, the Author of life, the Redeemer and Judge of man, the Arbiter of all the destinies and results both of the resurrection of life and the resurrection of damnation.

This was a wondrous sermon. Its texts are of an unfathomable meaning in vastness and glory. It was like taking up great mountains and throwing them into the sea. And indeed, with what an almost confounding weight must these disclosures of the two Resurrections have fallen upon the minds of our Lord's hearers! We can almost hear the fire-side report made by one of them as he went home to tell to his family what the great Prophet had been saying to the people. "He spake as never man spake. He told us that all things for time, death, and eternity, were committed into his hands, and that he, just as God the Father, had the power of life, death, and the judgment. He told us of the resurrection. He said that he himself was the Lord of it, and could raise the dead, and quicken whom he would. He told us of the resurrection of life, and how every one who would believe in God through his word should have everlasting life, and should pass from death unto life, and never more see condemnation. But O, he told us more than that; he told us of the resurrection of damnation; and when he told of that, it was with tones of such tenderness and sorrow, yet solemnity and awe, it was with such profound and overwhelming conviction accompanying the manner and the words in our souls, it fell from his lips upon us, not idly nor speculatively, as the Pharisees talk, but with such exceeding and eternal weight of truth and earnestness, that indeed it seemed as if the judgment had come, and Gehenna's gates stood open before us, and we were entering in. Yes, he told us of the resurrection of damnation; and I, who never before trembled at what our prophets have spoken, nor at what John spake of the fire unquenchable, when he warned us to flee from the wrath, felt this in mine inmost soul. The resurrection of damnation! The resurrection of damnation! The words still ring in mine ears. Oh what shall we do to escape the resurrection of damnation?"

Yes, even so, without all question: such was the preaching of Christ. The most burning revelations of hell and of heaven came from His words; and such, we doubt not, was the effect again and again produced upon the souls of His hearers. And here, again, we observe the reverberation of the tones and expressions of the Spirit of God from the Old Testament into the New, and from the New into the Old. Our blessed Lord was preaching simply what had been taught from the beginning of the revelation of God; and here, on this occasion, He had been referring to what was plainly set down in the Book of the Prophet Daniel. And when He said that all judgment was committed into His hands, because He was the Son of man, He referred to the description of the dominion of the Son of man coming in the clouds of heaven, seen in the night visions of Daniel. And when He spoke of the resurrection of life, and the resurrection of damnation, what was it but a Divine illumination and paraphrase of the great resurrection-text in Daniel, that they who sleep in the dust of the earth, shall awake, some to everlasting life, and some to shame and everlasting contempt; when they that be wise shall shine as the brightness of the firmament; and they that turn many to righteousness, as the stars forever and ever? In truth, the Old Testament declarations on this and other subjects were as the frame and canvas of a vast transparency prepared and sketched of God; while Christ and His Spirit and teachings in the New Testament are as the light from heaven, lighting all within, illuminating all the figures, and shining forth through them to all the world with such power and plainness, that he who runs may read.

Christ it was, and His Spirit indeed, that spake through all the prophets; but when Christ came on earth as the Word made flesh, then the Divine predictions in Daniel and all others became incarnate in Him, and the truth was seen and felt, no more in the difficulty or dimness of prophetic hieroglyphics, but living, moving, acting. The words that Christ uttered came as tongues of flame from the eternal world, touching men's souls as with fire; and all His revelations concerning the future retribution for the wicked assumed an awful distinctness, whether investing selected persons standing for classes of men, as Lazarus and Dives, and couched beneath the coloring and imagery of heaven and hell, personifying realities, or pealed forth in decisive language, as sharp and startling as the Archangel's trumpet, These shall go away into everlasting punishment; but the righteous, into life eternal!

Now, this powerful form of contrast adopted in the last sentence is familiar both in the Old and New Testament, but far more direct and startling in the New. Whatever of glory and blessedness there is known to be in the resurrection of life, we may and must, with certainty, conclude right the opposite in the resurrection of damnation. Experience, in both cases, deserts us, and we are thrown upon God's word. But there is a kind of predictive and corroborative experience, which we possess in each case, through the Spirit of God, and the revelation in our own consciousness, which is exceedingly powerful. The Spirit of God producing, in souls submissive and believing, a hungering and thirsting after righteousness in God's likeness, shows, beforehand, something of the glory to be revealed, in the event of an awaking in that likeness. The happiness arising, even in this world, even out of these desirés after God, is sometimes so great, that it is like an experience of heaven—like being filled with all the fulness of God. And just so the Spirit of God, and men's own convictions, together with their dread and foreboding of punishment, produce in the conscience of the wicked a sense of guilt, and a terror of coming wrath, which is sometimes insupportable; a sight of their own defilement and depravity, in the likeness of Satan, and in contrast with the character of a holy God, which produces some experimental demonstration of the terror of an awakening in the image of fiends.

To a mind that has any proper appreciation of the difference between holiness and sin, any true knowledge of the character of God, any sense of God's holiness, any true conviction of guilt, and sense of the evil of sin, there could be nothing more terrible than the contemplation of such an awakening, nothing so dreadful as the prospect or the fear of it in one's own case. There could be no description of the world of woe more terrific than this, that it is a world of unmingled and eternal depravity. And this is the least we can possibly make out of it, namely, that that depravity of our nature, which is here restricted, negatived, and neutralized, even with the worst, and made oftentimes to assume many insinuating, amiable and pleasing forms, will there be perfectly developed, without any restriction, any neutralization, any disguise. This is the world of seeds, of causes, and of tendencies; that is the world of harvests, of results, and of perfected and eternal consequences. There will be no mixture of causes or of character there, but perfect, defecated wickedness, purified from all mixture of good, and incurably, immutably, everlastingly evil. There will be nothing but the scum and dross of creation. It is rising to the surface here, and in process of development and of separation from the precious metal. It is mingled and separating now, because the very system under which we live, through the interposition of Christ, is that of probation and grace, for such development and separation, that character may be perfectly tried and known, that all who wish to become good, may, and that the righteous may be perfectly purified. But there the scum and dross will be gathered and flung away by itself, according to that significant declaration of the Psalmist, Thou puttest away all the wicked of the earth like dross. Many shall be purified and made white, and tried; but the wicked shall still do wickedly, and all forms of evil character will go on to fill up their measures of iniquity, and there must be an eternal separation, without any more combination. It must be so, for the defence of God's own character, for the sake of His righteousness and justice, and for the purity of heaven itself. Otherwise there would lie against God's government there, and against the possibility of unmingled blessedness there, the same objections that are brought here; according to that very striking passage in Jeremiah, where the prophet, describing the uselessness and misery of a state of society where justice is not executed, but the evil are permitted to mingle successfully with the good, corrupting and corrupted, observes that "the bellows are burned, the lead is consumed of the fire, and the founder melteth in vain, because the wicked are not plucked away."

But there will be nothing of this at the resurrection, but each world and system, of the righteous and the wicked, will be alone in its perfection. There will be no such thing there as a growth of character which is half tares and half grain, but all will be either tares or grain solely. The tares will be gathered into bundles to burn them, and the grain into God's barn. Here, a man going into the field, can hardly tell, sometimes, what is wheat and what are tares, and sometimes even the same ear will seem one side grain and the other tares; but it cannot be so at the end of all things, when character will be developed and discerned in infinite perfection. The angels shall come forth, and shall separate the evil from the good. The opposite and conflicting elements of character and of being will draw off to opposite extremes, opposite worlds, and there will be nothing but eternal and unchangeable fixtures of holiness and blessedness or of sin and misery.

Now, just as, if Christ be in you, though the body must die because of sin, yet the spirit is life because of righteousness, and He that raised up Christ from the dead shall also quicken your mortal bodies by

His Spirit that dwelleth in you; just so, if Christ be not in you, then, as the body must die because of sin, so body and soul must remain in sin, for there is no spirit of life to raise the body in Christ; but you are under the law of sin and of death, and yours is the carnal mind which is enmity against God, and the spirit in you is death because of wickedness. And as it is the work of the spirit of life to make a spiritual body, so it is the work of the spirit of death to make a corrupted and corruptible body. He that soweth to the Spirit shall of the Spirit reap life everlasting; but he that soweth to the flesh shall of the flesh reap corruption. And as the body of the resurrection of life is a glorified body suited to the character of the holy soul, and growing out of it, in the likeness of Christ, by the Spirit of Christ, so the body of the resurrection of damnation will be equally suited to the character of the sinful soul, growing out of *that*, by the spirit of death and of evil, a deformed and tormented body in the likeness of fiends. So that, although the awakening to shame and everlasting contempt spoken of beforehand in Daniel, seems a faint and mild form of the prediction of retribution, as compared with the figures and realities used by our Saviour, yet, interpreted by those, as it must be, and illuminated by the glare of that fiery corruption reaped from sowing to the flesh, it conveys a most terrific and tremendous meaning. What but a shame and everlasting contempt by us inconceivable can await the soul of the wicked, awakening in a body as deformed as the soul; in a body of infernal spirituality, which, with the same translucent power of a celestial body, will convey, and answer to, without any concealment or imperfection, the whole corruption of the soul, its real, undisguised, unmingled character of perfect evil.

For such it must be, to answer to that declaration of Christ, Depart ye cursed. For nothing, in which any mixture of good remained, could have such a curse from God; and anything bearing such a curse must be a terror and contempt to itself as well as a terror and contempt to the universe. And it is quite as impossible to conceive the overwhelming horror of surprise, in which a wicked soul will rise in such accursed deformity of utter wickedness in the resurrection of damnation, as it it impossible to conceive the overwhelming surprise of glory and blessedness, in which the holy soul will rise in God's perfect likeness. Take the case of the rich man given by our blessed Lord, as we have already taken the case of Lazarus amidst his sores, his sufferings, his wretchedness, on earth, with the dogs for his companions, to show how impossible it is for us to conceive the overwhelming surprise of blessedness and glory to him, when he found himself conveyed by angels, in God's own likeness, into the bliss of heaven; take the case of the rich man amidst his sumptuous living, his costly and splendid array, his crowd of waiting servants and of friends, all ministering to his pleasures, all praising his virtues, all treating him with marked and uninterrupted respect; and who can conceive the overwhelming surprise of horror with which he awoke on dying, and in hell lifted up his eyes being in torments? Who can conceive the awfulness of the man's terror and despair, in finding out his own character! No wonder that our Lord has said there shall be weeping and gnashing of teeth.

And let it be remembered that it is our blessed Lord himself who has said all these things. And though the carping unbeliever sometimes endeavors to countenance his attacks upon God's word by shooting his envenomed arrows at what he calls the hard and cruel things of the Old Testament, yet let it be remembered that for every threatening of evil to the wicked there, you will find incomparably greater terribleness and distinctness of retribution shrouded in the words of our Redeemer. Nay, not shrouded, but the shroud taken off, the covering in the Old Testament removed, and everything in the preaching of Christ made as if we stood ourselves on the burning verges of heaven and hell, and beheld, with our own eyes, their realities. For truth itself was incarnated in Christ, and as he was the Word made flesh, so the reports from heaven and hell in the Old Testament, coming through his lips, seem living and moving as incarnate forms among us.

Poor rich man! destined to such an awakening! could not some one, armed with the truth of heaven, have gone in at some of his grand feasts, and told him what was before him? Could not some earnest friend have said to him, Dear sir, you are close upon your mortal sickness, and you are not prepared for death, and when you die, from all this luxury you will wake up in unmingled wickedness, contempt and misery! But if there had been such a faithful messenger, one among a thousand, what would have been his reception? Have you no more manners, the rich man would have answered, than to bring your untimely croakings here in the midst of my company and pleasures? Away with your libels upon God and human nature, as if God were not a God who loves to see his creatures enjoying themselves! As if man were a being of so much wickedness as to be destined to the state which you call hell! Aye, but there stands Christ's own word, In hell he lifted up his eyes, being in torments. Poor rich man! had he no friends, nor warning messengers to entreat and save him. Oh yes! he had many! He had Moses and the Prophets. He had David describing to him his own state and danger. He had Daniel telling him of the resurrection of the wicked. He had God's word, God's providences, God's mercies, seeking to bring him to repentance; but all in vain.

Now, for what purpose are these disclosures? Have I any pleasure at all in the death of him that dieth? saith the Lord; and was it any pleasure to our Blessed Redeemer, to unveil the secrets of the world of woe? Is it not all in mercy, all in love, that he puts for us, in such vivid light, the resurrection of life on one side, and the resurrection of damnation on the other, and bids us choose?

The Work of the Angel Reapers.

In the mighty transactions of the judgment, how solemn and awful is the instrumentality of the angels of God! The Son of man shall send forth his angels. They are the angels of Christ; and as to their number, it seems to be intimated that all heaven, all the holy beings in God's universe, will be his ministers in the transactions of that day. The Son of man shall come in his glory, and *all* the holy angels with him. The Lord Jesus shall be revealed from Heaven with his mighty angels, in flaming fire, taking vengeance on them that know not God, and that obey not the Gospel of our Lord Jesus Christ. There was, in the antediluvian world, a prediction of the scene, and a foreshowing of the Lord's coming. For Enoch, the seventh from Adam, prophesied, saying, "Behold the Lord cometh with ten thousand of his saints, to execute judgment upon all, and to convince all that are ungodly of all their ungodly deeds which they have ungodly committed, and of all their hard speeches, which ungodly sinners have spoken against him." And at a later period, as an advancing step in this revelation, we have the sublime delineation in

Daniel. "I beheld till the Ancient of days did sit, whose garment was white as snow, and the hair of His head like the pure wool; His throne was like the fiery flame, and His wheels as burning fire. A fiery stream issued and came forth from before Him; thousand thousands ministered unto Him, and ten thousand times ten thousand stood before Him; the judgment was set, and the books were opened.

What multitudes on multitudes, countless, inconceivable, are here represented! Each as a flaming fire, each as the lightning, in power, swiftness, and glory! Who can conceive the unimaginable grandeur, the awful splendor of that day! All that ever went before, of God's judgments, were but faint symbols of this. God's coming on Sinai was terrible in grandeur, yea, of intolerable sublimity and glory; yet it was little compared with this. All the efforts of the human mind fail before the inconceivable magnitude and majesty of this final reality, this last whirlwind blaze, this ministration of flaming intelligences amidst material burnings, this manifestation and execution of the Divine attributes in the unrestricted fulness of their hitherto veiled and restrained glory, this final development of judgment and of retribution by the agency of all the brightest and mightiest holy beings in the universe of God! There have been dreams of these things; men have been visited in the night visions with appalling bursts of the light, the glory, and the terror of this last day, so that they have awaked in anguish uncontrollable; and some in words and images of fire have told the scenery through which their dreams have carried them; but no possible imagery can adequately realize this last transaction to the mind.

The angels of God, as presented in the parable of the tares, are the reapers of the final harvest. They are commissioned by the Son of man to gather out of His kingdom all things that offend, and them which do iniquity. They are thus to sever the wicked from among the just. They are to gather first the tares in bundles, preparatory to what follows. They are to make this great and final separation of the evil from the good, before they are cast into that world, in which the fountains of the great deep of retribution will be broken up upon them. They are supposed to know, instantly and unerringly, the objects of their search. There can be not a moment's doubt or hesitation. The tares and the wheat will both be disclosed in perfection. A good angel on this commission will have no more difficulty in knowing, as quick as thought, an evil being from this world, than he would have in discovering an angel of darkness from the bottomless pit. As in the resurrection, the awakening of the wicked will be to shame and everlasting contempt, in the character and likeness of unalloyed evil, while the good will shine out as the stars of the firmament in brightness, so in the change that will take place with all the living at the last day, all the growing tares then above ground will put off, with their mortal covering, all character but evil, and will develop all of evil that before was concealed. So that the passage of the lightning cannot be more swift, than the knowledge where the lightning should strike; and the angels that are to gather the tares into bundles, will have no more difficulty or uncertainty as to the indications of their work, in gathering out of Christ's kingdom all things that offend, and them that do iniquity, than those who are to gather the bright shining golden sheaves of wheat, to transport them into God's garner. What a harvest-home will that be, what a procession of glory, what songs of rejoicing, what melodies of heavenly blessedness, when the reaper's work is done, and the companies of white-winged seraphs convey their glorious sheaves, their gathered multitudes of the redeemed, into the presence of God and the Lamb! And on the other hand, what a harvest-home of misery, what a procession of terror, amidst weeping and wailing and gnashing of teeth, with the majesty and overwhelming glory of Halleluia anthems to the divine justice vindicated, when the reaper's work is done upon the tares, and the bundles of evil are carried to their own place!

And here we find, very clearly revealed, the principle of association, according to which the reaper's work is to be accomplished, when they bind the tares in bundles to be burned. The law of socialism, which men talk about so carelessly, may be, when fully realized and carried out, an infinitely terrible thing. These bundles of the tares mean, in all probability, that in the day of judgment and of retribution like will be gathered to like, forms of evil with kindred forms, peculiar refinements and hideousness of evil character with similar hideousness. This probability becomes quite a revealed certainty when we compare the note of the bundles in the parable of the tares with the category given by John in the 21st chapter of the Revelation, where he says that the fearful, and unbelieving, and the abominable, and murderers, and whoremongers, and sorcerers, and idolaters, and all liars, shall have their part in the lake that burneth with fire and brimstone; which is the second death; and also with the various notices, throughout the Scriptures, of the variety of degrees in which punishment is to be meted out of justice, and assumed by the sinner, according to the forms and degrees of his light and wickedness. And this makes a terrible demonstration of the nature of hell, considered as formed out of the combustion of the elements of sinful character, out of the necessary play and growth of principles of evil, out of the combination, concentration, and perfect development of specific forms of sin.

For if we will but apply this supposition even to our own world, we may see, by what it would be here, something of the tremendous reality of evil which it must be hereafter. Suppose that in this world men of similar evil dispositions and crimes were assorted and bound together, and left to the full development of those evil habits and tendencies. Suppose that all the murderers were gathered into one set, one community, and all the revengeful, cruel and passionate into another, and all the liars into another, and all the fraudful and dishonest into another, and all the proud, haughty, scornful and ambitious into another, and all unbelievers and corrupters of the truth into another, and all adulterers and sensualists into another, and all drunkards and intemperate into another, and all the profane swearers and blasphemers into another, and were thus left to themselves, and to the unrestrained growth and conflict of their respective depraved tendencies, chosen sins, vile, vicious habits, and abandoned, profligate practices. How unimaginably and intolerably dreadful and hateful would society become, even here upon earth! It is not so now, simply and solely because of God's restraining mercy in the arrangements of His providence and grace. He so governs the world, restraining its superfluity of wrath, that one passion in society modifies and confines another, even by the very selfishness of men. And it is just because every part of society is made up of all varieties of depravity, that depravity does not, in any one direction, go so far as to make our earth an absolute hell beforehand. But suppose all restraint withdrawn, and the associative principle in evil left to work itself completely out, in its fullest perfection and power, and then consequences would ensue, which might almost make the mind insane, even to follow them in imagination.

It was something like this idea that the poet Dante pursued with such terrific minuteness and horror of detail, in his tremendous delineation of the compartments of a moral and material hell. And the inscription, which that mighty poet has read, as traced in lurid fire over hell's portals, shows a theology deeper, truer, more scriptural, in his mind, and in the minds of multitudes for whom he wrote, in the middle ages, than that of multitudes of sickly sentimentalists since the Reformation. The theology of David and Paul, the one by eminence the inspired poet, and the other the inspired logician, of true Christianity, and thatof Dante and of Jonathan Edwards, the theological poet of the middle ages in Italy, and the theological logician of the modern world in New England, meet and coincide in that description. The united attributes of Divine Justice, Divine Power, and Divine Love, are recognized in the eternal punishment of all the incorrigibly wicked.

> "Through me you pass into the city of woe:
> Through me you pass into eternal pain:
> Through me among the people lost forever,
> Justice the founder of my fabric moved;
> To rear me was the task of power divine,
> Supremest wisdom, and primeval Love.
> Before me, things create were none, save things
> Eternal, and eternal I endure.
> All hope abandon, ye who enter here!"

And indeed all hope they must abandon, whose character of evil brings them into such a world. There the tares will grow on, everlastingly, forever burning, yet forever unconsumed. For wickedness burneth as the fire, and there is no stay to the onward progress of character, in a world of results and consequences. What it could have been, if it would have changed, what it might have been, had there been the disposition, the repenting will, under a system infinitely favorable for a return to holiness, has been offered, but not accepted; what it is, and must be forever, is all that remains. There can be nothing else. God gave the opportunity of what man *might be*, and the trial of what he *would do*, under the offer, nay, the urgency of pardon, regeneration, and eternal life through Christ; and now there only remains what man *must be*, and what God *must do*, man having passed, as a guilty being, through such an ordeal of the divine mercy, unchanged. And here we perceive that the object of the reapers work, the end of the commission to the angels, in binding the bundles of the tares, in severing the wicked from among the just, in gathering out of God's kingdom all things that offend and them that do iniquity, is just this, *to burn them.* "Let both grow together until the harvest, and in the time of harvest I will say to the reapers, gather ye together first the tares, *and bind them in bundles to burn them.* The Son of man shall send forth his angels, and they shall gather out of his kingdom all things that offend, and them that do iniquity, and shall cast them into a furnace of fire; there shall be weeping and gnashing of teeth." This is what God will do with the wicked. As to what, according to our ideas, he might do, ought to do, must do, we may reason, imagine, surmise, wonder; but as to all positive declaration of what he certainly *will* do, we are shut up, absolutely, to God's word. As to the inevitable consequences of sin, we not only may, but must, reason, and with the utmost certainty, out of God's word, as well as in it, knowing in ourselves that the wages of sin is death, and having also the light of God's judgments to guide us. But as to God's direct agency, as to his own execution of the penalty of his law, we must go solemnly, submissively, tremblingly, to God's word.

And here we are before it. And from the book of Genesis to that of Revelations we find this furnace of fire; find the wicked, according to that expression in Jude, suffering the vengeance of eternal fire. The last great prophet of the Old Testament closes his revelation with the announcement of this fire. "For behold the day cometh that shall burn as an oven, and all the proud, yea, and all that do wickedly, shall be stubble; and the day that cometh shall burn them up, saïth the Lord of hosts, that it shall leave them neither root nor branch." And the first great prophet of the New Testament opens his announcement of the gospel with the same fire. "Every tree, which bringeth not forth good fruit, is hewn down, and cast into the fire. He will gather his wheat into the garner, but he will burn up the chaff with unquenchable fire." And this same line and demonstration of fire is continued in our blessed Lord's discourses and parables with unparalleled vividness and power; so that sometimes, as in Mark, the sermon is one tissue of flame, and he repeats the warning of fire no less than seven different times, in as many verses, mentioning three times the fire of hell, and five times repeating the assurance that it never shall be quenched. And once he carries us into the eternal world, and sets us down in hell, with the rich man tormented in its flames, and tells us of the great immutable, impassable gulf between that and heaven. And in his very last sermon upon earth he leaves the wicked burning in that fire. His last words before the crucifixion, to a world of reckless sinners, open wide the doors both of heaven and of hell, and set before us the equally immutable awards of either. "These shall go away into everlasting punishment, but the righteous into life eternal."

Now, this is God's arrangement, God's work; this is what God will do with the tares, with the wicked; and the result in their case can be nothing but weeping and gnashing of teeth; the consciousness of guilt, the sufferance of deserved punishment, and the remorse of conscience, as the worm that never dieth, in the darkness of eternal despair. And with all this there will be the clearest sight and the deepest conviction of God's perfect righteousness and justice; nay more, of God's infinite love; a love abused, wasted, rejected on the part of the careless, obstinate soul, when God at the expense of the death of his son was interposing to save it from destruction, and it would not be saved; and a love now at length exercised for the guardianship of the universe, in eternal punishment demanded, made necessary, and absolutely drawn down upon the sinner by himself, in opposition to all God's efforts to the contrary.

The ordeal of Divine mercy through which the sinner thus forces his way to ruin, was a trial and a conflict on the part of God for man's life, man's salvation; it was a struggle on the part of man for his own perdition. Every way *was* tried, *is* tried, to induce men to flee from the wrath to come; but, in multitudes of cases, in vain. "How often would I have gathered your children, but *ye* would not!" In following out even the brief and simple course of this parable, into what an array of the Divine power, wisdom, and love for man's salvation, has the argument led us! What openings have we seen, through which heaven's light radiates on the earth as in a flood of demonstrations of Divine truth, in language not of words only, but of the mighty realities of the cross, and of God manifest in the flesh, and of the dying anguish of a Divine Sufferer, dying for man's sins; dying to demonstrate God's justice, that it might be possible, through such demonstration of it, for believing man to escape the realization and the sufferance of it; dying, in the exercise of God's compassion, that the guilty and the lost might live; and dying to show that if they do not live, if they *will* not live, through the merits of that death, they must die forever; dying to show at once the infinite depths of human guilt and ruin, and the infinite depths of Divine holiness and love; dying to demonstrate the meaning and eternity of both worlds, hell and heaven!

What openings of blazing light upon human character have we seen, *our* character, rendering its depravity and ruin, unless changed here, unmistakable, inveterate, irremediable! What movements of Divine providence have we seen, awakening, pursuing, enlightening, teaching; causing, as it were, the very fire from the eternal burnings to fly in men's faces, and to light upon their souls! What is there indeed, O careless, sinful, dying men! that God could do to awaken you, that He is not doing, has not done? You have been both entreated and alarmed, disciplined with trials and blessings, experiences of conviction, and promises of pardon; you have been pleased and disappointed, treated with indulgence and tenderness, and again brought into calamity; but in the day of your adversity, God has to complain of you, that you turn not to the hand of him that smiteth you; and in the day of your prosperity, your heart remains unchanged, hardened, and secure in sin. What now remains, after all this trial of the Divine mercy and love unavailing, but wrath against the day of wrath, and revelation of God's righteous judgment? What *can* be done? If mercy has been tried in vain, justice must follow. Under the Cross of Christ, God gives to sinful men the choice of just what attributes they will please to have displayed in themselves. He lets them experience all that they choose to experience of the Divine character, the Divine perfections. But in their guilt persisted in, all that they *can* experience, finally and eternally, is the Divine righteousness and justice; and therefore God points us to the Saviour, and Christ himself pleads with us, beseeches us, by His dying love and agony, that we would be reconciled to God!

The Power of an Endless Life.

It is a magnificent conception which is conveyed in this language, yet rarely do men pause and ponder before it. THE POWER OF AN ENDLESS LIFE! Life worthy to be called life; life holy, beatific, glorious, divine; life, participant of God's own holiness and blessedness; life, in comparison with which all that we have known of existence in this world is but as a sleep and a forgetting, or as a dismal dream, or as a terrible reality, the death of trespasses and sins. The power of such a life! endless, unchangeable, save only from accumulating glory; perpetual in its energy and freshness, with the boundlessness and security of infinitude before it, forever and ever!

It is this glory which is held out for our attainment. We, who are here in death, even the death of trespasses and sins, are invited to such a life. We know not, as yet, either death or life, absolutely, nor the power of either as eternal, but only in the embryo, or by an effort of imagination, in idea and not in reality. Soon we *shall* know, forever; shall know by experience what life is and what death is; what life is by possession of it, and what death is, by redemption from it; or what death is, by entering upon it, and what life is by the eternal loss of it.

It is to secure for us the redemption from such death, and the glory of such a life, that Christ came. He would not have come, had not both these inevitable consequences been eternal. He was made, not after the law of a carnal or temporary commandment, or necessity, or arrangement, but after the power of an endless life. He came *as* a Saviour, and came *such* a Saviour, with just that endless life in view, and just that salvation from an endless death; and he would not have come, otherwise. He was made, was constituted, not for any temporary purpose, plan, or ordinance, but in accordance with the necessity of an eternal salvation, an eternal life, for its accomplishment, after its power. Had it been a finite glory to be gained, or a finite misery avoided, a limited life on the one side, or a limited death on the other, a transitory heaven and a transitory hell, then a transitory High Priest and a finite Saviour might have answered. There had been no need for the Divine Word to be made flesh, nor any sufferance of such a sacrifice. But the penalties and powers concerned, the life and death, the guilt and the redemption, being boundless as eternity, and the government to be honored and sustained, the government of God, a Saviour must come in the glory and majesty of infinitude, possessing and answering to, the power of an endless life.

Such we take to be the argument in this grand and glorious passage, in Hebrews 7:16. The power of an endless life, and the might of a redemption into it, by the quickening and resurrection of the soul from the death of trespasses and sins, required and demanded such a Saviour, and for God's glory, justified such a sacrifice. A Saviour must be had, the benefit and power of whose atoning interposition would extend through eternity, would secure the universe through eternity from the incursions and the malignity of sin, would destroy him that had the power of death, would take away all guilt forever from the soul, and would confirm all redeemed and believing creatures in holiness and happiness, in God's love and under God's law, forever. Let us then look at some of the things included under this vast and mighty expression, The Power of an Endless Life.

And first, it is a perfect life. They who enter upon it are without fault before the throne of God. There is no sin, no defilement, no imperfection, no spot, nor wrinkle, nor any such thing, nor remnant, nor result, nor fear, of evil. There is not only no imperfection, but on the contrary, a purity and perfection so infinite, that it is just a participation of God's own holiness, a transformation and transfiguration into the righteousness of the Lord of life and glory. The glory and the bliss of such perfect, absolute, unspotted holiness, are beyond the possibility of our conception in this mortal state; and therefore the inspired Apostle himself is compelled to say that it doth not yet appear what we shall be, only this we know, that we shall be like Christ. And this perfection in his likeness will be of body as well as spirit, because he will change even our vile body, that it may be fashioned according to his glorious body; and the very example of his own resurrection is the pattern of God's mighty power towards those who believe, according to the working of that amazing power which he wrought in Christ, when he raised him from the dead, and set him at his own right hand in the heavenly places. This is Christ's own glory, Christ's own life, and we are complete in him, possessing and reflecting his glory. We cannot, in our mortal state, have any adequate idea of the infinite glory and blissfulness even of a perfect freedom from sin; but as to the positive glory of appearing in Christ's likeness, neither the heart nor imagination of man ever yet began the most distant conception of it, except as God deigns an otherwise incommunicable revelation, by his spirit. In Christ the perfection of Saints is an infinite perfection, and in him they enter on the power of an endless life in perfect oneness in spirit and in work with the infinitely glorious Jehovah, even as the Son of God, in his spirit and work, was one with the Father.

In the second place, it is a social life, in which all the communicative and companionable tendencies of our nature and powers of our being, will be exercised in an enjoyment ten thousand fold intensified by being reflected from, and shared with, the beatific experience of others. It is remarkable, as an indication of the glory of the social life of heaven, and the activity and blissfulness of mutual thought and affection interchanged and ardent there, that this same epistle to the Hebrews introduces us to the innumerable company of angels, and the general assembly and church of the first born whose names are written in heaven, and to the spirits of the just made perfect. We are come to such vast and glorious assemblages, as to scenes and objects transporting, even to be only looked at and admired, but how much more enrapturing to go in and out among them, holding communion with them. The very sight of others in glory will be infinite joy, a study of salvation, a rapture of delight. There will be so much to admire and love in every creature, every creature will be so full of glory, so ravishing a reflection of the glory of the Saviour, that eternity might be occupied in silently gazing, and adoring; and even so the Lord Jesus at his coming with His saints will be admired in all who believe.

But there will be infinite sociableness in heaven; that life will be the perfection of a social life, as truly as it will be a life filled with all the fulness of God. There will be the good and the glorious of all ages and all worlds to love and to rejoice with. There will be communion among angels and saints, sweeter than the conversation on the way to Emmaus, more frank and loving than ever could have been imagined, in ten thousand infinite directions and disclosures of mutual history and character, in the suggestion, investigation, and comparison of thought, amidst the providence, works, attributes and revelations of the infinite God. And indeed the power of an endless life would find full employment in the universe of God alone, and saints will find a boundless study of the Divine glory in angels, principalities and powers, even as to principalities and powers shall be revealed in the church the manifold wisdom of God. There will be mutual study, there will be social study, there will be nothing solitary in heaven, nothing exclusive or concealed, nor any need of guardian forms of courtesies, nor any distant or reserved civilities, nor any jealousy of honors claimed or due, nor any sense either of superiority or inferiority, all pride and envy being forever debarred from the possibility of entrance or existence there. Divine love is the atmosphere of heaven; they dwell in love, they dwell in God, for God is love, and in sweet forgetfulness of self, the happiness of others is as dear and delightful to each as their own.

But in the third place, it is a life of blissful activity. There will be employment enough in heaven, and they need no rest, day nor night, nor ever experience any exhaustion of their energies. All is harmonious activity, nothing conflicting, entangled, opposing, or out of joint. All the powers of the being are in concert, inspired with one mind and one spirit in the service and the praise of God. Every intellectual capacity will be carried to the highest possible exercise, in studying the divine attributes, and accomplishing the Divine will. The *individual* will, being in every respect one with God's, and the whole soul filled with His love, the activity of heaven in doing *His* will must be spontaneous and infinitely delightful, perpetual and unchangeable. And in whatever universe of God, or part of His universe, an intelligent being might be employed, there is everywhere a sense of God, a perception of His presence, such as in our mortal body we cannot have, but with which and in which there is, to the soul that loves God, the fulness of heaven's blessedness. God's will is the happiness of such a soul, and activity in doing it would be the irrepressible expression of such happiness. Would that it were so on earth; our meat and drink to do the will of our Father in heaven!

In the fourth place, it is a progressive life. And here it is that this phrase, *the power of an endless life*, comes into more immediate and definite exposition, at least the significance of it is more palpable. An endless life! the *power* of an endless life! The very idea of it is triumphant. The idea of the life of an antediluvian, a life of only a thousand years, is grand and imposing. Only a thousand years! What might not be accomplished in such a tract of time on earth, with energies unfettered and untired, a heart filled with God's love, and all the powers of the whole being employed and absorbed with inexhaustible spontaneous delight and zeal in His service! What progression, what acceleration would there be, and what accumulation of impulse and power from generation to generation! But a thousand years are as one day in the conception and incomputable arithmetic of an endless life. Our plans on earth are contracted, fragmentary, broken, and incomplete; but in the security and infinitude of an endless life there may be plans, even by finite minds, encompassing ages and worlds. And there will be nothing to prevent the execution of them, no fear of interruption by death, no doubt or indecision of mind, no inward conflict nor external foes, no enfeebling of the energies by sickness or unwillingness, nor distracting of them by temptation, nor crippling of them by want of means, nor any dividing of them, as in this world, between present and future, temporal and eternal, earthly and divine. There will be an infinitude of wealth in God's bounty to draw from, for all things are yours, children of this glorious adoption in Christ! whether things present or things to come; and ye are heirs of God, and joint heirs with Christ, and he that overcometh shall inherit all things. All fountains of strength and grace shall be yours to draw from, and with angelic skill and wisdom all needed resources will be combined, and with intuitive swiftness the best means will be seen and adopted. The understanding will be divinely illuminated, the mental vision seeing no more as through a glass darkly, but face to face, and the memory no longer treacherous and feeble, but capacious and retentive beyond all bounds. All past acquisitions will be secured, and nothing lost or wasted. There will be no haste, nor anxiety, but a divine and holy leisure and serenity of mind, even in the swiftest, grandest onward excitement and progress. It is only in the power and triumph of an endless life, that any creature from this restless world ever can be at leisure. But there you have eternity at your disposal, and all your plans, glorious and unembarrassed, may move on forever and ever! It is the power of an endless life.

There will be progression in holiness. There can indeed be no addition made to the righteousness of Christ, and that is what the believer is clothed with from the outset, and that is what every redeemed soul will reflect in glory everlasting. But as star differeth from star in glory, so in the reflection of that glory, which will be brighter and brighter the more the soul studies and knows of God and his holiness. The glory, the brightness, the worth of that holiness will continually be increasing in the creature, because it is infinite in the Creator, and the soul will forever be coming into nearer and nearer resemblance to God in Christ.

There will be progression in the power of holy habit. Think of the glory and the power of such habit in the soul, when ages on ages have made the life of love a nature so irrevocable, that by the very principles of an immortal constitution there shall be no more possibility of change, than in the nature of the Son of God! How glorious is this certainty! This is one element in the power of an endless life. It shall be a power of life that all the opposing powers in the universe might be let loose upon with safety; might war against it, and should not overcome, might labor with whatever native or permitted intensity and energy could be brought into the conflict, and yet should not start one impulse in the soul, or one thought or motive from its foundation in holiness, and its confirmed immutable fastening to the throne and being of God, and its direction in his love and glory! This is that great meaning, beginning in this life, and running on through ever, and yet no possible approximation be made to a limit, in the knowledge of God, in the study of his works and ways, in his kingdoms of creation, grace, and glory. All that is comprehended in the threefold division in that great promise of Christ in the Apocalypse, shall be given, as an infinite possession for the wanderings, and acquisitions, and visions of the soul. "Him that overcometh will I make a pillar in the temple of my God, and he shall go no more out. And I will write upon him the name of my God, and the name of the city of my God, new Jerusalem, which cometh down out of heaven from my God, and I will write upon him my new name." "Since the beginning of the world men have not heard, nor perceived by the ear, neither hath the eye seen, O God, besides thee, what He hath prepared for him that waiteth for Him."

And even the revelation by the Spirit is more the implantation or excitement in the soul of a longing, panting desire after God and his glory, than any actual sight or knowledge. We want the fire of inspiration, the winged fiery chariot of inspiration, to go careering on this vast immensity, this illimitable, unimaginable, incommunicable dominion of the divine attributes; and if we could give the widest scope and license to the grandest imagination ever created, as to the possibilities of glory to be encountered, we should fall infinitely below them. In the matter of merely material worlds, the career of journeying and investigation from one to another, the contemplation and the noting down, from universe to universe, of marvels, which it might take a thousand thousand ages of the swiftest possible motion to reach, and a thousand more to master and comprehend, present a sphere of mental activity and acquisition, boundless and eternal. What heart *can* conceive, what mind *can* measure, even in imagination, the infinitude of the riches of creative wisdom and love! But when you add to that the riches of God's grace, and superadd to that the riches of his glory, the kingdoms of creation, redemption and reward, piled one above another, in every direction an absolutely incomprehensible infinitude, you are confounded by the very attempt, and can only humbly cry out with the enraptured and yet baffled apostle, Oh the depths! the infinite depths! infinite on infinite!

And in view of such glimpses of God's glory, the heart that has been taught by His Spirit, the heart that has begun to know, in feeling and experience, the power of His love, is ready to exclaim, My God! it is enough! Thou art my all in all. Whom have I in heaven but Thee? and there is none upon the earth that I desire beside Thee. Oh! if I may but be made to know God, if I may but be taught to love Him, I want nothing else. My happiness is secure in Him. The power of an endless life is power to me, because it will let me study and love God to all eternity. The power of an endless life is glory to me, because it absorbs me in the glory of God, unfathomable, unsearchable, inconceivable, adorable, eternal. This is life eternal, this is the power of an endless life, to know Thee, the only true God, and Jesus Christ, whom Thou hast sent.

And thus, again, that life is eternally progressive in enjoyment, in delight, in happiness inconceivable, unutterable. Forever increasing with the increase of the knowledge of God in Christ, ages on ages shall witness an undiminished freshness and novelty in the glory still to be revealed, a capacity of bliss forever enlarging, and a reality of bliss forever accumulating. The bliss arising from the knowledge and the love of God not only never can have any limit, but, in the nature of things, must be positively and infinitely progressive. What raptures are produced, even now, even in this world, even in the midst of suffering and torture, by the manifestation of God to the soul! Take the case of such a man as the dying Payson, and see him racked with pain, yet swimming in a sea of glory; almost torn asunder with the spasms of bodily anguish, yet, in his inward spirit, visited not only of angels, but of God; almost entranced in the light and glory of God in Christ Jesus, and, under the communications of God to the soul, filled with serene, ineffable, ecstatic rapture and delight! Take the case of Dr. Scott, whose experience of dying was in these words: "This is heaven begun. I have done with darkness forever, *forever.* Satan is vanquished. Nothing now remains but salvation, with eternal glory—*eternal glory.*" This is of God—the presence, the power, the glory. It is a power and a mystery of bliss beyond the reach of mortal natural philosophy. Let reason, and naturalism, and rationalism, do the utmost with their forces—let them call in all the powers of science, art, nature, imagination, and they can produce no-

And thus, again, that life is eternally progressive in enjoyment, in delight, in happiness inconceivable, unutterable. Forever increasing with the increase of the knowledge of God in Christ, ages on ages shall witness an undiminished freshness and novelty in the glory still to be revealed, a capacity of bliss forever enlarging, and a reality of bliss forever accumulating. The bliss arising from the knowledge and the love of God not only never can have any limit, but, in the nature of things, must be positively and infinitely progressive. What raptures are produced, even now, even in this world, even in the midst of suffering and torture, by the manifestation of God to the soul! Take the case of such a man as the dying Payson, and see him racked with pain, yet swimming in a sea of glory; almost torn asunder with the spasms of bodily anguish, yet, in his inward spirit, visited not only of angels, but of God; almost entranced in the light and glory of God in Christ Jesus, and, under the communications of God to the soul, filled with serene, ineffable, ecstatic rapture and delight! Take the case of Dr. Scott, whose experience of dying was in these words: "This is heaven begun. I have done with darkness forever, *forever.* Satan is vanquished. Nothing now remains but salvation, with eternal glory—*eternal glory.*" This is of God—the presence, the power, the glory. It is a power and a mystery of bliss beyond the reach of mortal natural philosophy. Let reason, and naturalism, and rationalism, do the utmost with their forces—let them call in all the powers of science, art, nature, imagination, and they can produce nothing like this, nothing *of* this; neither can they account *for* this. It is God's own mystery, God's own glory, God's own gift, God's sole almighty power. Here are glimpses of what God can do, what the manifestations of God to the soul can do, even this side the grave, in a world of guilt and suffering. Who, then, can reach to any adequate conception of what God may do, what He has promised He will do, in a world where He himself dwelleth, in light inaccessible and full of glory? Who shall set any limits to the happiness of the soul in Him, in a world triumphant over all evil, where there is no more sin, doubt, darkness, unbelief, pain or suffering, but pure, clear, celestial, radiant light, within and without,—the region of the Paradise of God to dwell in, and the peace of God, which passeth all understanding, filling the soul and expanding it, as the air lifts up these heavens? O the power of an endless life! the power of an endless life! in the manifestation and discovery of God to the soul!

Many Mansions.

In His last loving address to the dear disciples, so sad, yet so consoling, our blessed Lord said, "In my Father's House are many mansions: if not, I would have told you. I go to prepare a place for you. And if I go and prepare a place for you, I will come again, and receive you unto myself; that where I am, there ye may be also."

My Father's House! How sweet a designation of locality as well as personal affection! My Father's House! And is not this vast universe the House of my Father, and where He is, there the very homestead of heaven, no matter where, if He be there? Oh yes! But that is not the thought that Jesus here suggests or intimates, nor that the form of truth that here He teaches to the faith of His disciples, for their joy and consolation. There is delightful definiteness here. It is not the dim incomprehensible universality of Omnipresence merely, but a place for our abode, as determinate as place is for us now, and with as intimate a home relation, as the dearest fireside on this earth can have, nay incomparably more intimate and personal and definitely local, in our Father's House in heaven.

It is that building of God, that house not made with hands, eternal in the heavens, to which the thoughts are here carried. We know that if our earthly house of this tabernacle were dissolved, we have that building of God; and this text of Paul in Corinthians may well be taken as a kind of paraphrase or guide to this, in John, for the interpretation of the expression, In my Father's House are many mansions. Thus, then, let us examine some of the glorious characteristics of that heavenly building, which is there our home.

In the first place, it is a building of God. God made it, with neither creature, nor created agency, intervening. It is God's own, immediate work. It is His work, as a different kind of work, and in a very different sense, from anything material. It is a building not merely of God, but as the expression may allow, a building proceeding forth from God, rather as an effluence from His own essence, than an ordinary exercise or result of creative power. It is said that God is light, also that God dwelleth *in* light, also that we ourselves, as the children of God, dwell in God; we are also called children of light. Now, if we knew the immateriality of light, we might find in that something more than a mere type of our Father's House in heaven. This building of God may be as different from all material constructions or creations, of which we have either knowledge or conception, as the light itself is different from the forms of material substance, which we see around us.

For, in the second place, it is a house not made

with hands, not capable of being so made. It is not constructed piece by piece, as all buildings here in this world are, but is one and indivisible, as if an orb in the heavens were constructed of one perfect diamond. Moreover, it is possessed and inspired with the attributes of a spiritual glory, so that we could get no more idea of it, nor of any likelihood of it, from anything of material growth or construction, than we could get an idea of the nature or appearance of this all-surrounding crystal atmosphere of heaven, from considering the doors of our houses, or the iron hinges on which they swing. All possible forms of architecture here are made with hands. The temple of God, built by Solomon, was so prepared, that there was neither hammer nor axe, nor any tool of iron heard in the house while it was in building; yet was it all built with hands, and its glory was to pass away and be forgotten forever. We can build out of God's material creation, structures of great beauty and grandeur; and we can imitate the very forms of nature, almost at our pleasure, using the materials placed of God at our disposal. Almost anything and everything in this lovely breathing world, the hand of man can imitate, with exquisite naturalness and skill; trees, plants, roses, feathers, flowers, birds; all the creations that the sun evolves or shines upon. The first Crystal Palace was a house made with hands. But its very idea sprung from the effort of a gardener to construct a large and peculiarly shaped glass covering for a strange, costly and wondrously beautiful lily from a foreign land. So with material substances, the architect wants but the idea, and the skill even of human hands can produce structures of vast magnificence and splendor. But life and light cannot be handled, cannot be put together, cannot be imitated, nor anything like them be made with hands, nor any approximation to them, nor any symbol, or forth-shadowing resemblance of a spiritual habitation. So this building of God, not made with hands, is thus presented as inconceivably superior in essence and in glory to anything suggested by our mortal frame, or the frame of this material universe.

It is also, in the third place, an eternal building. In this respect, again, it is different from anything in this world, anything in the visible universe. Everything that these eyes behold is transitory; not one thing that we are acquainted with is permanent. These spheres and orbs of glory, constructed with such infinite skill and grandeur, connected and revolving, and each in its own bosom creatively germinating, by laws of such infinite complication and harmony, by principles of such Divine wisdom and benevolence, are yet to be laid aside. This earth and these heavens are to be rolled together as a scroll, though so Divinely glorious; these elements shall melt with fervent heat, and all nature be dissolved in the chaos of a final conflagration. "Of old hast Thou laid the foundations of the earth, and the heavens are the work of Thy hands. They shall perish, but Thou endurest. As a vesture shalt Thou fold them up, and they shall be changed; but Thou art the same, from everlasting to everlasting!" And so is this building of God, not made with hands, immutable, imperishable, like His own eternity, the same forever and ever, indestructible, everlasting.

But, in the fourth place, it is eternal in the heavens. It is where God resides, in light inaccessible and full of glory; it is where God manifests the brightness of His attributes, in a display peculiar and endearing, intimate and local. My Father's house signified, even to the Saviour, a divine, beloved and heavenly abode, from which, for a season, He had departed, had laid aside His glory, had left His robes of Deity, as it were, lying there, thrown off upon the throne of God, till He should return to be reinvested with them, after having accomplished, by His sufferings and death, in human form, that infinite redemption which for guilty, dying sinners He had undertaken. My Father's house signified, even to Him, His home in the heavens. Did He not say so on earth? "I came forth from the Father, and am come into the world. Again I leave the world, and go to the Father." And again: "Touch me not, for I am not yet ascended to my Father; but go to my brethren, and say unto them, I ascend to my Father and your Father, and to my God and your God."

It is peculiarly the dwelling-place of God. That city of which we read in the Revelation of John—that holy city, New Jerusalem, coming down from God out of heaven, and called the tabernacle of God with men, having the glory of God, presents the most distinct and definite image under which it has pleased the Divine Spirit to shadow forth the place and nature of our house which is from heaven, my Father's house, in which are many mansions. The throne of God and of the Lamb is there; and His servants see His face, with His name in their foreheads. There is no temple there, for the Lord God Almighty and the Lamb are the temple of it. There is no need of the sun, nor of the moon there, for the glory of God doth lighten it, and the Lamb is the light thereof. And whereas, it is said of those who are before the throne of God in such glory, that they see His face, and then it is added, that His name is in their foreheads, this is to signify the completion of all those predictions and processes of grace unto glory, begun on earth and fulfilled in heaven; begun in beholding, by faith, as in a glass, even in this earthly tabernacle, the glory of the Lord, and being changed into the same image from glory to glory; begun here on earth, by having the life *hid* with Christ in God, to come forth there in heaven in the life revealed, seen and known, with Christ in God forever, according to the promise, "When He who is your life shall appear, then shall ye also appear with Him in glory;" begun by the burial and hiding of the life with Him and in Him here, and completed by and because of the sight of His face there, according to the promise and assurance, "We know that when He shall appear, we shall be like Him, for we shall see Him as He is."

The sight of Him as He is, in His Father's house in glory, will complete the fulness of perfection and of glory in His dear disciples, as they are in Him, in their many mansions in that house, in His eternal likeness. The sight of His face, without veil, without cloud, in the eternal glory, will bring out the fulness of His name in their foreheads—that is, in their whole conspicuous body, form, spirit and nature, —His whole name, the glory of His Divine attributes, His whole image, a perfect reflection of His holiness in their holiness in Christ, eternal in the heavens; the glory of God, and the glory of Jesus, and the glory of the city, all possessed and reflected in that name, in their foreheads, and flashing forth, when they see His face, even as the glory of the noonday sun would be flashed forth from a spotless mirror, with insufferable brightness, the moment you should turn the mirror to the sun. For the Lord of glory and of life hath said of him that overcometh, and is to see God, "I will write upon him the name of my God, and the name of the city of my God, and my new name"; and when they see His face, then will the whole eternal glory of that name shine forth in their whole being. They may be under a cloud now, as a pure and spotless mirror might be rolled up and covered round and hidden in a veil of dark cloth, so that even beneath the sun, you could not see that it is a mirror, could not see the sun in it; but the instant you unroll the cloth, take away the veil, and hold it up to the sun, then it is so flashing and glorious, that you cannot look at it. Just so, when these wrappings of cloth, these folds of earth, that veil the dwelling of the soul in this earthly tabernacle, are drawn away; when this tent is taken down, and the believing soul, without fault, without spot or wrinkle, or any such thing, is before the throne of God, and sees Jesus as He is, then will the soul itself be seen shining forth in Jesus' likeness, glorious in His glory.

But now, in the fifth place, there are many mansions. There is room for all, and all who are there belong there, and the house belongs to them, for they are heirs of God, and joint heirs with Christ. As being the sons of God, the dwellers in those mansions have received the building as their inheritance in Christ. For them he has fitted it up, and placed it at their disposal. "I go to prepare a place for you." They have their mansions in fee simple. They are no more tenants, but heirs, joint heirs with Christ, who, as a Son, with them as sons, abideth in the House forever. There is no incumbrance on the property, and never can be. There is no mortgage on our Father's house in Heaven, whatever there may sometimes be, even on his own house on earth, which there never should be. There is no debt upon it, nor ever was, nor ever can be; for the debts of the children in it, to whom it is freely given of God, were all paid by their suffering, dying Redeemer, and to them it is given, free, full, the title in Christ unquestioned, unincumbered, perpetual. So ought the house of God on earth to be in this respect some faint type of the freedom and glory of that house in Heaven. It ought to belong to God, and to be held by man simply in trust for him. And indeed, since he hath provided for us a habitation so glorious, his own free gift, with a perpetual title of heirship to it in Christ Jesus, it is but little that we can do for him, if, out of our abundance which he hath given us by the way, we put his house on earth into his hands unincumbered, for the glory of his kingdom, that it may be said in Zion, of this and that man, when he writeth up the people, These were born there. Oh truly we ought not to be willing to have God's house on earth in debt, where we are training for that house in glory, which he hath already put out of debt at our disposal.

Now, once more in our consideration of the building of God, if there are many mansions in our Father's house, and divinely glorious, there are to be glorious inhabitants also (as indeed we have already anticipated), and a great multitude of them, whom no man can number. "Ye are come," says Paul, "to an innumerable company of angels, to the general assembly and church of the first born, which are written in heaven, and to the spirits of the just made perfect." There will be the good and the blessed, from all ages and nations, the crowned and the glorified, all, whose robes have been washed and made white in the blood of the Lamb. There will be Paul and Peter and John, and all the beloved apostles and disciples, who walked with Christ on earth, and shared his personal sufferings. And there will be all those whom they were instrumental in bringing to glory. There will be the Ephesian, Philippian, Corinthian and Athenian converts. Joseph of Arimathea, and Nicodemus, and Dionysius the Areopagite, and Lydia the seller of purple, and Barnabas and Timotheus and Apollos, and multitudes of others from the Apostolic age, will be there together. There will be Phillip, and his interesting convert the Ethiopian, seen last on earth sitting together in the chariot, reading of their Saviour's sufferings, now beheld in heaven, gazing together on their Saviour's infinite glory. There will be Enoch and Abel, and Adam and Noah, and hosts of shining witnesses of oldest time. There will be Moses and Elias as on the Mount of Transfiguration. There will be Abraham, Isaac, and Jacob in the Kingdom of Heaven, with David and Job, Isaiah, Daniel, Jeremiah, and all the Prophets, and all who with them or through them died in faith, having embraced the promises. There will be the family of Bethany, and those dear ones who followed Christ with their hearts, and ministered to him of their substance. There will be that saint who washed his feet with her tears, and wiped them with the hairs of her head; and she too, who broke for him her box of Alabaster, and stood behind him weeping; and those who followed him to the cross, and watched him at the sepulchre. There, too, will be that poor widow whom Jesus beheld as she stole trembling to God's treasury, and threw in all the living that she had. Oh what a study of character will be there, and what a comparison of infinite reward of glory with little but precious sacrifices and services on earth! There will be the earliest noble army of confessors and martyrs. There will be the great companies of witnesses slain in the many persecutions of the saints. There will be the glorified forms of those Christian heroes, whose bones lie bleaching in the mountain snows, and those whose life wore out in dungeons, or who by racking tortures rode to heaven in fire. What a congregation of the good from every clime, and every nation! What spirits of the just made perfect, in assembled hosts, of men whose memory is sweet on earth, and around any one of whom, if seen again on earth in person, men would crowd in homage and admiration! Think of meeting them together! Think of being made *worthy* to meet them! Think of the only condition on which we *can* meet them, by a participation in the life and likeness of one common Saviour.

Dear friend, have you begun your acquaintance with Him? Is the power of his grace already experienced within you, and is your life so hid with Christ in God, that you can feel that he has gone to prepare a mansion for you, and that when he appears again, you also shall appear with him in glory? Happy indeed are you, if by the law of the spirit of life in Christ Jesus, setting you free from the law of sin and of death, this is your assurance. And ought not the possession of this assurance to be your constant aim and labor? Ask yourself daily, into what house you are going when you die. Do not imitate the fool, who spent his probation in pulling down his barns and building greater, but never in all his life made the least preparation for the dwelling of his soul in glory. Alas, there are many who take far greater care for a house for their carriages and horses, than they do for their own immortal spirits. Do not imitate the wretched being, who from his palaces, and magnificent furniture, and grand clothing and living, went into a house of flames. Oh see to it that you have this building of God. Give all diligence to make your title sure, your calling and election.

And another thing is evident, if you possess that building in the skies, your affections will be fixed there, you will sometimes long to go there, more earnestly than ever the owner of a lovely paradise in the country longs to escape from the city to the sweet open fields, when Spring and Summer are spreading glory and life over all nature. And again, if you possess it, you ought to know that you possess it, and to act accordingly, and never be much troubled by anything that befalls the walls of this earthly tenement, or you in it. You ought constantly to remember that this must be taken down, before you can be admitted to that; but though the taking down of this be painful, the being clothed upon with that—the hope and assurance of it—should make you resigned and happy, and your only anxiety should be, to be prepared.

The Building of God, for God.

In that passage in the second epistle of Paul to the Corinthians, to which we have already referred, as a fit commentary on the preceding passage in John, concerning our Father's house, and its many mansions, Paul says we KNOW that if our earthly house of this tabernacle were dissolved, we have a building of God, a house not made with hands, eternal in the heavens.

The language of this expression of Christian confidence is peculiar in respect both to the *intensity* of the confidence, as an absolute knowledge, and the *time* of the possession described, as the present time. We *know* that we *have.* Here is the intimation of a present experience as the ground of a future certainty. The experience in a Christian soul arises from what, under the grace of God, that soul has been and is now doing, the life, hid with Christ in God, which it has been and is living, the character it has assumed and is building up. If there be this well-grounded assurance of this glorious house, it is because, as the apostle continues in his argument, he that hath wrought us for this self same thing is God, who hath also given unto us the Earnest of his

Spirit. And the proof that he hath so wrought us, is to be found in the fact of our working in that same direction, by that same Spirit. Let every man take heed *how* he buildeth. Every man is building is *now* building for eternity. The manner in which he is building now, shows what will be the nature of his habitation in eternity. The building into which he is to remove so shortly, is preparing in this world. In many cases it is already decided; it is always so, if a man be truly a child of God; for when a sinner comes to the Saviour, and begins building for eternity, God is building with him and for him. "Know ye not that ye are the temple of the living God, and that the Spirit of God dwelleth in you? He that dwelleth in love, dwelleth in God and God in him. For thus saith the high and lofty one that inhabiteth eternity; I dwell in the high and holy place, with him also that is of a contrite and humble spirit. He that keepeth His commandments dwelleth in Him. And hereby know we that we dwell in Him, and that He abideth in us by His Spirit that He hath given us."

This, then, is the rule under which we are all advancing to meet God in eternity. By the manner of our passing through this world, we determine the manner of our residence in the next. It is just simply a question of character. They who work with God, and build their house as the Spirit of God directs, working out their own salvation by Him working in them both to will and to do, shall dwell with God forever. But if otherwise, if the master workman is Death, by sin, and Satan, every man's work shall be made manifest, for the day shall declare it, because it shall be revealed by fire, and the fire shall try every man's work, of what sort it is. It all proceeds just according to the rule that whatsoever a man soweth that shall he also reap. He that soweth to the flesh shall of the flesh reap corruption, but he that soweth to the Spirit shall of the Spirit reap life everlasting.

We see, then, if a man has so much to do in this world with the building of that house, if according as he builds here, such and so the building will be there, what madness it is to neglect this house, to make no provision in regard to it, or to be employed in constructing it out of materials that will not stand the fire. It must be of such materials that God can dwell in it, that we and God can dwell together in it. If God cannot dwell in it, then it can be no dwelling of happiness to us. For it is written that our God is a consuming fire. And when we bring such a text as that, alongside with that other from the Epistle to the Corinthians, that the fire shall try every man's work of what sort it is, it seems that we have a new light as to the kind of fire that is to try the building. Suppose it to be simply the fire of God's holiness, the fire of the presence of God. Can we stand that, if our building is made of such materials as cannot endure that light? It is said of all the wicked, that wickedness is in their dwellings; and it is also said, Thou art not a God that hast pleasure in wickedness, neither shall evil dwell with thee. But it is also said of all the good, The upright shall dwell in God's presence, and God hath said, I will dwell *in* them, and will be *with* them. The very essence of heaven, and the peculiarity of the building there, and the blissful certainty and immutable necessity of glory for the righteous there, is this, that they dwell in the very presence of God. But he himself is like the refiner's fire, and in the last revelation he will come in flaming fire, and the very work of the Holy Spirit in preparing submissive and believing souls for his presence and glory, is said to be that of the Holy Ghost and of fire; and therefore rolls forth the woe of the prophets against the men who build by iniquity, and in the very same breath we are called to mark that it is of the Lord of Hosts that such persons shall labor in the very fire. But who among us shall dwell with devouring fire, and who can lie down in everlasting burnings?

Now, a man may choose what materials he pleases; he may build for himself just what character he pleases; but let him remember that he is putting up a building, which is to meet God's inspection, and not only so, but if he has the least idea of eternal blessedness, it must be a building in which God can dwell.

Let us then suppose that a man having the command of all the elements, and of all the resources of science for their combination, and of all the agencies and materials for the construction of a splendid residence, should undertake to build a house out of a preparation of crystalized and solidified gunpowder, or whatever ingredients of mingled sulphurous, bituminous, fiery and explosive power, might be concentrated and hardened into beams, pillars, walls, roofs and rafters. He might also have his house furnished with wrought crystal furniture of the same material; brimstone couches, and chairs carved of solid nitre, and stuffed and cushioned with gun-cotton. The house is to be lighted with gas, and he has all the fixtures prepared accordingly, and gas-pipes of transparent asphaltum running through every apartment. It is a wondrous house indeed; the dreams of the Arabian Nights' Entertainments never imagined such a building; a splendid house, a most original and costly house; and if things were well adapted, if the nature of the materials would permit, it might be a most comfortable, useful, and lasting house. But there is one thing the builder has forgotten, or by a strange hallucination has overlooked, in thus consulting his own will, and building his house according to the freaks of his fancy; and that is, the inflammable nature of its materials, and the certainty that that which is necessary to light it, will also inevitably consume it; that which is requisite for the possibility of residing in it, will shroud it, from the foundation to the top-stone, in a sheet of fire. The instant the gas is lighted, or the fire kindled, the whole building is a flash of living inextinguishable flame.

Now, this is but a faint emblem of a man who builds up his character in this world without God, out of materials that are instinct with sin, and sealed with God's displeasure. His character thus wrought out, solidified, established here, is to be his possession and abode for eternity. Its materials are all chosen, not according to the reason of things, or the will of the great God of Eternity, but according to the freaks of his own fancy, the rule of his own appetites and passions, the indulgence of his own present pleasure. All the fixtures even for lighting up this abode, and making it comfortable, are according to the same law of present self-indulgence, wrought out of the same sinful ingredients; and the very atmosphere of the dwelling is of the same elemental stuff. Now, the house of a man's character, even thus constituted, may be all very grand, costly, luxurious, splendid in appearance, and may abide quiet for the present; but what will become of it the moment the fire tries it, the moment a flame is kindled in it, the moment that light, by which it must be lighted in eternity, if ever lighted at all, is let into it and upon it? What will become of it, when the light of God's holiness enters into it, flashes through it? Why, indeed, we have the answer to this question in the declaration of scripture, that to the wicked and the unbelieving, our God is a consuming fire. Such the Divine attributes must be, in the eternal world, to a man whose character is builded out of such materials, without Christ, without God, without prayer, without holiness, without hope.

For we know that we are designed to be, every one of us, according to God's rule, a dwelling place for God, a living temple, of which God shall be the happy life and soul. And the building built up in God and with God and for God here, and so formed that God can inhabit it forever, will be blessed in eternity, an immortal temple, a house not made with hands, eternal in the heavens. And unless so formed that God can enter it, can dwell in it, can be glorified by it, then the moment God touches it, the moment the light of God's holiness blazes upon it, surrounds it, flashes within, it will be all a flame of fire unquenchable. All the fixtures running to and fro in such a character are of inflammable materials, that will kindle with the fires of hell; all the furniture of such a character has only the seal of the self-willed maker, and of God's wrath. And the character thus formed in sin is of such a nature, that that very light which is necessary in order to light up and render happy any created soul, will inevitably consume it, the moment it meets it. That flame of purity and love, which alone can form the possibility of any man's blessed residence in the eternal world, will set the whole residence on fire, a lurid and conflicting fire, a retributive and self-avenging fire, forever burning, yet forever unconsumed, in the very materials out of which the soul's dwelling, nay, the soul's adopted nature, was constructed.

See, then, what you are doing, O man of sin! You wish to be saved, you wish to be received into heaven when you die. You wish by no means to be lost, you are not willing to contemplate *that* as your destiny, or to believe it possible. You wish that your existence in the eternal world may be a blessed and blissful existence, that for you there may be a mansion of eternal rest, that your name may be found in God's book of life, and that yours forever may be a place in the city of the righteous. Consider, then, what this wish really signifies. It means that you may be permitted to dwell with God, and that God would deign to dwell with you forever and ever. It means that you desire to have God's own abode within you, and to enter into an eternal and intimate communion with God, so that you shall be as cognizant and conscious of God's presence and inspection, as God is cognizant of your existence. It means that you desire a state of being, where every thought, wish, impulse and emotion shall be as clear to the eye of Jehovah, and you yourself conscious of it, as this material world and you yourself in it, or the men that walk upon it, or the trees and flowers that adorn it, are to your own eye. It means that you desire to meet God, and to have the blaze of all His attributes upon you and within you; that you desire to be forever fixed, where you can never for an instant escape the notice of His all-seeing eye, where your inmost being will be turned to Him as to the sun, where not a thought can arise, not a feeling be experienced, not a wish formed, not an impulse cherished, but it will confront the instant blaze of the Divine holiness; and where, consequently, unless you are one with God, your being will flash forth in hostility, just as the house of nitre, or of solidified oxygen, or alcohol, would kindle at the touch of fire.

Just consider, then, O creature of such tremendous responsibilities, if you be a stranger to grace, what it is that you are doing, while you are living in your sins, that is, while you are living in neglect of Christ Jesus, and of prayer, and without God in the world. For, to be without God is to be alienated from Him, it is to be without holiness, it is to be passing on towards Him, in the habitual formation of a character that cannot bear His sight, a character in hostility against Him. What are you doing to prepare your own heart, your own mind, your own consciousness, your thoughts and your affections, for the habitual presence of God? What are you doing to make your own being, with its spiritual furniture and habits, a temple for His indwelling, holiness and love? What are you doing in preparation for that meeting of your soul with God, to which, on the supposition of the least hope of a happy existence in the future world, you are advancing? What in preparation for that most intimate communion with God, and closeness of His inspection, which your very wish to be happy in the future world implies? What have you done already, supposing you should now die, just as you are, what *have* you accomplished in preparation for God's taking up His glorious and blissful abode with you? Alas, is there any joy within your heart at the thoughts of such a meeting, or do your thoughts draw back in terror as the reality draws near? Unless you are changed indeed, and possess a new spiritual character, unless you are submissive to God, and a partaker of His holiness, *could* God abide with you? Is there any such possibility? Can there be for you, in any such blissful sense, a building of God, a house not made with hands, eternal in the heavens? Would not the meeting of every prayerless being, every unregenerate heart, every sin-defiled soul with God, be just that of antagonist forces, incompatible, not to be united; that of infinite righteousness and utter sinfulness, infinite justice and uncancelled guilt, that of the Divine sovereignty and the sinful soul's habitual and supreme selfishness, that of the will of the creature and the Creator in uttermost eternal conflict?

It is one of the mightiest, most overwhelming truths of our existence, that we are all advancing into the immediate presence of God, all coming where we shall see him face to face, where the nature and operation of his attributes will be clearer to the soul, and more sensibly experienced, than the objects and qualities of the material world to the bodily senses. The meeting must take place. It is the great event to which we are all hastening. It is the event which is to determine our eternal destiny, according to the character with which we meet God. And one would think the sense of this truth, the remembrance of it, and a watchfulness accordingly, would never be out of our minds, but would inspire us with a spirit of incessant prayer. One would think that the knowledge of a meeting, so rapidly near, with Infinite Holiness, would arm us with such an energetic and instinctive terror and abhorrence of all sin, that we should recoil from the least approach of it, and start as from the upreared head of an adder in the way. One would think that the very breath of ceaseless prayer in our hearts, and the thought and the yearning co-present with all other thoughts, would be, Oh God! cleanse me from my sins, and make me like to thee! Oh Thou, whom I must shortly meet, and whose very love, if I be not a partaker of it, will burn me, like thine own holiness, as a consuming fire, take possession of me now for thyself, baptize me now with the Holy Spirit and with fire. Let the refining flame of thy love kindle within me, and never go out, but burn on, till every sinful thing shall be consumed, and every native faculty transfigured, and every impulse of will, feeling, and emotion baptized in that regenerating flame!

And how can such a prayer be answered, and to whom, if it be sincere, will it certainly bring the yearning heart and soul, that the whole being may be thus gloriously and forever transfigured, regenerated, and delivered from all sin? Oh! to Jesus, to the Son of God, our Saviour, to the great Physician of the soul! Behold the Lamb of God, who taketh away the sin of the world! There is the Being, to whom love will bring you, there is the Being, who will answer your love, and will fulfil, as he must have inspired, all blissful and heavenly desires within you. "Jesus answered and said, If a man love me, he will keep my words: and my Father will love him, and we will come to him and make our abode with him." "Lord, to whom shall we go, but unto thee? Thou hast the words of eternal life!"

The Family in Heaven.

THAT is a wonderfully glorious passage in the Epistle to the Ephesians, which reads thus; "Of whom the whole family in heaven and earth is named." The glory of the whole context is infinite, and this is but a sort of parenthesis before the prayer. But the full comprehensiveness and grandeur of this parenthesis, can be known only in the Redeemer's second coming, and final everlasting reign. As all beings were created by him and for him, so angels and archangels, principalities and powers of heavenly height and glory, as well as the redeemed from our fallen world, are named in him and for him, for he is before all things, and by him all things consist.

We have had occasion to refer to the manner in which God makes heaven our home; gives us a home locality there; throws around the idea of place there the same sweet associations that cluster in the heart and delight the imagination at the word *home*, here. But we are carried still farther. There is also the word *family* in heaven; indeed, the only time in which this word is spoken in the New Testament is here, in this mention of the *whole* family in heaven. There is a family circle there; there are family ties and associations dearer than all ties on earth; and if we should descend from the vast and mighty sweep of this whole phrase, "the whole family in heaven and on earth," which takes in all the redeemed out of every nation, and kindred, and tongue, and tribe, from the beginning to the end of time, and stop at the literality of the first clause; if we should cut out those striking words, the whole family in heaven, from their connection, and interpret them of one household, applying there in heaven something like the very thought and feeling of a loving family on earth, with its particular and strong affections, in which a stranger intermeddleth not, we should not perhaps be far out of the way. Nor can there be anything more delightful than the thought of a whole family in heaven. No doubt, there will be many such—many whole households, transplanted entire, not one left out or missing, from earth into the kingdom of heaven. There will be whole families gathered there, through the blessed instrumentality of one faithful and beloved member of the household, first brought to Jesus. There will be children gathered by the piety of parents, and parents gathered by the piety of children; brothers drawn to Christ by sisters, and sisters drawn by brothers; and whole families saved by the faith and prayers of one.

One of the two that heard John speak, and followed Jesus, was Andrew, Simon Peter's brother. He first findeth his own brother, Simon, and he brought him to Jesus. That is *one* example given us in God's own record of the manner in which He maketh up His jewels; how the endearments and affections of our family ties and duties sometimes lead on those of grace; the earthly affection brings the heavenly to bear upon the soul. And can there be the least doubt that in heaven itself, the tie on earth so strong between Andrew and Simon, and made the means of the salvation of the one, through the instrumentality of the other, and thus exalted and glorified, even here, will be recognized, will make the family there, in some sense, a family still? Why, we may learn something on this subject, even from the lost in the world of woe, as presented by our Saviour. We find the elder brother in the gulf of flame, trembling at the thought of meeting the family circle there; five brethren, whom he expected to meet, and to meet as brought thither partly by his own example, and in such a manner that the family on earth would be known as a family in hell.

That direction, also, of the Lord of the harvest, to gather the tares *in bundles*, and bind them for the burning, has a marked meaning here; for the principle of association and participation in sinful example, instrumentality and character, such as marks and attends an evil family all through life, will be one of the principles of association and relationship in an endless retribution. And the same principle of association in heavenly and holy relationship, character, example and influence, marking the families of redeemed on earth, will hold them peculiarly known and near in heaven. There will be trains of blissful causes, sacred instrumentalities, set at work in family circles here, the results of which will be seen, marked, traced, admired there, holding the same circle nearer and nearer through eternity, nearer and dearer in Christ, and in one another, in and through Him.

But if the whole family in heaven and earth is recognized, there are also the more particular representations, and representatives of the family there. There are children in heaven. There are babes in heaven, and there must be an infant's heavenly discipline there. Of such, said our blessed Lord, is the kingdom of Heaven; and we may suppose that he had in view not merely the childlike temper and disposition of a new-born soul in his kingdom here, but the fact that the kingdom of the redeemed there is made up, in so great a degree, of little children.

I shall go to him, but he will not return to me, exclaimed David, speaking of his own babe, that God had taken, and speaking of the child as at rest with God, in the presence of God in heaven. Thither the affections of David travelled; there his hopes were placed; there was his eternal dwelling-place and home. When he himself should depart from this world, he expected to be with God in glory. Thou wilt not leave my soul in hell; he could speak that promise of himself, as well as a prediction of the Messiah's resurrection. By the Earnest of the Spirit he was confident, for God had wrought him for the self-same thing, and he had the witness of the Spirit within him that he was a child of God. "The Lord is the portion of mine inheritance and my cup. Thou wilt show me the path of life: in thy presence is fulness of joy; at thy right hand there are pleasures forevermore. As for me, I will behold thy face in righteousness. I shall be satisfied, when I awake, with thy likeness."

But his child had gone thither, to God, before him. If there is anything clear in David's confidence, it is this, that his child was in heaven, and there in heaven he expected to meet him. I shall go to him. I shall rejoin him in God's good time, when it pleases God to take me also to my heavenly home. And the confidence has a personal and not merely a local direction. I shall go to him, not merely to the place where he is, but to him. It was in the heart of David to recognize his child again in glory; and the confidence does not seem to be set down as a mere imagination, springing out of a present fondness, or a mere desire that it *might* be so; but out of the darkness of his present sorrow it was the breaking forth of a great truth. It was an inspiration flashing from earth to heaven. As a sheet of lightning in the blackness of a midnight storm reveals instantly and vividly the whole horizon, so this confident declaration of David lights up the whole landscape, not only of heavenly realities, but of the Jewish belief in regard to them; not only throws a stream of sudden radiance into the revealed spiritual world, but shows the contemplation of a future existence habitual to the Hebrew mind, and that, too, on occasion of the death of an infant.

There was no surprise in David's servants, as though he had announced to them a new and most surprising, most overwhelming doctrine, such as it must have been if it had been new; but David enunciated it, and they received it, with the utmost calmness of a customary conviction, as a fixture of their own belief and instruction, to which they were to resort for consolation and submission under such a bereavement. Here, again, we have the scepticism and blindness of those who would dephlogisticate out of the word of God, in the Old Testament especially its living breath and flame of thought and knowledge in regard to a future world of rewards and punishments, put to shame and scorn. And out of the mouth of a babe, speaking as it were from the eternal world, God perfects truth and praise. Here we have a great prophet of God, speaking to the people over the grave of his own child, concerning a truth which they had all been taught from God's Word, as well as declaring out of his own impulse of Divine inspiration, I shall go to him, but he shall not return to me!

Now, as to the recognition in the heavenly world, it is to be marked that David himself did not die, did not depart to his heavenly home, to rejoin whatever loved ones of his family circle might be gathered there, till near twenty years after this beloved child had gone from its cradle to Abraham's bosom, to the companionship and glory of the celestial world. Twenty years the child would have been in heaven with Moses and Elias in glory, a lamb in the fold of Christ there, before his earthly parent would again see him; and could he be expected to know, in the bright form of a seraph, educated for twenty years in the presence and likeness of Jesus, his own departed babe? Why not, as well as Elijah, when translated to heaven, could be expected to know Moses, who had been dwelling in heaven five hundred years before Elijah went thither? There would be no more of mystery in the one recognition than in the other, but an equal delight and glory. That a Christian parent should recognize a child, passed into the skies, and educated there, is no more mysterious than that Moses and Elijah should recognize each other, or rather *know* each other, though they never met on earth, but only in heaven.

But whether that come to the mind as a mystery or not, there is something unspeakably delightful in following a little child, in imagination, into the heavenly world, and dwelling on the blissfulness and glory of its development there. There must be a nursery, an infant school in heaven, a peculiar training of these buds and blossoms of immortal being, which for all heaven may be a scene of greater rapture and delight, than perhaps any other of the infinite wonders of redemption, even in the heavenly world. What a sight must it be, that of the spirit of a babe, an infant, a prattling child, growing up in heaven, opening, developing, in the image of Jesus, perhaps beneath the guardianship and teaching of other angels—an employment how ecstatic, how divine!

For aught we know, there may be a form of glory, or degrees and qualities of glory, resulting from such a development in heaven, transcending all other manifestations of the manifold wisdom of God through the church to all ages. And as we have reason to believe that so vast a preponderating multitude of those transmitted from our world to heaven die in infancy and childhood, so the greater part of heaven is filled with just such scenes, and heaven might be conceived as one vast ecstatic holy school of youthful happy spirits. What curious, wondrous, blissful forms of the wisdom and love of the Creator, combined with the perfection of the work of our Divine Redeemer, may be seen in the evolution of the infant immortal spirit from the very bud of being,—who shall tell! Who has not felt, at times, an earnest desire to look into the invisible workings of an infant's mind, to see the dawnings of thought, reason, self-consciousness, to know the motions of this wondrous opening and dreaming soul, even as we know our own! Oh certainly, to see the growth of a mind in heaven, to watch its developings in Christ, above the brightness of the firmament, must be a process of glory so exquisite, that nothing which we now see in the grandeur and beauty of all this material universe can bear any proportion to its loveliness.

But we pass from the family to the name. Of whom the whole family in heaven and earth are named. It is Christ the Saviour. Not a creature of the redeemed of all our race, infant or aged, but bears his name. All are there through the virtue of his blood, and through that alone, without which no more the babe than the child a hundred years old, or the chief of sinners, could ever enter heaven. The whole family, young and old, are named of Christ, washed in his blood, clothed in his righteousness, and in him, and him alone, without fault before the throne of God. This is the certainty, and the only certainty, alike of the babe's salvation, and that of the matured, believing child of God. It is that Christ has died for the sins of the whole world, and that his blood cleanseth from all sin. It is that the child as well as the sinner a hundred years old, needs a Saviour, and that Jesus died for children. All that are in heaven bear his name, and only thus can any be in heaven.

It is as difficult for God to save a child as a grown person, equally a wondrous work of his Divine redemption; but it is also equally easy; for Christ has died, and it is not on account of any imagined or possible innocence or merit, that any human being, infant or aged, is ever saved, but only on account of the merit and the death of Christ. So the whole family in heaven and earth are named of him, though we have reason to believe the greater proportion by far of the members of the family at any one time, and at all times, passing from earth to heaven, are infant members. Their first lisp of language is his name, and the first exercise of belief into which their minds open, is faith in his blood, and the first and simplest feeling and emotions in which their hearts beat, intelligent and self-conscious, are of gratitude and love to him. And the first song in which their joy finds utterance must be the anthem, Worthy is the Lamb that was slain; and their infant melodies may be the sweetest of all heaven's melody, and the grandest part in those celestial services, that which they bear in the halleluiahs of redemption. Perhaps, indeed, it is this very thing, of which the Psalmist caught a view by inspiration, when he exclaimed, "O Lord! thou hast set thy glory above the heavens. Out of the mouth of babes and sucklings thou hast perfected praise!" No *literal* interpretation can be given to that passage in any other way. But if you translate it of the infant singers in heaven, it is a very natural window opened into the glories of the celestial world.

The assurance that little children, through the blood of Jesus Christ, are taken to heaven, should greatly mitigate the grief of parents and friends, when God takes them away. They cannot help sorrowing, for ever since Adam and Eve left the Garden of Eden and mourned the death of Abel, the loss of children has been and must be regarded as one of the severest of earthly trials; but they must not sorrow as those who have no hope. The sting of death is taken away, and the imagination and heart can follow the little one into a world of glory, where there are no conceptions of beauty and blessedness, in which they may not properly array it. All that ever they could depict to themselves, or by the Earnest of the Spirit ever foretasted, or could desire to experience, of holiness, radiance and happiness in the heavenly world, they may feel sure is outdone, is overpassed, by the infant cherubs that have gone before them. If the fancy in vain strives to paint the glories that surround the believer, when on rising from the river of death, the visions and realities of the celestial world burst upon the soul, still more impossible is it to conceive the beauty and happiness of a babe in heaven. What a privilege it is for parents whom God has bereaved, to feel that they have children there! What a privilege to have consecrated them to God, to have prayed over them, to have led them to the Saviour, to have offered them to God in baptism, to have claimed His promise for them, to have given them to Jesus as the members of His family, the lambs of His fold! And now, if God has taken them, from how many thousand evils, snares, temptations, dangers, sins, have they been snatched! Neither pain, nor sickness, nor sorrow shall they ever know more.

And what education could the most careful parents ever have given them, compared with that angelic and ecstatic discipline in which they are nurtured there in the perfect likeness and beholding of the Redeemer; or what care could the most anxious parents ever have bestowed upon them, compared with the care of that Saviour who has taken them to His bosom; or what fortune could the most indulgent parents ever have provided for them, though all the riches of the universe had been placed at their disposal, compared with that inheritance of which they are with Christ the heirs, those glorious mansions they inhabit, that blessed society where they rest? And we may add, what happiness could they ever have conferred upon the most delighted parents here, compared with that they are conferring in heaven upon myriads, who perhaps gather from the remotest dominions of the King of saints, to gaze upon their glory, and to admire with new love and gratitude, and new ecstasy of enjoyment and surprise, the glory of the Saviour revealed so ravishingly in them. If there is joy among the angels of God over one sinner that repenteth, oh what joy likewise over every babe received to glory!

But again, and more solemnly still, the consideration of this theme ought to make us think of the sacredness, preciousness and glory of the work of training up a little child for Christ and His Kingdom. How blessed the thought of a whole family in heaven! How precious, how delightful, the mutual communion, example, instrumentality, effort, faith, prayer, by which one after another, coming into the Christian life here, enter on the life of glory there, till all are gathered at length, a dear unbroken family before's God's throne! How infinitely important the work of faith, love, instruction and prayer, to be applied continually by parents upon the susceptible hearts and ductile minds of their little ones, that from the earliest period, the image and superscription of Jesus may be impressed and growing daily! We know not how rapidly they may be passing from the time, when, if they were suddenly taken, we might feel the assurance that Jesus has taken them to Himself in glory, to the period of conscious unbelief and voluntary neglect and rejection of Jesus from the heart. What fervent effort ought to be used, what earnest prayer, what affectionate persuasive instruction, that they may not enter upon that period, or if entered on it, that they may turn from it, and hasten to the Saviour, in faith, penitence and love, the youthful happy subjects of His sanctifying grace! Both the uncertainty of life, and the certainty that if habits of youthful piety are not commenced, the habits of procrastination and of sin are greatly and constantly strengthening, and the prospect becoming less and less favorable of a conversion to God, ought to impel every Christian parent to an earnest heartfelt, never-ceasing diligence, in pleading and applying the instructions and promises of the gracious Saviour, and the affectionate persuasive power of a heavenly example.

The Power of an Endless Death.

THE power of an endless death! Amazing and infinitely dreadful expression! Yet thus hath eternal life its infinite and opposite extreme; and little indeed could we know of either but by the disclosures of Divine Revelation. Accordingly, in one of the grandest chapters in the book of Job, we have the following sublime and impressive interrogation from the Almighty: "Have the gates of death been opened unto thee? or hast thou seen the doors of the shadow of death?"

And what mortal can answer it? Who hath ever gone down to those portals, or been admitted within the secrets of that prison house, and returned? What living man knows anything about death, even the death of the body, save as he sees some of the phases of departing life; but when it is gone, knows not which way it fled, nor how, nor whither? And as to the changing substance that remains, the mould, the worm, the putrefaction, the corruption of the grave, all *that* is no more a process of death, than the disintegration of a granite mountain by the rain, the light, the air, frost, fire and sunbeams. And whatever thou hast seen or known of disease or pain, dark-walking pestilence or noon-wasting destruction, fretting leprosies, plagues, lazar-houses, consumptions, fevers, poisons, wounds, or the bloodiest murderous carnage of war, if thou art yet alive, thou knowest nothing of death. So far from having entered the gates of death, thou hast not seen even the doors of its shadow.

THE DOORS OF THE SHADOW OF DEATH! Rightly considered, there is surely something exceedingly terrific and awful in this expression. Where are those doors? And if we were admitted within them, what is there *there* sending such shadow here? All that we see and know is *but* the shadow; and if such *be* the shadow, what must be the reality! and where is it? Sometimes God has caught us up as in a vision; once He stood upon the world, and bade us look down into the gulf, opening it before us; and always He makes us know that the substance, which sends, from the doors of the unseen, such a shadow, englooming the world, is infinite depths beyond the confines of time, filling eternity. And death here, Shadow or Skeleton, is the King of Terrors, because we know him not till we get beyond, within those unseen portals, whence this vast, wide, creeping, desolating shadow issues and enshrouds us.

DEATH! Its shadow covers the world, darkens it, and fills all hearts with gloomy fears and forebodings. All their lifetime, through fear of death, men are subject unto bondage. Its shadow is here, but its substance and its power are the power of an endless life, life in death, and death in life, conflicting forever. The reality of death is in eternity.

And that death is called in scripture the SECOND death. This is that, of which the first death is but the shadow. This is the last, and, in some respects, the most terrible designation of it in God's word—the second death. There is nothing after that, but that holds on, perpetual, eternal. And it is under this designation that we must examine it. It is appointed unto men once to die; but that death is scarcely worthy of the name of death. The death that comes after the judgment—the death of the soul—the death of sin, and of retribution *for* sin—the death eternal—that is death indeed, that is the second death. Salvation from that is indeed salvation. Anything less than that would be but the purchase of a lease, that would of itself inevitably run out. Redemption from the second death was a work worthy the interposition and atoning sacrifice of the Son of God; but nothing less than eternity made it so. Nothing less than the power of an endless life, on one hand, and the power of an endless death, on the other, demanded, for a High Priest and Saviour, the Almighty, the Word that was with God, and was God.

Under this view, let us examine it. We have to set out with the great fact of scripture and of our own experience, that death is death in sin, and that only. Dead in sin, dead in trespasses and sins, and such like expressions, are some of the forms conveying the description, or announcing the reality, of this state. The sting of death is sin, and the strength of sin is the law,—expressions which carry us at once beyond the grave, not referring merely, or by any means mainly, to that shadow of death under which this body passes to the tomb, but to the reality and power of death in eternity; and that reality and power is sin. The first thing, then, to be noted of the substance of death, under the power of an endless life, is, that it is perfection in sin.

It is not until this corruptible shall have put on incorruption, and this mortal, immortality—not till after the passing of the shadow of death, and the raising of the body from its dominion into the glorified body—that, in eternal life, the saying is brought to pass that is written, Death is swallowed up in victory. Oh death! where is thy sting? Gone forever, because sin is gone. And, therefore, in the last description of the blessed in Christ, the all-embracing proposition is, that there shall be no more death. Over such the second death hath no power; for there is no sin, but an eternal victory over it, eternal, absolute, perfect holiness, in the imparted and participated nature of the Redeemer.

And on the other hand, it is not till the absolute, unmingled mastery of sin beyond the grave, not till the destruction of both soul and body in hell, that life is swallowed up of death, and death is seen and known, as sin is seen and known, by and in eternity. In this view there is a tremendous emphasis in the declaration that sin, when it is finished, bringeth forth death. When sin is finished, the whole being is alive with it, in a living, positive, active death, perfect, unmingled, unalleviated. There is no good left. It is absolute evil, unbalanced, unmodified, unmitigated. Perfection in sin is the negation of all good, and the active despotism of all evil. Neither of these can be without the other. John says, even in this world, He that loveth not his brother, abideth in death. He knoweth nothing of life, nothing of God, nothing of heaven. In this the children of God are manifest, and the children of the devil. In the absence of all good, all evil reigns. Even now, the carnal mind is enmity against God; it is not subject to the law of God, neither indeed can be. But enmity against God is the parent of all other enmity. Our blessed Lord said, Whosoever committeth sin is the servant of sin; and again, by the Apostle John, Whosoever committeth sin is of the devil. And again, our blessed Lord, Ye are of your father the devil, a murderer from the beginning; and by the Apostle John, He that hateth his brother is a murderer.

Now here is the dominant spirit of heaven, and the dominant spirit of hell, love on the one side, and hate on the other, and each in infinite perfection. To be ruled by the spirit of hate is to be by nature the children of wrath and children of the devil. When that nature is given over to itself, then there can be nothing but despair, no more possibility of good, no motive for good, no desire towards it, no possibility of ever communicating aught but evil. And as the happiness of heaven consists in the knowledge of good, so the misery of hell consists in the knowledge of evil. In both directions the measure is infinite. Approximation towards God, in His knowledge, likeness and love, is the rule in heaven, distance from Him, and enmity against Him, is the rule in hell. And there is no half-way, but a perfection in both extremes. This is the nature of things in a world where all tendencies, both good and evil, will be left to a perfect development. The points of starting are separate and absolute, and the directions opposite, and so the course in either case runs on, according to the judgment pronounced in the shutting up of God's own word, He that is unjust, let him be unjust still, and he that is filthy, let him be filthy still; and he that is righteous, let him be righteous still, and he that is holy, let him be holy still.

This then brings us to a second manifest point in the power of an endless death, that it is *progression* in sin. As it is the power of an endless life, that it is progression in holiness, in the knowledge and likeness of God, and consequently in happiness inconceivable, immeasurable, so it is the power of an endless death, that it is a living death, and a progressive death, in the increase of wickedness, the knowledge and experience of evil, and consequently the endurance of misery. Here we are on simple and plain ground. Character is progressive, unalterably so, even in this world, in one direction or the other. And here, also, character would be exclusively bad or good, and sin with the sinful would go to an instant entireness and supremacy, if it were not for the interposition of a Saviour, which has made this world a world of restraint and grace. Even under all opposing, preventing and reclaiming influences, evil character, if not changed by grace, exasperates and grows, even to the end.

Character accumulates and shoots onward. There is nothing that gathers such strength, and at length acquires it even from opposition. This is the power of habit. The progression of the mind in evil is tremendous, and wickedness burneth as a fire. There comes a time, even this side the grave, when the power of habit is absolutely irresistible, and passion is like a forest conflagration. Yet here there is vast and constant restraint. What then will it be, when all restraint is taken away, and what when ages on ages shall have passed, and all the while the habit growing, and the evil nature becoming more and more permanent and predominant. Then will passion be seen in its omnipotence, and the will in its immortality and inflexibility as the slave of the passion, yet one with it, as the regent of a hurricane, bound to it, and madly driving through eternity. Progression in sin is as inevitable as progression in holiness.

In the third place, there will be communion in sin; a community, and yet anarchy, a fellowship, and yet repulsion, nearness, and yet malignity. Heaven is a social state, a state of perfect love; hell is an unsocial state, and yet a community; but of perfect wrath and hatred. The conception is fearful beyond expression, of a world of intelligent beings, demoniac in nature and by habit, abhorred of one another, repulsive and repelled, and yet, by very wickedness and hate compelled into proximity, suspicious, angry, raging, tormenting and tormented, living in malice and envy, hateful and hating one another. Fearful as the conception is, it may be in a great degree realized, even in this world; and in fact the last expressions used, are just merely descriptions by the Apostle of a state of society on earth, of which he and his friends had formed a part. It was a state of society little better than that of Sodom and Gomorrah, the state of all bad passions dominant, with little restraint save that of fear, hatred and revenge. The description of such a state on earth is to be found in the first chapter of the Epistle to the Romans; a description of human beings, filled with all unrighteousness, fornication, wickedness, covetousness, maliciousness; full of envy, murder, debate, deceit, malignity; whisperers, backbiters, haters of God, despiteful, proud, boasters, inventors of evil things, disobedient to parents, without understanding, covenant-breakers, without natural affection, implacable, unmerciful; who, knowing the judgment of God, that they which commit such things are worthy of death, not only do the same, but have pleasure in those that do them.

What have we in this account, when all restraint is removed, but the very elements of hell in depraved human nature? And we have only to carry forward the evil which we see here, to a progressive social perfection there, a perfect unrestrained development; we need only take what we are by nature, in our depravity, and let it run on at natural compound interest, and no hell of revelation could disclose more dreadful realities. We only need to take a wicked community, and endow that community with the power of endless life and progression in wickedness, that is, with the power of endless death.

The good are all drawn off to a better world. There is left only in the seething mixture the dross of the universe. It is one of the descriptions of God's justice and goodness in the word of God, Thou puttest away all the wicked of the earth like dross. It is the scum and corruption of this universe that will form the social state of hell. The universe is to be purified, and its dregs, its impurities, as dross, when the scurf rises to the surface from the crucible, shall be thrown away, shall be gathered into one place. The wicked shall be driven away in his wickedness, and the strongest spirits in this seething mass of demoniacs will still be uppermost, and there will be plans of evil carried careering over ages, ambition towering upon ambition, empires and shoals of evil natures driven on over the depths of hell, and chasing one another like waves as wide as the ocean. Raging waves of the sea, foaming out their own shame, clouds without water, carried about of winds; trees whose fruit withereth, without fruit, twice dead, plucked up by the roots; wandering stars, to whom is reserved the blackness of darkness forever! Such are some of the expressions in scripture descriptive of the character of those who shall compose this fraternity of perfect, progressive sin, and absolute despair. Separated from the good they must be, and gathered into one place they must be, by the very necessity of God's goodness and love as the guardian of his universe, no more to permit the combination of evil with the good, nor the spread of temptation, nor the power of bad example. How terrific is the thought of such a community! How fearful the imagination, how dire the prospect, for an immortal intelligent nature, of spending eternity in such companionship! Yet such are the very terms of judgment announced by our blessed Lord beforehand, "Depart, ye cursed, into everlasting fire, prepared for the devil and his angels." What remorse, recrimination, angry despair, weeping and wailing and gnashing of teeth, must constitute the materials of social intercourse there, we can more easily in silence contemplate and shudder at, than openly express.

In the solemn providence of God, in the deep valley of Hinnom, outside the city of Jerusalem, there was of old a place of infinite abomination, where the carcasses of animals, and the dead bodies of malefactors, were thrown together, and an incessant smouldering fire was kept up to consume them. It became an emblem of the place and state of everlasting torment of the wicked. The glorious predictions of Isaiah close with it: "They shall go forth, and look upon the carcasses of the men that have transgressed against me, for their worm shall not die, neither shall their fire be quenched, and they shall be an abhorring unto all flesh." That outcast and detested place, that vale of death and putrefaction, where carcasses were festering with fire and worm together, day and night unquenchable, the energies of corruption always going on, and the elements of consumption always administered, that dreadful place God chose, to be some emblem, and indeed a most lively and terrible emblem, of the everlasting corruption and conflagration of the soul in sin, in the world of retribution and despair, where their worm dieth not, and the fire is not quenched. And may not these two agencies have been chosen on purpose to signify, the first the nature of sin as a corruption and undying worm in the conscience and the soul; and the second, the external kindled fire, to signify the retributive and guardian justice of God, a fire which He will never quench, which never indeed *can* be quenched, being as eternal as his own goodness. Not once, nor twice, but many times, and sometimes with vast and mighty array of circumstantial imagery, our blessed Lord took up the same emblems, and wrought them, with solemn, awful, deliberate intensity of truth, into his appeals to the soul against sin and temptation. "If thy hand offend thee, cut it off; it is better for thee to enter into life maimed, than having two hands to go into hell, into the fire that never shall be quenched. Where their worm dieth not, and the fire is not quenched. And if thy foot offend thee, cut it off; it is better for thee to enter halt into life, than having two feet to be cast into hell, into the fire that never shall be quenched. Where their worm dieth not, and the fire is not quenched. And if thine eye offend thee, pluck it out, it is better for thee to enter into the kingdom of God with one eye, than having two eyes to be cast into hell fire. Where their worm dieth not, and the fire is not quenched."

This then brings us to the last point, as to the power of an endless death, its absolute endlessness. It is eternity in sin. It is that, or it is nothing. It is that, or the shadow of death has no substance. It is that, or the system of redemption is a mockery, and the Bible the falsest, most deceitful book in the world. The wages of sin is death; but the gift of God is eternal life, through Jesus Christ our Lord. The death is the opposite of life, and wages are paid to a living intelligence. Forever, and forever, and forever! The death itself of Christ for us, demonstrates the endlessness of death without him, the eternal ruin of the soul, had he not died, and the everlasting destruction from the presence of the Lord, and from the glory of his power, of those who obey not the gospel.

And we are thus taught, with an exceeding and eternal weight of solemnity, the dreadful meaning of that declaration of our blessed Lord, "If ye believe not in me, ye shall die in your sins." To die in your sins is to be buried to all eternity in them, beneath the experience and power of an endless death. But as there is no possibility of redemption from them but in Christ, no possibility of having them removed but by his Spirit, who but must feel the infinite importance of an immediate application for his mercy? There is no time to lose. The law of sin and of death in our depraved natures is every day growing stronger, while we stay away from Christ. It can never be overcome but by him; it will soon become the power of an endless death, if we do not go to him. It can be broken now, but only in him, only by the law of the spirit of life in Christ Jesus, working in our souls. If it be *not* broken now, it cannot forever. If you die in your sins, under this law of sin and of death, there will be no more change, but from wickedness to wickedness.

How *should* there be? Are there any conceivable motives that could be tried in that world, that have not been tried in this, under a far more hopeful state? There can be no new atonement, there remaineth no more sacrifice for sin, but if there could be, it would be only a new world of probation, and the law of sin and of death there, would act with still greater certainty and power than here, keeping the soul from Christ. But the neglect and contempt of Christ in this world is the very thing that shuts the soul out of heaven in that. On the supposition of the possibility of a change there, it must be by the power of motives, as here; but no motive can be imagined, none can possibly exist, of greater power than that derived from the knowledge of an endless hell on the one hand, and heaven on the other, and from the knowledge of the way of salvation. But these motives have already been presented, and failed, in a world of probation and restraint, where guilt and habit were neither so great nor powerful; and how should they ever be effective, in a world of unmitigated rebellion and depravity.

There must be again in such a world the announcement of hope, and the moment there is hope, then again there is all the balance of disposition and indisposition, willingness and unwillingness, as in this world. And the discovery of there being still hope in that world, after all revelations to the contrary in this, would cut off all possibility of belief in eternal misery at all, so that the only motive that could have the least power against the habit and the love of sin would in reality be destroyed, and all possibility of change would be destroyed with it. All appeals would cease to be of any avail, and onward the soul of the sinner would be carried in the career of increasing and perpetual evil.

But the whole question is set at rest by God's word. There is no room for any speculation on the subject. The wicked are driven away in their wickedness, they die in their sins; and these shall go away into everlasting punishment, and the righteous into life eternal. If we notice the broaching of any other speculation, it is only to show, by the place where it lands us, that a sinful character itself, unchanged, constitutes and creates an essential and inevitable hell, even were there no other retribution than the last law announced in God's word, "He that is filthy let him be filthy still." And in the nature of things, the guilt, the power, the horror of such a hell must go on increasing. There could be no end.

We revert, then, to the necessity of an immediate application by faith, in prayer, in repentance, to the Lord Jesus. We see clearly what, in our sins, we are coming to. Yet in point of fact we are not so much coming *to* the promised wrath, as carrying its elements in our souls, to their place of full development, to be there lighted, to be there set on fire, and left to burn on uninterrupted. What, in such a case, shall be done? Who, that stays away from Christ, that defers for one single hour the outcry of the soul to him for mercy, is not guilty of a madness that cannot be described?

Continued Wickedness, an Endless Death.

THE proverbs of the Hebrews are radiant with spiritual life. They are not merely a poor man's almanac, or a "pocket piece" of prudence for this world, or sagacity in making money. They are set deep in Divine sanctions, and the beginning of their wisdom is the fear of the Lord. How vast and solemn is that definite retributive disclosure to which we have referred, "The wicked is driven away in his wickedness, but the righteous hath hope in his death."

This text of "picked words" was a commanding, well-known proverb of the nation, and is one of the plainest and most pointed sentences in the word of God. It deals with great principles, announces great principles. It is not a mere maxim of economy or prosperity in this world, or of guidance for this life, which indeed it does not touch, but springs at once beyond it, and reveals the rule and nature of an eternal existence. The idea of a future endless life of happiness or misery underlies this utterance, and bears it up, as the earth bears up its mountain ridges, and the sea its waves. There could never have been this mighty utterance, were it not for that idea, and not as an idea merely, but belief, deep, vast, authoritative. Out of no economical calculations, or processes, or rules, of the wisdom of this world merely, could this flash of light have sprung, irradiating the eternal world, but out of the intelligence of a well-known and acknowledged revelation.

This is an important consideration. When great principles pass into proverbs, it is proof that the universal heart is filled with them; when a great meaning is condensed into a proverbial expression, and conveyed in it, as one of the intellectual and moral coins of society, it is manifest that there is a general understanding of it; that it appeals to deep and well-known convictions in the soul, and is, indeed, a record of such convictions. Such condensed and universal utterances are like the spark that has run through a succession of electric batteries, gathering strength in them all, and at length discharging itself with irresistible energy. And this great proverb is just such a discharge of truth, just the accumulating lightning of truth, deep-working in the soul, established by the attributes and laws of Jehovah, expressive of the eternal reality of things, and exploding in an utterance for all mankind, in all places, in all ages.

The doctrine enunciated is as clear as the day. Its significance and application rush instant into eternity. It does not stop; cannot be restricted to a temporal existence, to the fears of a retribution, or the expectations of a reward, this side the grave; or to any effects, either hoped or dreaded, in this world, from any earthly agencies, principles, or combinations of circumstances or events. It has nothing to do with this life, except as bringing in the powers of another life to act upon this. It takes a plunge with the soul at once into eternity. It is a flight beyond the grave into the realities of a retributive existence after death; and there is no other meaning that can be given to it, no other light in which it can possibly be taken, no other sense in which any sane mind can contrive to understand it.

The wicked shall be driven away in his wickedness. If the proverb had stopped there, if there were no other clause following it, and belonging to it, with a clearer elucidation of its meaning, a clenching of its argument beyond the grave, then the company of sceptical, self-blinded critics, in their desire to blind others, handling the word of God deceitfully, might have said that it simply means that the wicked shall be expelled from court, shall have no employment or honor from the King, shall find no entertainment or support in His presence, or by His officers, or in His dominions. Some such critics have contended, (and immense learning in such a case may be blinder than ignorance, as one may see by looking into Hengstenberg), that when David, in the seventeenth Psalm, said that he should be satisfied when he should awake in God's likeness, it meant simply and merely that David intended to awake early enough to be up in season for morning prayers!

And the same critics might have contended concerning the first clause of this proverb, that it merely means a temporary fine with a banishment or transportation of some few years to some Oriental Botany Bay; intimates just a residence for some year or two in the Bridewell of Judea, but afterwards a reformation and restoration to favor. But the succeeding phrase puts a stopper upon all this, and so establishes the scope of the passage, that there is no denying or evading it: "The wicked shall be driven away in his wickedness; but the righteous hath hope in his death." The passage has precisely the same sphere of application for the wicked, that it has for the righteous; and if an immortality of existence is referred to for the righteous, so it is for the wicked. That it is such a future existence for the righteous which is here signified, and nothing earthly, nothing limited to this world, is absolutely demonstrated by the only quality predicated of the righteous, or as belonging to him, being that of hope in his death, that is, hope of something after death, the hope of a life of happiness in holiness beyond the grave. But right the reverse is predicated of the wicked; and the words *driven away*, in the first clause, answer precisely to the word *death* in the last clause.

And the little particle *but* is of amazing force in the connection of the two affirmations. The wicked dieth in his wickedness, and therefore without hope; but the righteous hath hope in his death. It is as certainly the lot and sphere of the wicked after death here referred to, as it is the lot and sphere of the righteous after death. Moreover, the language in reference to the wicked has a prolonged scorpion power, a demonstration of continued existence in misery, which might have been sophistically evaded, or at least the way might have been more open for attempted escape from its evident meaning, if merely the word death had been used in the first clause; if merely it had been said that the wicked shall disappear out of existence; but it is said that the wicked shall not merely cease to exist, but shall be driven away in his wickedness, shall continue in his wickedness, thus driven away. The form of expression is strikingly similar to that in Job concerning the wicked: "He shall be driven from light into darkness, and chased out of the world."

It is beyond all question the lot and sphere of the wicked after death referred to in this proverb. There is no possibility, by any twisting, or screwing, or distortion, or blinding, or critical perversion, of getting any other meaning out of it. Interrogate it how you please, with whatever cross-examination, or brow-beating of the witnesses, or sophistical torture of the testimony, you can make it speak only this thing; that in his death, and after death, the wicked man still lives, and that he not only still lives, but is driven away in his wickedness, which secures and renders inevitable his misery. In opposition to the *hope* of the righteous in *his* death, the wickedness of the wicked constitutes hopelessness in his; nay, it is the certainty of perdition, it is absolute despair.

The whole proverb is just precisely a counterpart of that passage in the New Testament, "The wages of sin is death; but the gift of God is eternal life, through Jesus Christ our Lord." One paragraph of stumbling-block, and gives the lie to any such assertion as that of the absence of the teaching of a future retribution in the pages of the Old Testament. What can be made of this passage, if this great doctrine is not in it? How could any but an idiot, any man that can put two sentences together, perceive the connection between them, and reason from the one to the other, see anything *else* in this passage, any *other* meaning in it, but just this of an unending retribution beyond the grave? What other significance can even be imagined for it? There is nothing in it, if that meaning be not there; it is absurd unintelligible jargon otherwise.

And what, in the face of such a clear indisputable announcement, recorded as a proverb of the nation, and passed into circulation as one of the established coins of its habitual admitted thought, and acknowledged genuine truth, would we say of the impudent assertion that a people that had such central, outshining truth as this, for their daily currency of intellect and heart, knew nothing of the doctrine of immortality, and were never influenced by the expectation of future rewards and punishments, nor were ever dealt with by Jehovah on such grounds?

Let us suppose that we heard the proverb uttered in English, or had met with it in a book, *penny wise and pound foolish*, and that some sage critic should tell us that the people among whom this proverb originated, and where it was in vogue, knew neither the meaning of *penny* nor *pound*, nor ever had any coined money in circulation, nor ever transacted any of their business through any such medium stumbling-block, and gives the lie to any such assertion as that of the absence of the teaching of a future retribution in the pages of the Old Testament. What can be made of this passage, if this great doctrine is not in it? How could any but an idiot, any man that can put two sentences together, perceive the connection between them, and reason from the one to the other, see anything *else* in this passage, any *other* meaning in it, but just this of an unending retribution beyond the grave? What other significance can even be imagined for it? There is nothing in it, if that meaning be not there; it is absurd unintelligible jargon otherwise.

And what, in the face of such a clear indisputable announcement, recorded as a proverb of the nation, and passed into circulation as one of the established coins of its habitual admitted thought, and acknowledged genuine truth, would we say of the impudent assertion that a people that had such central, outshining truth as this, for their daily currency of intellect and heart, knew nothing of the doctrine of immortality, and were never influenced by the expectation of future rewards and punishments, nor were ever dealt with by Jehovah on such grounds?

Let us suppose that we heard the proverb uttered in English, or had met with it in a book, *penny wise and pound foolish*, and that some sage critic should tell us that the people among whom this proverb originated, and where it was in vogue, knew neither the meaning of *penny* nor *pound*, nor ever had any coined money in circulation, nor ever transacted any of their business through any such medium what would we say of such an impudent fool? Suppose, to make the two cases more similar, that two thousand years hence a book of our English literature should be found, with just this proverb in it, penny wise, and pound foolish, along with others of like tenor, such as *time is money*, or, *a penny saved is a penny earned*, or, take care of the shillings, and the pounds will take care of themselves; and suppose that some sagacious German critics of those days should undertake, in the face of such proverbs and declarations, to affirm and maintain that neither the English nor the American nation knew either the nature of gold or silver, or ever had any of those precious metals in their possession, or ever carried on any of their commercial affairs of trading business with pieces of stamped money of known and determined value. Would any credit be attached to any such speculations? Would not men stamp the critic's own mind as that of a blinded, credulous, unbelieving fool, or rather would not such a critic be treated, if not avowedly intending a hoax, as a perfect lunatic in literature?

Yet just this is the boasted wisdom with which some learned critics have put their confounding eye glasses to the Bible. Just with this stupidity, just with this mixture of credulity and unbelief, have men come to the consideration of some of the most explicitly and undeniably revealed truths in God's word. Just thus impudently have they denied the plain and inevitable meaning on many a passage, and with the same stolidity have closed their eyes, their minds, their hearts, against doctrines revealed in such unmistakable fulness and power, that the wayfaring man, though a fool, need not err in regard to them. In such cases God at length does not unfrequently give the man over to strong delusion to believe a lie. And such cases realize the declaration in Isaiah, "He feedeth on ashes; a deceived heart hath turned him aside, that he cannot deliver his soul, nor say is there not a lie in my right hand?" And the words of the prophet Jeremiah receive a new fulfilment, "The wise men are ashamed, they are dismayed and taken; lo, they have rejected the word of the Lord, and what wisdom is in them? Every man is brutish in his knowledge, and the spiritual man is mad."

And furthermore, we see the *reason* of such lying criticisms, so profoundly, palpably false, and covering the plainest book in the world with such Egyptian darkness. It is because of the threatening and repulsive nature of such announcements to men that will indulge their sins, and still hope for heaven. It is because such principles as those announced in regard to God's dealing with the righteous and the wicked, and revealed in such passages as this explicit proverb, *cover the whole ground of an eternal retribution.* They arraign man as guilty before God, and accuse and condemn the sinner as deserving of nothing less than hopeless, and therefore everlasting banishment from God's presence, and an immutable confinement and permanence of nature in that wickedness which he has chosen.

If a man chooses to live in it, in it he will die; and if he chooses to die in it, (and at his own choice it is whether to die in it or be redeemed from it,)—if he chooses to die in it, in it he will be driven away; and no matter where, if he be still the same. It might be a province in the precincts of heaven; but if he carries that wicked nature with him, in which he is driven away, everywhere in the universe it would be misery. No outward change could be a change within.

Now, in this view, this Proverb is just exactly counterparted by our blessed Lord, when he says, "If ye believe not that I am He, your predicted and appointed Messiah and Saviour, ye shall die in your sins." The manner of this announcement by the Lord Jesus presents this perdition of dying in your sins as the climax of horror, beyond which no imagery nor reality could go. It is the announcement of an eternal destruction. But as from the Lord of life and glory comes this new announcement of the terror and certainty of everlasting death, so from him, and him only, comes the offer and assurance of a possible deliverance, the promise of an everlasting redemption to any and every man, whosoever he may be, that will sincerely trust in him. Such an one shall not die in his wickedness, but shall be redeemed from it, shall be released from its bondage, purified from its defilement, delivered from its condemnation, and set free from its power. Sin and death shall have no more dominion over him, but even now, the very moment of the beginning of his faith, he shall begin to live an indestructible eternal life. Believing in Christ, he hath passed already from death unto life, and over him the second death hath no power, and the first death is but a release for him into the blissful presence and likeness of his Saviour. He hath hope in his death, such a hope as fills the whole valley with light, such a hope as in Christ Jesus takes away the sting of Death, and sings out of the heart, as from an organ, the dying anthem, "O Death, where is thy sting, Oh grave, where is thy victory!" "He that believeth in me," said our Lord Jesus, "though he were dead, yet shall he live; and whosoever liveth and believeth in me, shall never die."

We see, in this Proverb, some of the reasons why our blessed Lord affirmed that if the men of his day would not hear Moses and the Prophets, neither would they be persuaded, though one rose from the dead. The light is so clear, the doctrine of future rewards and punishments so explicit, that there is no escaping from it, except by an insensibility, blindness, and unbelief, that would remain unmoved, even if a man came from the dead to bear witness to the secrets of another world. The evil is in a sinful heart.

But we also see, on the comparison of this passage with answering passages in the New Testament, an example of the climax from one to the other, from the lower to the higher, from the dawn to the perfect day, from the vestibule to the inner temple. This passage in the Old Testament is translated, transfigured in the New. In the presence of Jesus, it appears as Moses and Elias appeared, in a new glory, in garments that shine like the sun, in the overwhelming power and radiance poured by him upon all truth, and reflected from Eternity realized.

And so again we see our heightened responsibility and duty. The greater our light, the greater our guilt, if we neglect or reject it. The more advanced and precious our privileges, the deeper and more terrible our ruin, if from them we pass to everlasting woe. Nearer in Jesus to the highest heavens of glory; nearer also to the deepest hell, by the possibility of a perdition, through neglect and rejection of that blessed Saviour, more intolerable than that of Sodom!

Dead and Lost.

WHAT contrasts, what lights and shades, what depths of extreme worlds, what inconceivable experiences, till experience itself has given the reality, in that simple announcement, "Was dead, and is alive again, was lost, and is found!"

We know but little of death, still less of life; in another sense, we know but little of life, still less of death. Something we know of both; enough on the one hand, for some computation of the power of an endless life, enough on the other for some prophecy or forewarning and assurance of the terribleness of eternal death. Something we know of life, in our experience of physical existence, and the exercise of intellectual capacities exceedingly limited. But in our native state, untransfigured by Divine Grace, not quickened by the Divine Spirit, we know nothing of life in its positiveness, its joyousness, its greatness, its glory. We are sinful; and sinful beings can never know what life is, till the law of the Spirit of life in Christ Jesus has begun to set them free from the law of sin and of death. And even then, in this world we know but little of life; it is always life under a veil, life in a prison, life in a body of death, life imperfectly understood, imperfectly developed, manifested often mainly in groanings that cannot be uttered, and in the earnest expectation of the creature, waiting for the manifestation of the Sons of God. What can we know, here on earth, of the boundless freedom and glory of the life of heaven?

But we are quite as ignorant of death, although death has passed upon all men, for that all have sinned, and this is an article of as universal experience as life. Yet because even under this penalty, grace has interposed, and our world is suspended between life and death, of death positively we know almost nothing. Change we know, decay we know, the decline and departure of life, the body mouldering in the grave, some of the concomitants and circumstances of death; but death in its reality, death positive, death spiritual, death eternal, we know little of that, because the ravages of death are suspended, and we are held back from the experience of it, by the very nature of the system of mercy and grace in Christ Jesus. Perhaps we know less of death eternal than we do of life eternal; for life eternal is a gift, through Jesus Christ our Lord, and the earnest of it is already conferred; but death eternal is only the wages of sin, and the wages are not paid till the day of reckoning and of retribution.

And although in some terrific cases there has seemed to be, even on earth, the commencement of an experience of the world of woe, yet no living man ever had the gates of death and of hell opened before him, ever entered into their secrets. A tortured conscience reveals much in the way of forewarning and prediction; and the anguish of despair, so far as there be despair this side of the grave, sometimes almost draws back the parting veil; but still, except by the declarations of the word of God, we know almost nothing. By those declarations we may know; but they demand faith, and we must take them on God's authority; and if we will not believe them, there is nothing in us, or about us, that can supply the place of faith, or be to us beforehand a realization of the things revealed in God's word. The wrath of God itself is revealed from heaven against all unrighteousness and ungodliness of men; but we have nothing as yet in our own experience, or in the course of the world, to make us know to the full what the wrath of God is, what it must be to suffer that wrath in hell.

The *revelation* is *given*, on purpose that we may *avoid* that wrath; for the wrath is future, and the hell is future, and we are commanded to flee from it; and faith in it is requisite, *before* the experience of it, that we *may* flee from it. If we do not take it on God's assurance, and at His command apply to Jesus Christ for redemption from it, then we are lost; if we wait for the experience of it before we will believe it, then, when the realization of it comes, it will be too late for that faith in Jesus which might have saved the soul. There will be the eternal knowledge of that wrath for those who wait to be thus convinced of it, but no longer any possibility of fleeing from it; and therefore that wrath is directly pointed against unbelief itself, against that state of mind which renders a man insensible to God's warnings, and prevents him from fleeing at once to Christ. "He that believeth not the Son shall not see life, but the wrath of God abideth on him."

The most vivid images of scripture, therefore, are but faint and inadequate shadowings forth of the reality; they demonstrate and unveil it, as far as possible, but they require belief. Our blessed Lord makes His appeal to our very senses, as far as it can be made. He takes the torture which is most terrible to us, that from which our sensitive nature shrinks back with the greatest horror and repugnance, and constructs a world out of it, and carries us into the midst of that world, as in the tremendous colloquy between Lazarus in heaven and the lost man in hell; so that we see the flames, we hear the wail of souls tormented, we observe the anguish of despair.

But all this is still only an appeal to faith. We have not yet ourselves gone into those torments; and this powerful rhetoric of heaven is adopted, that we might *not;* and it is like placing angels with drawn swords before the entrance to that world of woe—it is like piling crags of burning coal before the gates of the prison of God's insufferable wrath—that we may not enter.

But all this requires faith. Perhaps it comes the nearest to the demonstration of experience to which the Lord God of our salvation could bring it, and yet not break down our freedom; not render faith impossible; not destroy the liberty of will, the possibility of a voluntary choice; the nearest to a physical and moral compulsion to which God could bring mere truth, and still leave us free agents, still leave it as a matter for ourselves to decide, by our own preferences, whether to seek God's mercy in Christ or not, whether to believe or not.

The strong representations, the overwhelming appeals, the vivid realities of God's word, almost force conviction, almost take away the *opportunity* of faith; and yet they are powerless *without* faith. If a man who never knew what fire was, never had experience of the sensation of burning, should stand before a pool of molten lava, about to plunge into it, what could you do to convince him of the madness of such a step, except assure him that it would be instant and inevitable destruction? You might thrust his hand into the flame of a candle, or touch his bare arm with a live coal, but still, as to the pool of lava, he would have to exercise faith; you could go no farther in your demonstration. Anything farther is the very thing, the very experience of perdition, from which you would pull him back; but, after all your attempted demonstrations, you can give him no adequate idea of what it would be, if he should plunge into a sea of burning lava.

But much greater, of necessity, is the inadequacy of all truth, and all mere imagery, to set forth the reality of what is coming in the eternal world. It goes beyond all our experience, and *must* have *faith.* If we shall ransack the universe, and combine all its agencies and capacities of representation, or of appeal to the imagination, we could contrive no demonstration that would answer in the place of experience, or obviate the necessity of simple faith in

God. There must be that faith as to what we ourselves are, as to our present condition, as well as what we are to be; that faith as to the nature of our present ruin, as well as the means of our redemption from it. The combinations of human language, and the appeals of resemblance from what we do know to what we do not know, make some little approximation; but still, as to experience, we know almost nothing.

Deep calleth unto deep, death bears testimony to death, the King of Terrors is God's artist, with his pencil dabbled in the grave's corruption, to draw our character, and we are said to be dead in trespasses and sins. But the moral death infinitely transcends the physical, and passes out of reach, beyond all conception, all comparison. For when the physical death ends, the moral death begins. Nay, the physical death may be said to be the first positive symptom or demonstration of the moral death, for until the physical death is realized, the moral death is suspended, its positive agencies are held back from operation. What we call death is but the close of mortal life, and it is only when life ends that positive death begins. The passions and faculties of our being do not, this side the grave, enter upon their eternal elemental war. Nor is there anything that can adequately shadow forth that state, nothing positive, nothing negative; nothing but the agony of a wounded conscience ever begins to make the soul realize the truth.

There are tremendous images. The shock of furious armies, the crash of falling avalanches, mountains overwhelming cities, volcanoes in action, herds of wild beasts, confined and roaring in the dungeons of the Coliseum, making the whole structure shake with their bellowings, then all at once let loose, and with a fierce conflict of hunger and rage grappling with one another; the elements in wild affright and uproar; earthquakes, conflagrations, floods, pestilences, wars; all these are dire images of terror, ruin, desolation, destruction. But all these, and even the stars dropping from heaven, as when a fig-tree casteth her untimely figs, and the whole universe beaten together in chaos, or shrivelling as a parched scroll; all these come short of any representation of an eternal death; they all fail, they are mere transitory syllables. The moral death is unapproachable by any such representation. And so is the greatness of the moral life, and the glory of a moral regeneration.

For if we were to see all these things in perfection, all these events and images of death and chaos, in utmost perfection, and then witness an instantaneous restoration from death to life, from destruction to reorganization, from rage to serenity, from desolation to peace, from chaos and ruin to order and beauty, from pain and misery to comfort and happiness; all this would go but a little way towards symbolizing the change from spiritual death to spiritual life, from sin to holiness, from hell to heaven. If we were to behold a decaying human body suddenly rise out of the coffin in all the beauty and freshness of youthful life and health, it would be a change of solemn, overwhelming, supernatural power and glory. If we should behold a marble statue, as we gaze upon it, walk living from its pedestal, endued suddenly with the powers of vitality and motion, it would be a wondrous, overpowering miracle. Could we have stood by the grave of Lazarus, and seen the dead man, the decay of whose body in the tomb had already commenced, come forth at the word of the Lord of life and glory, bound hand and foot with his grave-clothes, *that* had been a most stupendous spectacle. But all this is nothing to the contrast between a dead soul and a living soul, dead or living forever and ever.

A dead tree is a striking object, a gigantic, dead, withered oak, or sycamore, or maple, for example, dry, leafless, blasted, amidst a living forest; and if we should see such a tree instantaneously clothed with verdure while we are looking at it; or still more, if with gradual but rapid progress we should see the buds start and open into leaves, and new sprigs shoot forth fresh and waving; such a change and innovation would be an amazing phenomenon. The winter of our world is a solemn season, and the resurrection of all nature in the spring is a miracle of such unlimited power and exquisite beauty, that the scene arrests, with vast influence, every reflecting mind. But all these illustrations are deficient, incapable; and neither the death nor the life of nature is any adequate exponent of the death or the life of the soul.

If now, quitting all these images, we should take a man like John Newton, and follow him closely, with a perception of his qualities and character like that of Omniscience; if we could bring a vivid perfect view of the man in his early, increasing, and uttermost depravity, and contrast it with an equally vivid and perfect view of the man in his greatest purity and most exalted life, *that* would be something. But in such contrast it is only the faint beginning on both sides, the dark and the bright, that we see; it is only as the evening or the morning twilight; the one verging to a darkness and a death, that if it went on to its perfection, would be the blackness of darkness forever; the other but the dawning of life, which is to open into perfect day only in the world of heavenly glory.

We can have no absolute realization beforehand, either of the heaven or hell of character carried to its extreme, and perfected in good or evil. The anguish of a wounded conscience, a sense of the burden of unpardoned sin, as we have already intimated, does something in the way of personal experience. And if men would look into their hearts and lives, more frequently than they do, and compare them with the holiness of God and the requirements of the Divine Law, they would have knowledge and experience enough of death and hell to drive them to most earnest and unceasing prayer for God's mercy. There is proof enough, demonstration enough, imagery enough, and vivid and powerful to the uttermost possible degree, and yet falling immeasurably short of the reality.

Neither is there anything in that other image, lost and found, that by any illustration can reach and expound the infinitude of an eternal ruin and salvation. It can only shadow it forth dimly, darkly, but profoundly; for that word *lost*, applied to the soul, is perhaps the most tremendously expressive word in our language; and in every man's own thoughts it distances instantly all possibility of approximation by images or illustrations of things lost here; and the very use of such illustrations is not so much to convey any new revelation, or open up any deeper depth of meaning, or more absolute realization of infinitude, but rather to set the mind more vividly at work, to quicken the play of its activity, to inspire and energize its sluggish imagination, to carry it brooding over the deeps of hell. And when the mind becomes thus active and heated on the subject, the word itself, when the ideas of heaven, hell, eternity, are quickened from their slumbers, will do more than all possible illustrations.

And, indeed, such illustrations can be only and remotely relative. For there is nothing in all the universe that ever can be actually and absolutely *lost*, except the soul. God knows where every lost thing is, and can lay his hand upon it in an instant. And although things may be withdrawn from the sight and hidden from the knowledge both of angels and of men, for a season, by and by they may come into view again, and God could bring them into view in a moment. The constellations that have vanished from the sky, God knows where they are, and what use to make of them. The lost knowledges too, in men's minds, can be revived. The sciences and arts, that have gone out of existence, are as absolutely true and possible as ever. The lost manuscripts, and burned libraries and parchments, could all be restored at a motion from the Almighty. The lost tribes could be discovered, the lost navigators disentombed, the lost ships brought up from the bosom of the deep. Every missing coin of gold or silver is somewhere still, and though rust-eaten, or gone back to its original elements, could be produced. Everything mislaid may have its place again and its use again. Nothing is really lost, that is not lost by sin. But a lost soul is lost even to God.

Nothing is lost that is lovingly known to God. A holy angel might be lost for a season, in our common sense of the word, wandering among the worlds of God, might lose his own way in the wilderness of God's infinitude of glory in this universe, as a little child is lost in a pathless forest; but he would be sure to find his way back again; and even the sense of such bewilderment would be no trouble or anxiety to him, for he could not go where God is not, and though he should be wandering a thousand years, they would be wanderings of bliss and glory. But a lost soul is lost from God, from heaven, from the universe, from all good, from all blessedness, in all evil, in all woe. A lost soul is lost by sin, by corruption, by enmity against God. A lost soul is good for nothing, and fit only to be burned, fit only to show the infinite misery of sin.

Oh, who can tell, who here can imagine the infinite horror in that word *lost*, applied to the ruined soul, the soul forever dead and lost in sin! And who is there that can be willing to hazard such loss, such ruin? If not, then hasten to the cross of Christ, for as in the sufferings and death of the Redeemer you have the greatest possible demonstration beforehand of the value of the soul, and the infinite wretchedness of its ruin, so in the mercy of that Redeemer you have the only possible deliverance and refuge from the wrath to come. In His grace, His willing grace, freely offered to all; His dying grace, dying to make it possible; His sanctifying grace, ready to renew and save the soul; in Him, His love, His grace, is our only possible redemption. And oh, to be found in Christ!

The Argument of Ruin, from Salvation.

THE very casual droppings from the honey-combs of Divine mercy and truth in God's Word are full of infinite principle and argument. Take, for example, that declaration from the heart of Divine love, on occasion of the conversion of Zaccheus, in Luke 19: 10. "For the Son of Man is come to seek and to save that which was lost."

There are in this passage three distinct and grand elements of thought, bearing upon one another, balancing one another, elucidating one another. They are as the quantities in an algebraic equation; given, the one, the other is determinate, is certain. They are attributes and relations of personal and moral infinitude, and the connection between them, and the conclusions among them, are profound and mighty. So infinite indeed is the passage in its reach and application, that these three questions, Who it is that came? how He came? and for what He came? contained in it, constitute a volume of theology embracing heaven, earth and hell. When we proceed to investigate these points, we find a power and profoundness of connection and conclusion among them, so close and inevitable, that the strongest mathematical demonstration could not be more irresistible; a logic and a sweep of internal mutual evidence and significance, so vast and majestic, that when we begin thoroughly to comprehend it, the mind is overwhelmed by it. Simple as are its terms, the compass and sublimity of the passage, in the investigation, Who it is that came, how He came, and for what He came, are past measurement, past utterance.

There is a grand reciprocal argument between the dignity and glory of a Divine Saviour, and the character and ruin of the lost, whom he came to save. The one reveals, illustrates, determines, the other. Especially is this the case, in reference to the guilt and misery of the creature. We must look first at the great blaze of light in this direction, produced by the determination of the question, Who is it that came, and the manner of his coming. We are not left to the least uncertainty or doubt in regard to it. The Son of man is the Creator and Lord of the universe, by whom and for whom all beings and things have their existence. He is the Word, the Being, who was in the beginning with God, and who was God. In his original glory being in the form of God, and on an equality with God, he nevertheless took upon him the form of a servant, and became obedient unto death, even the death of the Cross. In this humiliation, suffering, and death, he became an offering for sin, set forth of God as a propitiation, a sacrifice, through the Eternal Spirit, by his own blood, for the obtaining of an eternal redemption, that God might be just, and the justifier of him that believeth in Jesus. For this purpose the Eternal Word was made flesh, and dwelt among us, with all the fulness of the God-head bodily, God manifest in the flesh, justified in the spirit, seen of angels, preached unto the Gentiles, believed on in the world, received up into glory. By virtue of his own possession and manifestation of supreme Deity, he became an eternal and unchangeable High Priest and Saviour, not after the law of a carnal commandment, but the power of an endless life, having offered up himself once for all, a sacrifice, whose efficacy is to all eternity, for deliverance from eternal death, and the gift of an inheritance in life everlasting. Even such a Divine Almighty Saviour was necessary, that he might be able to save to the uttermost all that come unto God by him, seeing he ever liveth to make intercession for them. Such is the being who came, and such the manner of his coming, to seek and to save that which was lost.

What, then, is the measure and peculiarity of significance, the exceeding and eternal weight of meaning, accumulated, by such a preparation, upon that word LOST? What is the conclusion forced upon it, and what the definition wrung out, or the impossibility of definition, because it is found to be illimitable and immeasurable, in the same way as eternity itself is unsearchable, and yet known, absolute, unquestionable? From the previous terms of the equation given, you are flung into an infinitude of disclosure, a boundless abyss of undeniable, yet tremendous truth, the last, and the most terrible, that the mind can know or be employed upon. What is this light, this sudden blaze far round illuminating hell, this penetrating revelation of the unseen and the eternal, by the person and the cross of Christ? What light does the announcement of God manifest in the flesh for human salvation, the Word made flesh, and suffering, dying, throw upon the character and condition of the lost? How lost, in what manner, in what nature, to what extent, to necessitate, or justify, such an interposition?

For, if there is a necessity of justification for God's pardoning the guilty, there is also a necessity of justification for God's offering up his own Son. How could he do it, without an infinite and eternal reason? How could he do it for any expediency or necessity short of infinitude? How could he do it, but under the sanction, which indeed he has revealed to us, of the power of an endless life, for guilty creatures, on the one hand, if redeemed, and the power of an endless death, inevitable, on the other hand, if *not* redeemed?

The redemption is in Christ Jesus, whom God hath set forth, a propitiation through faith in His blood, to declare His righteousness for the remission of sins. The infinite God declares the necessity of such a sacrifice for such a justification. Now, then, we may turn the equation; we are compelled to do it. If God hath set forth Christ crucified, the Son of God incarnate, suffering, dying, that God might be just, and the Justifier of him that believeth, and the Redeemer of the soul from an eternity of sin and misery, then also, at the other end, there must be set forth such an eternity, such an infinite reality of guilt, of death, of ruin, to justify the offering up of the Son of God as a sacrifice; a reality having in it the weight of eternity, and deciding at once for the universe—not as a dream, not as a pageant, not as a transitory show—the infinite necessity and justice of the measure, for the purposes of infinite love, as a measure in the highest degree worthy of Jehovah, and illustrating the infinite glory of His attributes. God can do nothing inconsistent with those attributes; and behind such a sacrifice as that of Christ, the Son of God, there must be the sanctions of eternity; and we are justified in saying that there must be, because God has declared to us that there are.

This word lost, then, has a meaning never possessed by any significance that we give it in regard to any interest in time, or anything limited or transitory, missing by us, or separated from us. The lost whom Christ came to seek and to save are not entities or intelligences, mislaid merely, and sure to be found again, and restored uninjured as before; they are not merely wandering about bewildered, as a lost child in the wilderness, or as one that has mistaken his way. Not for that would the Son of God come down from heaven—not for that was any such interposition necessary as that of Christ upon the cross. This word *came* embraces the whole transaction of redemption, the incarnate Son of God suffering and dying. But not to find mislaid souls, or to guide mistaken ones merely, was that sacrifice demanded. An angel could have done that—a being of limited knowledge could have done that, could have ransacked the globe, yea, the universe, for everything lost, and found it; could have found it, and brought it back to God. Indeed, there is nothing really lost, in that sense. God knows where everything is hidden, is wandering, is mislaid, and can in a moment bring it to light, if He pleases. There is no sacrifice upon the cross needed for *that.*

Infinitely different from anything like this, is the loss of lost souls. It was a loss, in the manner and the nature of it, from which no created being or power could recover the sinner. It was a moral loss, a spiritual loss, a loss of immortality, a loss forever. It was a death in trespasses and sins, and therefore an eternal death. It was an alienation from the life of God, and enmity against him, and a penalty and power of endless duration, under the law of sin and of death *in* the soul, and of retributive wrath *upon* it. It was a death, and a ruin, and a loss, by the terms of the law, The soul that sinneth, it shall die, and by the terms of the gospel, He that believeth not the son shall not see life, but the wrath of God abideth on him.

And being such a loss, it was eternal. Nothing but such a loss could be eternal, and such a loss could be no other *than* eternal. It was not a loss of time, not a loss for any limited period of duration; for that would have brought its own cure, its own redemption. The end would have come, and the restoration. The finding again, and the recovery, at the close of the fated period, of whatever length it might be, would be as certain as the loss.

Nothing could be said to be lost, in that sense, which merely had its period to run, and then would come back into heaven again, by as known and immutable a necessity and certainty, as it ever went out. There would be no need of a Saviour for that. It would be indeed a work of supererogation to set up an atonement by the sufferings of the Son of God for the recovery of a guilty race, which, left to itself, would assuredly and inevitably work out a salvation for itself by its *own* suffering.

The essence of salvation by mercy is, that it could have been had in no other way; and that certainty alone secures its being a spiritual, abiding, eternal salvation. A salvation indeed could not be infinitely prized, which could have been possible in any other way. What security would there be against the spirit of pride, ingratitude, and rebellion, even in heaven, if it could be ever said in answer to the claim of supreme allegiance and everlasting gratitude, "What do we owe to you? We should have been saved at any rate, and by our own suffering." And who can imagine the result, which yet would be inevitable, when the time of ruin, suffering, and loss, on the part of those *not* saved, should have been lapsed away, served out, and the banished, punished crew of rebels and of unbelievers should return from their transportation in hell, literally saved so as by fire, with the scars of the thunder of divine retribution upon them, to take their place in heaven, singing the glory of their own personal sufferings, side by side with the company of the redeemed, amidst anthems to the Lamb that was slain! In very truth, the idea of salvation at all is inconsistent with the idea of any temporary or limited perdition. If the lost are saved, it is because they were lost forever. If they were not lost forever, they were not lost at all, but were only taking one necessary step to everlasting blessedness.

Furthermore, if the loss were not a loss eternal, were not known to be such, the power of habit in sin is so despotic, so irresistible, the preference of sin instead of holiness in depraved natures is so omnipotent, that a sinful man would say, "Rather than have all this labor of salvation, rather than encounter all this self-denial and renunciation of sin and its enjoyments, I will let the ruin take its own course; the disease shall be in its own Saviour; since it is not forever; and I will even try the experiment of the appointed ages in the purgatory of hell-fire. They will come to an end, and all will be well at last, and I shall be saved at any rate." Proclaim such a theology, and let the result show how many creatures of sinful nature and habit its indefatigable preachers will ever succeed in turning from their iniquities. No man will renounce his sins, who, by continuance in them, is sure at last of entering heaven.

Neither, again, can this word "lost" mean annihilation, the extinction of being, the cessation, forever, of thought and feeling. There can be no punishment in that, nor retribution, nor wrath abiding, nor wages paid, nor second death, nor anything, indeed, that needs a Saviour. A new race of souls could be created, that should amply supply the place of those dropped from existence, without any atoning sacrifice, or any diminution of the happiness of the universe. God could as easily create new souls, as he could new worlds, without any interposition of a Saviour.

Nor was it any bare negation, or form of negation, but a positive, absolute perdition, of which no words can convey any adequate sense or measure; a perdition without end, and a loss therefore of souls in sin and death eternal. It was a loss of immortal beings, from the purity and enjoyment of heaven, to the guilt and misery of an endless hell. It was the loss of lost souls, in a perpetual death of enmity against God, and in the consequent inevitable endurance of everlasting punishment. That presents a case, worthy indeed of the interposition of the Saviour; for salvation of a world from such ruin, the Son of God might justly die, and the Father's infinite love might justly be exercised, even at such an expense. And it is declared that the Lord Jesus came to save his people from their sins, to seek and to save the lost in sin, the lost eternally.

This is the very argument of the Apostle, and it is irresistible. Because we thus judge, that if one died for all, then were all dead; dead in sin, in a death that kills beyond the tomb, in a death that is undying, a mortality that is immortal, a death in trespasses and sins, of which the habit itself, and the nature, is death, and the penalty everlasting punishment. This indeed is a ruin and a misery, demanding the interposition of an Almighty Saviour, and justifying God in such a sacrifice. Thus it is that God *has* interposed. "Unto you first, God, having raised up his Son Jesus, sent him to bless you, in turning away every one of you from his iniquities. This is a faithful saying, and worthy of all acceptation, that Christ Jesus came into the world to save sinners. He shall save his people from their sins."

He only *can* save them, and in God's appointed way. There is no other name. If ye believe not in Him, ye shall die in your sins. We must be saved from sin, or we have *no* salvation, even in Christ. Whomsoever Christ does *not* save, that soul is lost in sin forever; and such a loss of the soul is a calamity, in comparison with which, it were better for a man that he had never been born. What shall it profit a man, if he gain the whole world, and lose his own soul? Or what shall a man give in exchange for his soul? Christ came *to* save, because, if *not* saved by Him, the ruin of the soul would never end. Had it not been so, Christ would never have come, but would have let the ages roll on, and produce their fruit, and bring at length their promised and inevitable renovation. But the demonstration of eternal death, from the offer of eternal life through Christ, is unquestionable.

In this view, the coming of Christ, and the offer of salvation through Him, is a most awakening and alarming advent and interposition. Though an interposition of infinite mercy and love, yet is it as a burst of thunder on the sleeping careless soul, and as a glare of lightning in midnight, disclosing both our guilt and danger. It startles the soul from its false security with that impressive question pressed by the Apostle Paul, "How shall we escape, if we *neglect* so great salvation?"

On the one side there is manifested by this light the greatness and dreadfulness of our ruin, on the other, the greatness and glory of our redemption; both are measured by the character and the cross of Christ. We learn, on the one side, the profoundness and terribleness of our despair, native, eternal, if left to ourselves; on the other, the mightiness and all-sufficiency of our hope in Christ. Without Christ, the depths of our despair are unfathomable and eternal. But in Christ, if the soul flies to Him, the greater the guilt, the greater the hope, by the very appointed argument of supplication, "For Thy name's sake, pardon mine iniquity, FOR it is great." God loves to show His power and glory in such a salvation,—the power of an endless life from the power of an endless death,—a translation all the way from hell to heaven. It is beyond all possibility of question, that having given His Son to die for us, God is ready to save us, desires to save us. We *are* in a desperate condition; but if we only feel it, and lay hold on Christ, then, the more desperate, the more hopeful, and the deeper our despair, the stronger our encouragement. Because, Christ came not to call the righteous, but sinners to repentance, and the greatest sinner first, as the most needy, and the chosen object of mercy. So did he choose Paul as a pattern.

And we see clearly that Paul was in the right. when he counted all things as worthless, if he might be found in Christ. Paul, as lost in sin, made it the aim of his whole existence to be found in Christ, and what else, personally, should be the perpetual business of our existence? We are lost, whom He came to seek and to save. Has He found us? Is He carrying us home rejoicing? Are we folded in His arms, as the careful loving shepherd of our souls? Are we found of Christ? All the lost souls ever found will be found in Him. When God searches for souls saved, He will look nowhere but in Christ. If you are not in Him, no matter where or what you are, or may have been, you are lost. Even God cannot find you, out of Christ; even God will overlook you, out of Christ. No matter if your name were in all the church records upon earth; no matter if you died receiving ten thousand sacraments; if you are not in Christ, by a living faith, God cannot find you; you are lost.

Yet now the Saviour himself is seeking for you to save you. Suppose you were a wounded wandering sheep upon the mountains, lying helpless, almost insensible; yet if you heard the voice and footstep of the shepherd, seeking you, you would, even by moanings and bleatings inarticulate, show him where you are. When the blind men sat by the way-side, and Jesus passed by, they no sooner heard that he was near, than they cried out, with so great an outcry, that the angry bystanders told them to keep their peace. But what cared they for the bystanders, so they could only be found of Christ? Oh, that weary, worn, way-side wanderers now would use the same diligence for salvation! The anxious, loving, compassionate shepherd is on the mountains. Come forth, ye wandering, dying, lost, yet heedless souls, come forth from your graves, your tombs, your darkness, your insensibility, your despair, come forth and see your Saviour! It is night, dark night upon the mountains, yet he is there, looking for you. Will you give Him no sign that *you* are there, will you make no outcry, that he may snatch you from ruin, and carry you home rejoicing?

The Argument of Ruin, from the Joy of Heaven.

THE argument from the *lost* is connected with another, of equal, irresistible power and glory, from the state and relations of the *found*. These are somewhat opened in the declaration by our blessed Lord, "That joy shall be in heaven over one sinner that repenteth; joy in the presence of the angels of God, over one sinner that repenteth."

There is illimitable grandeur in this representation. It embraces and illustrates many things, the vastest in God's universe; and is indeed like a flash of lightning, or a shaft of steady golden light, from one end of the universe to the other. Let us look at it first as the representation of an absorbing interest in heaven, of which we ourselves are the subjects, but of which we should have known nothing, had it not been for this declaration of our Saviour. "There is joy in heaven." It is a great fact which is here noted, something like the fact that at the creation the morning stars sang together, and all the sons of God shouted for joy. It is an impulse and movement, powerful and simultaneous throughout God's holy universe, that is here noted; for nothing less than this can be comprehended in the designation heaven, so far as place or infinitude are concerned, and nothing less can be comprehended in the term joy applied to the inhabitants of heaven, so far as intensity of emotion is concerned. That which, amidst the perpetual inconceivable ardors and raptures of enjoyment, in the celestial world, can arrest attention as a new and sudden impulse of joy even in heaven, must be deep, intense, and blissful beyond conception.

Let us consider this. It takes much to move a world. An event, indeed, must be of some note to move even one large city in a world, so deeply that the movement shall be simultaneous and universal. We remember once reading an article in an English periodical, saying that there was but one man in the kingdom, whose death would really make a sensation all over the city of London; a thousand others might die, and all the people in the city would not even know it, much less care for it. That one man was then the Duke of Wellington.

And so of events. It must be an astounding event indeed that would move a city of fifteen hundred thousand inhabitants to its centre. But how much vaster in magnitude and importance must the event be, much to move men's minds simultaneously to any great extent all over the world. The fall of a mountain in Switzerland, burying a whole village, would create no stir at the Antipodes, perhaps would not even be noticed. A great battle in India, involving the loss of thousands of lives, and the fate perhaps of empires, is announced without creating any deep feeling. If the thing be near us, of course we feel it more. The burning of a steamer on our own waters may affect us more than the second engulphing of a city like Pompeii in the fiery lava. We are affected but little by things at a distance, even on the surface of our own native world.

Carry this principle to other worlds, think of a distant planet, and the intelligence that a whole globe had gone from the sky, with all its inhabitants, would produce scarcely any excitement. How much less the fate of one individual among many millions of inhabitants. Suppose it were proclaimed in this world that a creature in the Star Sirius, who was under sentence of death, had repented and was pardoned. Would it produce the least sensation? Would any notice be taken of it? Not so much as the rise of stocks five per cent., or the sudden reception of half a million of gold from California, or the intelligence of the failure of a great banking-house in London.

Now, apply these facts to the actual relations between us and heaven, to the effect of intelligence from this world to that, as made known to us. Heaven is illimitable; its inhabitants are innumerable; its interests and its objects of interest are infinite and transporting. Its transactions are of a grandeur and glory, compared with which perhaps the building or burning of our whole globe would be a minute thing. And yet there is anxiety in that world respecting intelligence from this. The countless inhabitants of heaven take so absorbing and thrilling an interest even in one soul in this world, that when it is told in heaven that here on this earth one sinner has repented, there is a sensation there; there is a universal sensation, there is joy in Heaven, as over an event of glory, important to the whole universe of God.

There is such an intimate connection and communion, and such a fervent sympathy, between that world and this. And yet that celestial region where this sympathy is felt, and where this benevolent concern and joy are manifested, may be farther distant from us in locality than the farthest point of the universe to which the telescope has ever carried our vision, or of which any astronomical computation has ever rendered our knowledge possible. And that glorious celestial region is the place where the inhabitants see God; where there is the personal presence and glory of the Saviour; where there is no night, nor any mechanism of a material universe needed; neither sun nor moon, nor hanging worlds of flame; but where the Lord God Almighty and the Lamb are the everlasting light and the all-surrounding temple. Would we have supposed it possible for the inhabitants of such a region, in the midst of their absorbing and glorious employments and enjoyments, to have leisure for a thought upon a world like this? And yet, between that inconceivably exalted and glorious region and this wandering, distant orb on which we dwell, there is this intimacy of sympathetic interest so close and thrilling; an interest turning exclusively upon the welfare of the soul, and absorbed in the one question of its repentance—joy in heaven over one sinner that repenteth.

Now, what an amazing difference between the interest of heaven towards us, and our destitution of interest towards heaven!—the intense benevolence and sympathy in that world, and the intense stupidity in this! There is but one way of accounting for it, and that is the great fact revealed in scripture, that ours is a fallen world, under a scheme and possibility of redemption;—there is but one way of accounting for it, and that is made known in the same passage that announces this heavenly joy, as a joy over one SINNER that REPENTETH. There is stupidity here, and a lack of all right interest towards heaven, because this is a world of sinners in rebellion against God, in whom the very beginning of life, and of the manifestation of sympathy with heaven, is in repentance. And there is this absorbing interest *there*, for the same reason, because this is a world of souls in rebellion, and repentance is the redemption of a soul from this rebellion and ruin, and the inhabitants of heaven are perfectly benevolent.

They have none of our defect of sensibility. A vast interest loses none of its greatness with them by distance, and their judgment of things in principle does not depend, like ours, upon circumstances. They see and know the value of the soul. The ruin of the soul in consequence of sin is eternal, and they see and know that. We are this side that demonstration; they are on the other. We know it by faith; they know it by sight. We know it by God's word, in order to avoid it; they know it not only so, but by beholding it. We are *warned* of eternal realities; they are in the midst of them.

It is joy over one sinner that *repenteth.* The whole emotion of heaven turns on that. That is the one only point in the life of mortals that excites any interest in heaven, and *that* commands the interest of *all* heaven. Without that, men are of no worth; they are the cast-off lumber of creation; they are fit only to be burned; they are good for nothing but to illustrate God's justice; they are of no more interest than the fallen angels. But while there is a possibility of repentance, they are objects of interest and of affectionate ministry to all heaven; and the moment repentance begins, so soon as in any lost soul that light is seen breaking out of darkness, then there is joy in heaven. It is as if all heaven's inhabitants were gazing towards a dark quarter of the universe, where God is going to light up a point hitherto black, dreary and unknown, with the sudden blaze of a new created world in glory. When the light flames out into the void of chaos, the morning stars shall sing together, and all the sons of God shall shout for joy. So is the joy over one sinner that repenteth. The repentance is the flame of a new radiant lustre hung up in God's universe; it is the light of a new creation of God. The repentance is life out of death, light out of darkness, holiness out of sin, bliss out of guilt and misery, love out of enmity and rebellion, heaven out of hell. There is nothing but this in the life of a sinner that can make him the subject of a blissful interest in heaven—nothing but this that makes a soul worthy of the notice of heaven—nothing but this that can awaken joy in heaven. If you would ever produce joy in heaven, or be the possessor of joy yourself, then *repent!* This is the only possibility of your salvation.

It is joy over *one* sinner. If there were *but* one in all the guilty part of God's universe, that would be enough to produce this joy, enough to illustrate God's glory, the Saviour's love, the wonders of redemption; enough to create an eternity of blessedness out of an eternity of woe. Nothing could more strikingly demonstrate the infinite worth of the soul, the dreadfulness of its destruction, the importance of its salvation; *one* soul, no matter whose, for there is no respect of persons with God, and the soul of the poorest beggar is of the same infinite worth as that of the greatest philosopher or monarch on his throne. It is one sinner's repentence, one sinner's salvation, that stirs all heaven. Amidst the truths of doctrine flaming out from this great fact there shines prominent the truth that repentance *is* salvation; that God will never leave a soul once penitent to fall away and perish. Such souls are *kept* by the power of God through faith unto salvation. Otherwise the joy of heaven would be a mistaken joy, and the sympathy of heaven a mistaken sympathy. But it is joy there, even while the soul is yet struggling here. It is joy there, as for a glorious certainty, even while in this world there is yet doubt and darkness. It is joy there, because, when a sinner repents, a sinner is saved. Hell is despoiled of a victim, and heaven is enriched with a soul in the image of Christ.

Furthermore, the repentance of the soul is the thing for which Christ died, Christ, the Son of God Incarnate, and the accomplishment of that object is infinite joy. This is the object of His mission on earth, and the inhabitants of heaven know it. They know well that Christ came to seek and to save that which was lost. They know the amazing instrumentalities and agencies put in motion to accomplish this object, and the mighty transaction planned from eternity and finished on Calvary, and in heaven itself, by that sacrifice through the Eternal Spirit, that stupendous work of Love, the foundation of the possibility of repentance. And that for which Christ died, occupies the attention and engages the activity of heaven. It cannot be otherwise. Of the angels of God it is said, Are they not all ministering spirits, sent forth to minister to those who shall be heirs of salvation? A great, yea, a truly astonishing passage, opening to us, as through a wide-flung gate, a sudden view of the rushing activities of all heaven in this work of human redemption; the incessant holy ministries of angelic beings waiting upon His movements who is King of saints, and who hath at His control, as the Captain of salvation, all principalities and powers, and every agency and name that is named or is active, either in this world or in that which is to come.

The great passages in Daniel 7: 10, and in Revelation 19: 11, and onward, are similar disclosures as to the work that absorbs the active ministry of heaven. It could not be otherwise than that that object for which Christ incomprehensibly emptied Himself of that Divine glory which He had with the Father before the world was, and as it were absented Himself from heaven, and became incarnate, and died upon the cross to bring it about, should command the attention and engage the activity of heaven. It could not be otherwise than that angels should glory in its accomplishment. And whatever incomprehensible mystery there might and must be to the intellect, to the intelligence of all heaven, in the incarnation and the crucifixion, it would all serve, not to distract the attention of angelic minds from the great end of this mystery, but to raise that object into more commanding attractiveness and brightness, and to fix the instant gaze of souls with more intense interest upon it. Incomprehensibility there must be, to them as well as to us, in the mystery of the incarnation. The goings forth of Emmanuel from heaven, the veiling of that Divine Person in human flesh, the process, whatever it might be, alluded to by the Apostle Paul in the second chapter in the Epistle to the Philippians, when He who was in the form of God, and for whom it was no robbery to be equal with God, made Himself of no reputation, and took upon Him the form of a servant, and was made in the likeness of men, is to us entirely inconceivable, and must have been to all heaven incomprehensible. He, by whom all things were created, visible and invisible, worlds and creatures, thrones and dominions, principalities and powers; He by whom all things consist, and who must be omnipresent to all beings and things of His dominions; He to whom it was said, Thy throne, O God, is forever and ever; He of whom, and of whose glory in the heavens, amid the worship of the holy seraphim, Isaiah had that glorious vision, recorded in the sixth chapter of his prophecy, when one cried to another and said Holy, holy, holy, is the Lord of hosts, the whole earth is full of His glory; He, the object of that worship, the Creator and Lord of those angelic beings, with their thundering halleluias, wondrously withdrawing Himself from that worship in heaven, and passing into the form of a servant on earth, entering into an eclipse, so to speak, of which the first portion of the veil visible must have been the form of the Babe in Bethlehem.

O there was a mystery in that, more incomprehensible to them, heaven-ward, than the sight of the Babe, and the revelation of incarnate Deity to us earth-ward. For to us the man Christ Jesus is seen first, and we travel from that sight to the revelation of His Deity. But they had seen only the Divinity, seen their own God and Creator, seen Him, of whom the first annunciation in his essential glory, before yet the angelic minds of heaven had been created, is the ultimate declaration, beyond which the thought of created beings either in heaven or on earth cannot go, that, "In the beginning was the Word, and the Word was with God, and the Word was God. All things were made by Him, and without Him was not anything made that was made."

Well! to see Him, their Creator, dying away from that infinite glory, of which His was the mastership, the ownership, and theirs the adoration and the service, to see Him passing into the form of a servant, making Himself of no reputation, to see Him entering into that veiling, that INCARNATION, the reality of which is the certainty of human redemption, the central revelation of God's plan, and the invisibility of the Deity becoming visible; this must have been to them a greater incomprehensibility than it ever yet has been to us. We feel as though no word could have been uttered in heaven while this was taking place, as though the inhabitants of heaven must have gazed silently, in submissive adoration and awe. But when He bringeth in His first-begotten into the world, He saith, "Let all the angels of God worship Him!" and something of the glory of that worship was made visible to the shepherds, when suddenly there was with the announcing angel a multitude of the heavenly host, praising God and saying, "Glory to God in the highest, and on earth peace, good will to men!"

But now, this is to be marked, that the greater the incomprehensibility of these transactions in heaven, the more immeasurably did it enhance and exalt beyond all conception the greatness of the end for which, as to earth, as to mankind, these transactions were taking place, the repentance of the ruined sinner, the salvation of the lost soul. So far from being turned away from that, or distracted into idle questionings by the incomprehensibility of the stupendous scenes of the incarnation, the minds of angels were turned by it to more adoring views of God's love, and more exalted conceptions of the magnitude of the interests at stake, the infinite greatness and worth of the object to be accomplished; and they were fired with more intense desires to be in some measure instrumental in accomplishing that purpose. They saw, by the mystery of that incarnation, the worth of the soul, the certainty and awfulness of the penalty of God's law, the dreadfulness of sin, the eternal ruin of man without a recovery from sin, the glory and blissfulness of one sinner's repentance. They saw the glory of the Saviour manifested in that; the glory of God in the display of all His attributes. They saw the glory of the Divine Word, which had been veiled for this purpose, coming out from that veiling, that eclipse, into a brightness transcending the most transcendent of all previous manifestations of might, majesty and loveliness. They saw the happiness of the redeemed soul, the awfulness of the hell of sin and wrath, from which the repenting sinner is rescued, and the ravishing excellence, glory and beauty of that perfect image of the Saviour, into which, by faith, through the power of the Eternal Spirit, the rescued soul is transfigured. All this in the regeneration of one sinner that repenteth! All these elements of blissfulness in the tide of joy that as a ground wave rolls through all heaven at the salvation of one repenting and returning sinner!

Now, there are some glorious and blessed lessons out of this survey of things through the window of this grand revelation; and, first, that which makes joy in heaven calls for joy on earth; and that which commands the activity of heaven, in blissful ministry, with seraphic fire, demands the activity of earth. The hearts of Christians should be on fire here, as the hearts of angels are on fire there. There is no other object that can be put into comparison or competition for one moment with this of the sinner's repentance, or that does not sink into insignificance, or pass into absolute wickedness, beside it. It justifies all the activity of our being in the work of revivals of religion, all our efforts to win souls to Christ. It puts the mark of reprobation on all indifference to this great interest. It shows, in the most striking light, the sinfulness and wonderfulness of such indifference, and how buried in sin men must be, to remain insensible to transactions involving their own eternal welfare to such a degree and in such relations, as on that account alone to stir the heavenly world to its centre. All heaven is anxious for earth, astir for earth; but earth is heedless for itself, and careless both of hell and heaven,—a combined blindness and madness of infinite malignity and destructiveness.

But again, that which commands the belief of heaven should command the belief of earth. The blessed creatures of the heavenly world do not draw back from plainly-revealed truths or facts, because of real or alleged incomprehensibilities; nay, the incomprehensibilities attending the incarnation of the Son of God for our redemption only deepen their sense of the necessity of such an interposition, and confirm their knowledge of all the plain facts of sin and of endless retribution. But here in this world, sinners on trial for their eternal retribution put the incomprehensibilities of God's triune or incarnate existence as a breast-work of unbelief against the plainest truths of the gospel. The blind, unbelieving moles of creation look out from their dirt-hills, and deny the things which they cannot understand, or take, by virtue of speculation about them, a release from truths as plain as the noonday.

And such truths are those of an eternal retribution, as illustrated by the cross, and by this very joy of heaven over souls repentant at the cross. And therefore, furthermore, that which excites the dread of heaven should excite the dread of earth. The terror of heaven on our account is the wrath to come; the anxiety of heaven on our account is deliverance from that wrath to come, by our repentance. And shall there be no corresponding anxiety here? Shall there be stupidity here, while all around us in God's universe there is a stir of anxiety, activity and sympathy, both in heaven and hell; for hell itself is moved to destroy us, as heaven to save us.

There is no defect of warning here, no more than there. We are in rebellion against God, and we know both its wickedness and its consequences. The riot act has been read ever since the creation; it is read in God's word; it is read in men's own souls. Conscience reads it perpetually amidst the mob of a man's wicked thoughts; and still men rush on to perdition. They themselves together make such a stunning noise in their rebellion, their ten thousand activities of sin, their hubbub of earthly vanities, that they will not hear God's voice; and multitudes of them, when they do hear, do not believe, or endeavor not to believe, that God will ever carry His threats into execution. "Oh," they say, "the guns are only loaded with blank cartridges!" And because sentence against an evil work is not executed speedily, therefore the hearts of the sons of men are fully set in them to do evil.

But whose fault is all this unbelief and insensibility and ignorance? And when the great guns of God's promised justice are fired in upon the masses of the rebellious, then how terrible will be the conviction, the consternation, and the misery!

Character and Consequences.

THE beginning of evil is in man's departure from God; the perfection and immutability of evil is when God departs from man. The essence of happiness and misery is in character; a man sinful in heart shall be filled with his own ways, and the good man also shall be satisfied from himself. The determination of character is in man's own power; for he may get from God what elements of good he pleases, and may have whatever of evil he pleases taken away. The good is of God, and if a man sows *that*, he shall eat the fruit of it. The bad is of man and Satan, and if a man chooses *that*, he shall eat of the fruit of *that*. The warning against it and the salvation from it are of God. The misery consequent upon it is of the sinner's own self, and not of God; though God is the security, both to the righteous and the wicked, of having their respective wages paid to them. I will bring evil on this people, says God, even the fruit of their thoughts, because they have not hearkened to my words, nor to my law, but have rejected them. Say ye to the righteous that it shall be well with them, for they shall eat the fruit of their doings; but they that plough iniquity and sow wickedness shall reap the same. This throws all consequences, even for eternity, back upon character. Character produces consequences, and is the great lord of destiny forever.

God tells us that character formed according to His word, by His counsel, is safe, and forms a security of happiness for eternity; but otherwise, it is a security of shame and misery, the shame and misery being the inevitable result and production of an irreligious character. Now, if this requires faith in order to believe it, it is faith in God, which is the highest exercise of reason, and moreover it is not a faith without corroboration in experience. By seeing what vast and dreadful consequences wait often upon guilty character and upon single acts of crime, even here in a world of probation, we see continual proofs that a man's misery in the eternal world may be wholly from himself, and wholly the natural result and working of inevitable consequences.

Now, all great demonstrations of these principles in this life, are important. They ought to be examined and pondered. The history of wicked souls is a history of wretchedness, up to the last point at which you can trace them; and if you think that wretchedness shall stop in eternity, it must be because the character of the soul stops, which is impossible. But even if it did stop, still there is the fruit of character, and the fruit of the sinner's doings, to come back to the sinner as his harvest; and how he is to shake off that, how he is to get rid of that, no man can tell. But how the harvest may come, how it does come, how certain it is, may be known even by experience in this life, and often is known, in extraordinary instances, which are like the thunder before a storm, like the warning signs of an earthquake, and which the human soul should make the most of, for its admonition.

All great crimes and great virtues are public property. They are warnings of evil, and examples of good. In the Word of God a man who commits a great crime, be he Cain, David, Peter, or Judas, is marked, and the case is held up, in clear light, without any disguise, for the world's admonition and instruction. The position and family of the man make no difference; there is the sternest impartiality and openness. The repentance of the man, if he have become penitent, is recorded; and repentance makes a great difference in the divine administration with the man. Repentance in faith is the very condition of forgiveness. He that confesseth and forsaketh his sins shall find mercy, however black and enormous those sins may have been. But God is no respecter of persons. Neither wealth, nor respectability, nor position, nor family, are regarded by Him, except as aggravating the guilt of the offender. If a man is guilty, he must bear the consequences; and the higher his position in society, and the more involved and vast and important his social relationships and responsibilities, the more terrible are those consequences, and the more important is that example. So that while in one view, as respects those who suffer from another's crime, the greatness of their interests and affections, so dreadfully sacrificed, deepens the public sympathy; in another view, in respect to the guilt that disregards and sacrifices such interests and affections, it increases, or ought to increase, the public hatred of the crime and indignation against the criminal. In proportion as the consequences of his crime are felt by others in misery, they ought to be felt by him in punishment. And if *they* have to bear *their* share in the consequences, *he* certainly will have to bear *his*. And a great part of his guilt, and what indeed he will have to suffer for, besides the direct crime, is the bringing such consequences upon others, the disregard of his responsibilities, the sacrifice of the interests entrusted to his care. For no man liveth to himself, and no man dieth to himself. In another sense besides the Christian sense, this is true. A man cannot live, without living for good or evil to others; a man cannot die, without dying for good or evil to others. When he is born, other interests are born with him, and dependent upon him; while he lives, other interests live with him, and are affected by him; and his sun can neither rise nor set, but with others, experience of its lights and shadows.

Therefore God always makes great far-shining harbor-beacons out of great virtues, and great lighthouses on desperate reefs out of great crimes and great criminals. Some men are very willing this should be done in respect to virtue, with unregenerate men; philosophic virtues, moral virtues, public spirit and philanthropy; but the virtues of grace and the characters of grace, they despise, and set down such men as hypocrites. And in respect to crime, if they can catch a professedly religious man in such a snare, they are glad enough to make an example of such a one. They are very willing to harangue the world about *David's* murder, but if you speak in the same terms about any other murderer, they accuse you of cruelty, and of a want of sympathy with an unfortunate criminal. We have known men go to the verge of blasphemy in consigning the whole character of David to the deepest damnation, who would perhaps shed tears of sensibility over the same guilt, unaccompanied by David's repentance. There are men who so hate religion, that they cannot endure it, even as the cure of crime.

Now, society are bound to get all the good they can out of great crimes as well as great virtues. Upon the criminal, the government must execute the deserved punishment, for the good of others, for the protection of society, for a warning to the world. If a man will sacrifice both himself and others in the indulgence of his own passions, then both God and man must bring all the good that is possible out of that evil, must make use of the warning, must hold up the lessons. And God, by the freedom with which he lets consequences come down even in this world, which confessedly is not the world of retribution, but of restraint, shows us what may be expected, when consequences shall have their full swing and development, when complete justice shall be administered, and men shall be judged according to the fruit of their doings, as well as the nature of their character. For if God spared not the angels that sinned, but cast them down to hell, and delivered them into chains of darkness, to be reserved unto judgment, and spared not the old world, bringing in the flood upon the world of the ungodly, and turning the cities of Sodom and Go morrah into ashes condemned them with an overthrow, making them an example, then the Lord knoweth how to reserve the unjust now and in every age unto the judgment to be punished. And if those consequences here in this world, on the commission of crime, were so tremendous, what will they be when the fountains of the great deep of justice shall be broken up in the eternal world, and God shall let all the consequences of sin unrestricted come to pass? All present consequences are in one sense mere warnings; all present experience of the evil of sin is but a prediction of what is to come; and all present sight and demonstration of what sin can do is but a foreshadowing and forewarning symbol of what it must do in eternity, when God lets loose his hold of consequences, and adopts the consequences as part of a just retribution.

In the Tyrol mountains a band of patriots preparing against an invading army, loosened an immense mass of huge fragments of rock and soil upon the brow of perpendicular precipices under which the invaders had to pass, and then lay in ambush above, ready at an instant's signal to topple down the ruin. The invading army rolled on, glittering and secure, till it got within the heart of these fastnesses, and not an obstacle was to be met, nor an enemy to be seen. And in that deep defile there was something ominous and awful in the loneliness and silence. Suddenly there echoed through the pass a clear ringing voice from the heights, "In the name of the Holy Trinity, cut all loose!" And instantly the vast and irresistible rock-cataract rolled down into the defile, crushing and burying almost the whole army. The souls of sinners pass through such defiles sometimes even in this world, and consequences come rushing down upon them like a torrent. But this is nothing to what shall take place in the Eternal World when the time of suspension is ended, and the voice is heard through the universe, "In the name of the Holy Trinity, cut all loose!" Consequences now are tied up, under the power of the Redeemer's sufferings and death, while mercy is offered, and a salvation is possible both from the guilt and the consequences of sin. And God's messengers and mercies do, as it were, stand at the mouth of those eternal defiles, and warn men away; there are passes, which if you enter, you are lost, there being a time, when all that keeps the ruin from descending will, in the name of the Holy Trinity, be cut loose.

At present, God is satisfied with warning men of the consequences to come. Afterwards, when the time for warning and escape has gone by, there will be the consequences beheld and experienced; and if you now will not be warned by consequences reported to you as coming, others will be warned, when consequences are adopted as retribution; and the whole universe will be warned by your very sufferance of these consequences. God will get this good out of you, even if you continue his enemy; you shall glorify the divine attribute of justice, and serve to keep others from sin, even in the endurance of that penalty, which you affected to deny, or were too heedless to regard, or used no endeavor to escape. At present, the experience is that of mercy, and the question is whether you will be insured against consequences by taking hold upon the mercy, whether you will flee to Christ, and be insured against the penalty by forgiveness and grace in Him. At present the character is forming, its fixedness for eternity being determined by the choice you make in reference to Christ; by the manner in which you live and the state in which you die, in relation to Him. Afterwards come the results of life and character. And when they come, they will be very different from the warning.

But results even here are sometimes so astounding; and when they come even partially in this world, they bring upon the sinful soul such a huge overwhelming anguish and sense of guilt, that it is easy to forsee, let but every act and principle of life be visited in a similar way, what an infinite weight and train of evil the soul will have to encounter in Eternity. Our sins in the light of their consequences merely, to say nothing of the light of God and His holiness, would be a terrible array; the view would be intolerable. Consequences, when they are known, arm the conscience with a new authority, and create a new and peculiar sense of sin. Sometimes, in this world, an act of bare carelessness, attended with fearful consequences, agonizes the mind with a remorse like that for murder. We have seen the description of such anguish in a man appointed to the charge of watching the lanterns on board a beacon-ship. The ship was moored upon a dangerous sand-bank, to keep up a floating light as a warning, and it was the duty of the keeper to see to it that by night the lights were always burning. One stormy night, shortly after he began to take charge of the beacon, he fell into a profound sleep while watching upon deck. From this he was awakened by shouts and cries from the sea, which was raging furiously. The lamps in the lantern had all been extinguished while he slept, and for want of the beacon, a large ship had run a-ground, and the waves were then breaking over her with great violence. When the lantern was lighted again and hoisted, the vessel could be seen breaking up, and the people crying, struggling and sinking among the billows. They seemed every one to upbraid the keeper of the light-ship, whose untimely sleep had been the occasion of their untimely end. Nothing could be done to save them, and the scene of their death haunted the man night and day. The masts of the wrecked vessel projected above the surface of the sea for several months after she was lost, keeping him in recollection of the night in which so many human beings perished in consequence of his neglect and carelessness. It almost made him mad, the memory of that one night of horror.

Now, in this world, we are able to trace consequences but a very little way, and in very small part; and there may be a thousand results from our habits and actions, our sins of omission and of commission, which we do not yet see, for one which we do see. As, for example, the ramifications of the consequences of that night's carelessness would extend through all the relationships and responsibilities of every human being lost that night, through many a circle of interests unseen, unheard of. And in view of this fact, who is not ready to exclaim with David, "Who can understand his errors?" Who can know the full nature and extent of his guilt, till he sees, as God sees, how far his guilt has worked, and what it has accomplished? And hence God says that he tries the reins and the heart, in order to give to every man exactly according to his ways, and according to the fruit of his doings. The fruit of his doings! That is a tremendous computation, of which eternity alone can reveal the sum. No man knows as yet either the infinitude of his influences and responsibilities, or the depths of his heart; neither what things may be let down into it, nor what may be brought up out of it. No man knows to what desperate courses temptation might lead him; into what snares, that look now too infernal to be thought of, his own heart, left of God, might precipitate him.

There are tendencies in that heart which even now, under God's warnings, are burning on, like trains of wet powder with slow matches, leading to magazines in the centre of great mountains. There is no knowing what trains of passion there may be, nor how near they may have already burned towards the catastrophe, nor what tremendous magazines of consequences, what rock-galleries of evil to be exploded they may lead to. Sometimes, God in His Providence cuts a ditch, as it were, across the train, and so stops it. Sometimes great calamities intervene, to save the man, by losses and disappointments here, from ruin in eternity. Just as, in a great devouring fire, in a large city, whole streets of buildings are sometimes torn down or blown up, to stay the conflagration, so the dearest earthly interests of men have to be demolished, for the sake of their eternal interests. Sometimes the experienced consequences, even of great crimes, in this world, are thus the means of staying the conflagration. The very sentence of death for murder may be the means of a preparation for forgiveness and life everlasting; the consequences experienced in this world of a particular great crime against God and man, may lead to a salutary deep conviction of sin, all sin, in the sight of God, and heartfelt sorrow for the same, deep conviction of the soul's ruin, and a hearty penitent search for the divine mercy and grace in regeneration.

But all providences and all consequences are unavailing without this. All the ditches digged in a man's path, to stop his career, all the houses blown up to stay the conflagration, will be of no use, no efficacy, without the spirit of God received into the soul. The fire will still burn on underground, or at some unexpected point it will leap clear across the ditch that was digged to stop it, and on it goes, careering towards eternity, where the gulf of death itself will not stop it, but will only give a clear uninterrupted sweep to its devouring energies.

Sacred and solemn are the lessons and admonitions, from such realities. As sinful beings, it is clear that we have put so many things in train for explosions of evil, that there is no evil which can be imagined that may not at any time burst upon us, unless we seek safety in Christ, and seek it in season. As sinful beings, we are under all the penalties of God's law, and all the principles of an eternal retribution. We walk beneath a firmament of upper, nether, and surrounding fires. Beneath the glorious and merciful restraint of the atonement, God holds them in, and bears them back, on every side, from hurting us, for the present time of probation, and during the present offer of salvation in Christ. But they are the realities of things, the certainties of the universe, the inevitable upshot of consequences, the penalty, the principle, the necessity, of law and government. God holds them in, during a world of probation, so that things in such a world, appear to be really upside down, and are not as they should be, according to eternal law and righteousness, which is against all sin, and connects all sin with suffering. Yet now and then, even here, the reality, the penalty, the principle, breaks out. There are, as it were, safety valves, here and there, in this iron firmament above and around us; this firmament of God's restraint, that for the present holds off the fire from us; and now and then one of those safety valves or demonstraters flies open, and lets down a jet of flame, a spout of hideous combustion, a sheet of fire like that which consumed Sodom and Gomorrah. Men gaze at these things with momentary horror, but still go on. Perhaps they pick up the falling lava, when it has got a little cool, and speculate about its origin, and its meaning, and the extent of pent-up fires that it may be supposed to indicate, and whether the firmament itself will ever fall. But few believe the danger, and secure themselves against it. They are too busy to take care of their souls, too fond of self-indulgence to listen to God's warnings. They want none of his counsel, and despise all his reproofs. Therefore shall they eat of the fruit of their own way, and be filled with their own devices.

THE PROVISION.

Forewarned, Forearmed.

Consequences are always a tremendous subject, with eternity in view; but there is nothing in the utmost reach of consequences unveiled before us, which gives the least shadow of a reason for complaint against God, were it only because His attributes and system of government and our relations to it, the tendencies of things and our responsibilities, are fully and fairly laid before us. We are not only informed of the good and invited to it, but are told of the evil and warned off; and therefore, if we madly incur the evil, it is our own choice, against God's choice for us. We shall now consider first the danger and the evil before us, as God warns us of it, as it lies in the nature of God's retributive system, against which if we run, notwithstanding all God's warnings, it is certain that instead of God bringing the evil upon us, it is we who bring the evil on ourselves. And second, we shall consider the danger and the evil as to the voluntary habits of character which we form in sin, in the disregard of God's warnings, and the neglect of prayer, by which habits and tendencies of character we ensure a shipwreck to the soul.

I say, then, that we are not in the midst of those evils and dangers which surround us, without the provision of a perfect security against them, if we choose to avail ourselves of it. We can foresee the evil and hide ourselves; and if we hearken to God, He himself will hide us.

We say, *Forewarned, forearmed.* It is a proverb of deep meaning. A man warned of an evil, which is not inevitable, may avoid it; he has the means of avoiding it, if he will apply them. It may cost effort, watchfulness, diligence; it requires forecast, arrangement, the application of his faculties and energies in earnest, to prepare for the crisis, the emergency. But if he will prepare for it, he may; he may be ready to meet it; he may secure himself against it. Forewarned, he is forearmed. The weapons are in his power, the armor of defence is round about him. And even if the evil be inevitable, yet still, being forewarned, he is forearmed, and may be prepared to encounter it, so that when it comes he may bear up manfully, and by the provisions he has been enabled to make, in the time given him for such preparation, may come forth, if not absolutely triumphant, yet not destroyed, nor fatally injured. Nay, the wise and earnest grappling with inevitable evil, and the patient endurance of it when it comes, the preparation for it as foreseen, and the discipline in passing through it, may be a great benefit to his character; and on the whole, the evil, he being forewarned of it, and having acted the part of a wise and noble nature in meeting and bearing it, may be an absolute blessing. He may ride out the gale, though he cannot escape it. But a sudden hurricane, uuexpected, unknown, or a storm for which, though he knew it was coming, he made no preparation, may carry him to the bottom.

When the signs in the heavens forewarn an experienced navigator of the approach of a sudden tempest, he instantly takes in sail, makes all fast, battens down the hatches, sets every man at his post, and so waits the bursting of the hurricane. Forewarned, he is forearmed. A sudden fall in the barometer, while he was sitting in his cabin, when the heavens were as yet cloudless, and the air serene and clear, may have been his first warning, and he alone, of all in the ship, may have seen it; and it may have been observed by him at that particular moment, merely because he happened, without the intention of an observation, to turn his eye towards the instrument; or it may have been observed, because, being in a latitude where sudden storms were not unlikely, he kept an unwearied vigilance, and consulted, every few moments, the indications of that faithful sentinel of tempests. But, however that may be, when the warning comes, it no sooner forewarns than it forearms him. He may neglect the warning, and thus refuse to use the armor; but he might have used it, and was bound to do so; and when it came, it threw upon him the whole responsibility of guarding against the predicted evil, or of all the consequences, if he went on to meet it unprepared. The evil is inevitable, the tempest must come, but if he calls all hands at once to action, lets them know what he knows, puts every man on guard, and the ship in storm-trim, then when the gale rages, though the ship may labor and plunge, and be in great peril, yet she rights again, by God's blessing on human watchfulness and effort, and rides out the storm in safety. Forewarned, the Captain was forearmed. But if he had been heedless of the warning, or had counted upon time enough by the next watch, or the next morning, if he had been seated at a table with a merry party of passengers, or at a game of cards, which he was unwilling to interrupt, and so had taken for his own and their amusement the time given him to prepare for the safety of the ship, then the storm bursting, finds everything loose, and all sail set, and comes like the crash of an earthquake. The masts go by the board, the ship founders, and every soul perishes; and the whole responsibility of every life lost comes upon the Captain, heedless of the warning, which it was his office to know, and his business to obey. Forewarned, he was forearmed, and he might have been prepared; and in that view, it was not the storm that did the injury, but his carelessness. If he had put to sea without a compass or a rudder, or with a supply of provisions so insecure and insufficient as to produce a famine, it would have been his own heedlessness, and not the laws of nature, nor the violence of the waves, nor the ungovernable will of the winds, nor the pathless wilderness of ocean, that produced all the evils consequent on such a course. And just so, if his ship is wrecked because of his delay or heedlessness in not preparing for a storm of which he is warned, or if he runs upon a reef, laid down in his chart, of his nearness to which he was ignorant because he had not taken the observations which he was bound to take in order to ascertain his latitude, it is neither the storm nor the reef that wrecks his ship, but his own heedlessness.

Now, apply this to our spiritual destiny. For, even thus, it is not the laws of God, that wreck and ruin our souls, if we run against them, but our own iniquity in disobeying them. It is not the reefs of evil, eternal though they be, that bring us up, and destroy us, but we, who madly, and against all warning, run upon them. It is not the bursting, overwhelming hurricane, that sends us to the bottom, but our wilful heedlessness in rushing into it, our madness in meeting it unprepared, our self-indulgence and indolence, taking that time for gratifying our own passions, which was given us, with full warning of what was to come, that we might avoid the evil. The sinner himself, and not God, is the author of the sinner's destruction. The prudent man foreseeth the evil and hideth himself; the wicked pass on and are punished. God utters His thunders and flashes His lightnings across the path of the sinner, but he disregards them. On the sea of life, not only the barometer in his own soul tells him of the coming tempest, and he neglects the warning, but even when the clouds roll up angry and heavy before him, with the roar of the thunder and the lurid play of the lightnings, he steers his ship right into them. God warns him off, but he minds not the warning. There is never an inevitable storm, but he has time to prepare for it, full notice of it, and might ride it out in safety. There is never a reef rising, nor a dangerous shoal, but it is laid down in his chart, and the means given him to know his position, so that he might give it a wide berth, and steer clear of it completely, without even coming near enough to see the breakers. There is a barometer in his conscience, and a chart and compass in the Word of God, which, if he would go by it, would keep him clear of all danger; and even when he is entering into danger, the elements themselves act the sentinel for him in season, and the moaning winds, and the agitated waves, and the big beginning drops of rain, forewarn him, if the storm be inevitable, to prepare for it. It never need find him unprepared, nor come upon him unawares. But if he will not mark these signs in heaven above and in the earth beneath, if he will not regard these warnings of God, neither in his own soul, nor in God's Word, nor in the Divine Providence, nor in the gathering elements of wrath and ruin, but will pass on and be punished, so be it, since that is his decision; he must eat of the fruit of his own way, and be filled with his own devices.

Forewarned, forearmed. The proverb applies not only to the external dangers and evils on our course through life, and to the appointed penalties of courses of disobedience and folly, if we enter on them, but also to the responsibilities of our being, the dangers in ourselves, the tendencies, principles, and elements of retribution or of blessedness with which we are laden. We are fearfully and wonderfully made, with capabilities, powers, and faculties, that in themselves can make a heaven of hell, a hell of heaven. Now, knowing all this, knowing beforehand the power of habit in character, being told plainly by the Lord God, besides knowing it by our own experience,—that we are daily treasuring up, in what we make of ourselves, in our favorite and indulged elements of feeling, of thought, of action, in our whole natures, as formed and worked in a world of probation,—that we are daily treasuring up what we are forever to be and to experience, and daily setting in motion trains of tendencies and influences, which are to be developed in their consequences,—and those consequences belonging so exclusively to our voluntary being, that by them and in them we are to abide forever—knowing all this, what course do we take in setting forth this being of ours into life, daily, as it were, launching anew this ship of existence with all its activities and responsibilities? Under whose care do we place it? Into whose trust do we commit it? What officers do we put in command? By what principles do we determine they shall be guided? What and whose chart do we provide, and with what security that it shall be faithfully consulted? Who makes the barometer that we hang in the cabin? What kind of compass is it that we put in the binnacle? And into whose charge do we put the care of the engine? All these things are for us to determine, and we do determine them, and we must abide by the consequences. We know that the result of these things is life or death, eternal misery, or eternal blessedness.

If all these things are under the guidance and command of God, if it be with reference to what He has taught us, and with a simple single-hearted regard to principle and duty as marked by Him, that we arrange all these things, if we commit the care of our mind, heart, life, habits, and whole character, to the Lord Jesus Christ, if we go to His Word as our chart and compass, if we take our conscience, our inward barometer, to Him, to make it right, if we commit heart, conscience, understanding, and life to His spirit, to mould and guide us according to His will, then we are sure of success, and can meet with no evil. There shall be no wandering from the way, no mistake, no darkness, no running upon reefs through intoxication, or wilful ignorance, or heedlessness, no explosion, nor sudden hurricane, unprovided for and ruinous, but a safe passage, and an eternal harbor in heaven. But if a man neglect all these things, if he say within himself, To-morrow shall be as this day, and much more abundant; there shall no evil come, or before it comes, I shall have prolonged time to prepare; thus far, all has gone on well, and no shipwreck, though I have been in many seas; then, as his time past of security or exemption is no assurance of safety for one day to come, but on the contrary is itself a consideration why he should suppose the threatened evil more likely to come the very next day,—so in fact it will come, suddenly and unexpectedly, and will cut him asunder at an hour when he looked not for it.

And thus heedlessly do men go on. Because sentence against an evil work is not executed speedily, therefore the heart of the sons of men is fully set in them to do evil. It would seem, in many cases, in spite of all the forewarnings of God, to be fully set in them to *secure* evil, and to render it inevitable and eternal. Men put into their characters, and cultivate into perfection, evil elements, as sure to come out in eternal consequences, as the spots of the leopard's cub are sure to be found in the full grown creature; tendencies and habits are fostered, by which the soul is sure to make shipwreck; and the shipwreck, when it comes, and comes without remedy, is the man's own work, and not God's; it is the man's own work *against* God's. If a man will put his soul under charge of sin and sinful passion, instead of God's grace, as the pilot; under charge of self-will instead of God as the commander; then the consequences are of his own making.

Suppose that a man building a steam-ship should supply it with a store of ardent spirits, and put it under charge of a drunken engineer, or a man in the habit of using intoxicating drink. With all this, the vessel may possibly make several voyages without injury, and the man, on being expostulated with as to his folly, may say and think that things are not so bad as they are said to be; the vessel has gone well thus far, and no calamity, and another voyage may be just as successful as the last. To-morrow shall be as this day, and much more abundant. Such a man goes on in a headstrong, sinful, obstinate disregard of consequences; and now when the consequences come, he must be held responsible for the whole of them. If the vessel is wrecked, as she is likely to be wrecked, in consequence of the owner's recklessness, and if the lives of a hundred passengers, who were persuaded to embark, because of confiding in his prudence and in the good qualities of the steamer, are sacrificed in the shipwreck, certainly the sacrifice lies at his door, and the guilt comes upon him. The responsibility has various steps, and if it lights on the intoxicated engineer first, it lights next and largest on the owner or commander, who continued him in their employ, and supplied the means of his dangerous vices. He may be as the entrusted agent, but they are as the wholesale dealers and principals in the ruin, and on them the responsibility of the ruin falls.

Just so it is in reference to eternity. Men go on, voyage after voyage, year after year, with materials and officers in charge, that must, some time or another, inevitably wreck them; but because the ruin does not come now, they think little of the danger. They are forewarned, but it does no good; they take no heed to the warning. On the contrary, they take the very steps that are sure to realize the warning, to bring down the predicted consequences. And in such a case, when the result comes, it will come like a whirlwind, realizing the prediction in God's Word, and sweeping everything before it.

Now, there is a salvation from all this, or God would not have been at the pains to spread out all the warnings in regard to it before us in His Word. There is a deliverance in Christ, both from ourselves, and from God's retributive justice; and it is hard to say which is the greater salvation; for we carry within ourselves, in the elements of an unchanged sinful character, the very essence and assurance of perdition, the very elements of everlasting misery. Unbelief and sin in the soul are as unfailing a well of everlasting death, as faith and love, and the Lord Jesus Himself in the soul, are a well of everlasting life. And the question is, Shall the depths of death be exhausted and closed up by the Redeemer, and made to give place to the unfailing spring of life everlasting in Him? This may be done; the fountains of evil in the soul may be sealed, the tendencies of evil all removed and destroyed, the disposition to sin may be exterminated, and nothing but the life of Christ remain abiding in the soul, and a will as sweetly subdued to His will in meekness and lowliness as His was to His Father's, till the soul be presented without spot or wrinkle or any such thing, spotless before the throne of His glory with exceeding great joy. Thus sin gives place to holiness and hell to heaven, wherever the Lord Jesus takes up His abode. The sting is taken from death, and from every other evil, and what before was evil and only evil continually, a complication and accumulation of evils, from which there was no possibility of being extricated, becomes now a train of God's ministers for good, a chariot of fiery and glorious discipline, to which Satan himself is harnessed, if God pleases, to do

God's bidding; and life and death, and angels, principalities and powers, adversity or prosperity, temptations, trials, distresses, tribulations, things present or things to come, are bound to that chariot, and reined in by the reins of that promise, that all things shall work for good to the soul that loves God.

This is our salvation in Christ; an infinitely perfect and glorious salvation; and therefore let no man complain of any the darkest and severest terms and colors, in which the depths of our depravity are unveiled before us, and of the hell to which that depravity is carrying us; nor let any man complain of the endeavor on the part of God and his servants to make us realize the intolerable burden and hatefulness of our guilt; for if that process of rebuke will but open our eyes, will but take away our insensibility, will but carry us, yea drive us to the Cross, and compel us to flee in anguish and self-despair to the Saviour, the severest treatment is the greatest mercy. An utterly false benevolence is that which shrinks from making known our guilt and ruin; a lying sympathy is that, and a most reprehensible and contemptible dread of giving offence, which fears to mention hell to ears polite, which sheaths the sword of the spirit in flowers, and never discloses the terror of the Lord, but with apologetic circumlocution. God's greatest severity is man's mercy, and the Lord Jesus is never more tenderly compassionate than when He says, "He that believeth not the Son shall not see life, but the wrath of God abideth on him."

Surely, considerate men would much prefer that God and His ministers should let them know their danger plainly, rather than suffer them to rush on blindfold into the midst of it.

Faithful ministers of the Gospel have sometimes been accused of gloom, darkness, and terror in their delineations of the nature and consequences of human guilt. What would such critics say, if men like Jonathan Edwards stood in all our pulpits, and rolled the thunders of God's law upon the guilty conscience? Let men consider, if the bare *description* of the realities of guilt and perdition be so terrible, what must be the realities themselves? Who can dwell in the devouring fire? Who can lie down to everlasting burnings? Let those who dread even the announcement of such terrors, hearken to the merciful warning in God's Word, and flee to Christ Jesus while they may. God be praised that we have the possibility, the opportunity, of such a refuge! God be praised that Jesus is an Almighty Saviour. It is omnipotence and infinite mercy that we need, and now, while the Almighty arm is stretched down to us from heaven, let us take hold upon it. Now let us cast ourselves upon God's mercy in Christ, praising Him that out of the depths of such an abyss of ruin as ours is by character and retribution, He can raise us by infinite grace and love!

The Ultimate Warning.

THE passage in the Epistle to the Hebrews, on which the preceding chapters are founded, pours its vast and solemn train of thought and warning on the soul, as follows: "For it is impossible for those who were once enlightened, and have tasted of the heavenly gift, and were made partakers of the Holy Ghost, and have tasted the good Word of God and the powers of the World to come, if they shall fall away, to renew them again into repentance, seeing they crucify to themselves the Son of God afresh, and put Him to an open shame."

This passage of God's Word, solemn and pungent as it is, has, we doubt not, in cases almost innumerable, failed of its proper application and effect, by being restricted to a supposed particular and small class of sinners. It belongs to all, who have ever enjoyed the privilege of fully hearing the gospel, being enlightened by the Word of God. There is not one specification in it which may not enter into the Divine Indictment against the whole multitude of men in Christendom, who from Sabbath to Sabbath have heard the Word of God proclaimed and expounded. They are fully enlightened, they have tasted of the heavenly gift of the Gospel, and all its blessings have been placed at their disposal, they are made partakers of the Holy Ghost, according to the sense of this passage, if not in its fullest sense, just as the Jews were, who, according to the charge of Stephen, had received the law by the disposition of angels, but had not kept it, but being stiff-necked and circumcised in heart and ears, did always resist the Holy Ghost. But all men, under the Gospel, are made more largely partakers of the Holy Ghost, than under the law; his ordinary influences are more abundant, and the sin of resisting and rejecting those influences is more common. The gifts of the Holy Ghost are larger and more varied, and all are in one sense partakers of them, who have been instructed in the fact of their having been given for the accomplishment of the work of God's mercy in the redemption of mankind. The gracious influences of the Holy Spirit continually accompany the Word of God, and all who hear it are aware of God's promise to give the Holy Spirit to those who ask Him, and by His Spirit and with His Word God strives with men, so that they do really grieve the Holy Spirit of God, by continued impenitence and sin. They have tasted the good Word of God, the Word which is quick and powerful, and able to make them wise unto salvation through faith in Christ Jesus. They have experienced also the powers of the world to come; the whole revelation from God, especially in the New Testament, is a manifestation of those powers, and a grappling of them, like great grappling irons, upon the alarmed hearts and consciences of men. "Knowing the terror of the Lord," says the Apostle, "we persuade men, and are made manifest in men's consciences. And knowing the glory and joy of the Lord, we persuade men. There is hope laid up for you in heaven, and a blissful and glorious inheritance, even the inheritance of Saints in light, and a crown of righteousness, and rest from sorrow and from sin, in the likeness and presence of the Saviour, when the Lord Jesus shall be revealed from Heaven with His holy angels, in flaming fire, taking vengeance on them that know not God, and that obey not the Gospel of our Lord Jesus Christ, who shall be punished with everlasting destruction from the presence of the Lord, and from the glory of His power, when he shall come to be glorified in his saints, and to be admired in all them that believe."

Now, in this very last quotation from Paul, this compact and comprehensive burst of revelation, are the powers of the world to come; powers of eternity, powers of hell and heaven, powers of promise and despair, powers of attraction and of fear. And they who hear them, taste them; they cannot but have some recognition of them; and oftentimes, beneath the working of the Spirit of God with them, they are powerfully affected by them; they are wrought upon to such a degree, as to feel, if they do not exclaim with Agrippa, "Almost thou persuadest me to be a Christian." And yet, after all this, in multitudes of cases, despising the riches of God's goodness, forbeasance, and long-suffering, and not recognizing the fact, not remembering it, not laying it to heart, nor considering its solemn consequences, that the very purpose of this goodness of God is to lead them to repentance, arrested and awakened men, even after having thus heard and tasted the powers of the world to come, and the good Word of God, do nevertheless return to their carelessness and insensibility, and after their hardness and impenitent heart, led by that, following that, and not obeying the powers of the world to come, and the good Word of God, and the strivings of the Holy Spirit, they treasure up wrath against the day of wrath, and revelation of the righteous judgment of God; who will render to every man according to his deeds; to those who by patient continuance in well doing seek for glory and honor and immortality, eternal life; but unto those who do not obey the truth, but obey unrighteousness, indignation and wrath, tribulation and anguish, upon every soul of man that doeth evil, of the Jew first, and also of the Gentile; but glory, honor, and peace, to every man that worketh good, to the Jew first and also to the Gentile, there being no respect of persons with God.

Here, again, in *this* passage, this compact and comprehensive delineation of God's ways with man, and of careless man's neglect, ingratitude, and madness with God, and of the consequences coming, we have the powers of the world to come, and the manner in which many a hardened and impenitent heart treats them. This good Word of God, sharper than any two-edged sword, and these powers of the world to come, are the rod and spur for a sleeping conscience and insensible heart; they convince of sin, they alarm the soul with a sense of danger. These powers of the world to come are as the broom of the Divine Law; they perform the work of sweeping; sometimes for a season they sweep the habits by an enforced moral reformation; they frighten men from their sins, they almost persuade them to flee thoroughly and truly from the wrath to come, by submission to the Saviour, by receiving Him into the heart, as its everlasting life and possessor.

But now do we wish for a description of the result, precisely corresponding to the text, if they do not thus admit the Saviour, thus cast themselves on Him? We may have it in the words of Jesus Christ, which, if they had been written after the great and solemn passages from the Epistle to the Hebrews, and in illustration of it, could not have been a more pointed and enlightening commentary. "When the unclean spirit is gone out of a man, he walketh through dry places, seeking rest. And finding none, he saith, I will return to my house, whence I came out. And when he cometh, he findeth it empty, swept and garnished. Then goeth he, and taketh to him seven other spirits, more wicked than himself, and they enter in and dwell there; and the last state of that man is worse than the first."

Or, again, do we wish from another Apostle, a similar commentary, an equally powerful and solemn explanation? We may have it from Peter, concerning those, who for a season, by the power of the truth and of conscience, driven into just such a temporary reformation, seem clean escaped from those who live in error; but not truly fleeing to Christ, nor trusting in His blood, His grace, nor receiving Him into their hearts, they still are the servants of corruption, with all their promised and imagined liberty. "For of whom a man is overcome, of the same he is brought into bondage. But if, after they have escaped the pollutions of the world through the knowledge of the Lord and Saviour Jesus Christ, they are entangled therein, and overcome, the latter end is worse with them than the beginning. For it had been better for them not to have known the way of righteousness, than, after they have known it, to turn from the holy commandment delivered unto them. But it is happened unto them according to the true proverb, The dog is turned to his own vomit again, and the sow that was washed to her wallowing in the mire."

The powers of the world to come are elevating powers, reforming powers, impelling powers, persuasive, mightily argumentative and constraining, when believed and felt. Beneath their influence men are naturally drawn upwards towards heaven. They are sometimes taken by these powers, as by angels, and laid down at heaven's very threshold, where one step would be an entrance. But if from thence they turn away from such a glorious salvation, and from such a mighty agency, and from beneath such an impression wrought upon them, and such an almost persuasion effected in them, then there are no other powers, and no other agencies, that can raise them again to that vantage ground of mercy. That good Word of God, and those powers of the world to come, and those precious influences of the Holy Spirit accompanying them, have lifted them into a condition, in which salvation was accessible, and very near. But, if from all these advantages, these pinnacles of opportunity, these ladder-tops of means and grace they fall away, or if under all these influences and privileges they remain unmoved, unconverted, then there is no more hope. What possibility remains, after all the round of God's applied expedients is run through, and is ineffectual? Light, knowledge, love, warnings, threatenings, promises, invitations, commands, arguments, entreaties, gifts, powers, providences, the Word, the Spirit, convictions, awakenings, the Cross, the sufferings, the death of Christ, and the glories of Heaven, and the terrors of Hell, all applied in vain! What is there left, what more powerful, what as a last resort? What is there of hope or possibility, to throw yourself back upon, after all the agencies of mercy in God's universe have been tried in vain?

A last resort! Here we come upon the mighty and closing reason for the "impossible," in the appeal to the Hebrews. It is impossible to renew them again unto repentance, seeing that they crucify unto themselves the Son of God afresh, and put Him to an open shame. They crucify Him unto themselves. They do it on their own account, their own responsibility. Instead of accepting His crucifixion for them, and gratefully trusting in it, pleading it, claiming it as their redemption, as the atonement for their sins through His dying love, they renounce it as God's work of mercy, and renew it as their own work of contempt. Sinful, unbelieving, unconverted men in our day do this in some measure as the Jews did, but more knowingly, more deliberately, and unto themselves, as their own private choice, as a thing which they accomplish alone, and wholly for themselves, no other participating with them. The Jews of old did it as a nation, and while they did it thus, they ignorantly fulfilled their own prophets and the will of God, and crucified Christ for their own as well as the world's salvation, that is, for any and all who would believe, Jews or Gentiles; and many of themselves, individually, were brought to repentance and faith in the crucified Redeemer, by that very act being charged home upon them. But when men, after knowing the purpose and meaning of the atonement, and receiving its propositions, still reject Christ, and remain impenitent, they crucify Christ *unto* themselves. They crucify Him, even in that sense in which Paul says that by the Cross of Christ *the world* was crucified unto *Him*, and He unto the world; just so *Christ* is crucified unto *them*, and they unto Christ, his love having no more power over them, and they no more interest in Him. They render themselves dead to Him, and His Cross dead to them. They render His death of no more efficacy for their salvathan if they had never heard of it. Nay, that is not all. They invest it with a dreadful efficacy in their own guilt, and for their own condemnation. It is a savor of death unto death, instead of life unto life. It shall be more tolerable for Tyre and Sidon, for Sodom and Gomorrah, in the day of judgment, than for such. This rejection of Christ constitutes an impossibility of repentance and of salvation, because, beyond Him, His sacrifice being neglected, there is no way of removing guilt.

And this brings us to another profoundly solemn commentary and paraphrase of our whole text, that parallel passage in the same Epistle, which we have purposely reserved to this point, because it lifts up to a startling manifestation and preëminence both the reason of the impossibility and the dreadfulness of the sin. "For if we sin wilfully after that we have received the knowledge of the truth, there remaineth no more sacrifice for sins, but a certain fearful looking for of judgment and of fiery indignation, which shall devour the adversaries. He that despised Moses' law died without mercy, under two or three witnesses. Of how much sorer punishment suppose ye shall he be thought worthy, who hath trodden under foot the Son of God, and hath counted the blood of the covenant wherewith he was sanctified, an unholy thing, and hath done despite unto the Spirit of grace?" See, adds the Apostle afterwards, that ye refuse not Him that speaketh. For if they escaped not, who refused Him that spake on earth, much more shall not we escape, if we turn away from Him that speaketh from Heaven. Truly, this is the last limit and degree of warning in the Word of God. It is the last terror, even the terror of the Lord, the terror of the guilt and condemnation of rejecting such authority, such a Being, such an interposition, such a Saviour. The warning is clothed in language and embodies ideas, that, rightly pondered, could not fail to awaken every man from his insensibility, who hath not yet fled to Christ Jesus from the wrath to come. And yet, terrible as this passage is, it is announced, in its very opening, as belonging to those simply, it is dedicated to just simply those, who sin wilfully after receiving the knowledge of the truth. Now, who that has heard the gospel has *not* received the knowledge of the truth? And who that turns away from it does *not* reject it wilfully? Who that remains impenitent under the light of the gospel, is not employed, every time that the offers of salvation and the claims of Christ are passed before him, in doing despite unto the Spirit of grace, and treating with contempt the Cross, the sufferings, the death of Christ, the blood of the covenant, and the person of the Son of God? Last of all, He sent unto them His Son, saying, they will reverence my Son. When this last of all expectations, hopes, efforts, interpositions, is proved in vain, there can be no other possibility of salvation, there remaineth no more sacrifice for sin.

Now, when this guilt of a despised and neglected gospel is analyzed, as it has been in these passages by the Holy Spirit, and is presented as God's own indictment against the sinner, in so many separate and dreadful counts, and conscience begins to see a little what it means, the expressions are terrible indeed; there is a lurid glare in them, a flashing of the bottomless pit. The drawing up of the accusation is terrible, the terms are terrible, the personality, malignity, and wilfulness of the sin are terrible, and the charging of it from God Himself as a treading under foot of the Son of God is terrible. And men would fain imagine that it is not *their* sin that is meant in such an indictment, but some horrible, gloomy, daring and desperate apostasy, like that of Judas. They cannot see, they will not acknowledge, they do not feel, that they themselves are thus personally insulting the Son of God, and putting Him to an open shame. And yet, the analysis of this passage shows, and the demonstration of the nature of unbelief shows, that it belongs to just those who, under the light of the gospel, obey not the gospel, those who, at the call of the Saviour, come not to the Saviour, those who, at the invitation to the King's marriage supper for His Son, make light of it, and turn away from it to their farms, their merchandize, their pleasures.

They could not well show contempt more clearly than by such a course. And it is contempt that touches the dignity, authority, and paternal throne and government of God at a very tender and jealous point. It was said of old, Kiss the Son, lest He be angry, and ye perish from the way, when His wrath is kindled but a little. Blessed are all they that yet trust in Him And by the Son Himself it is said, "He that believeth on the Son hath everlasting life; he that believeth not the Son shall not see life, but the wrath of God abideth on him." He that, after an intelligible and repeated manifestation of the claims of the Son of God upon his faith, his gratitude, his affections, still withholds his whole nature and will and heart from those claims, and forms the habit of such reluctance and resistance, is under the whole of this fearful condemnation. There remaineth no more sacrifice for sin. There is no sacrifice, there can be none, that, when the offer of the one atoning sacrifice in the blood of Christ is for the last time rejected, and its efficacy despised, can atone for the sin of such wilful and deliberate rejection both of God's authority and mercy, or prevent the consummation of such a choice of everlasting destruction from the presence of the Lord.

And therefore this whole subject shows, in a most vivid light, the greatness of the sin of unbelief in Christ, above all other sins, and the profound depth and solemnity of meaning in the question of the Apostle, How shall we escape, if we neglect so great salvation? It shows the necessity of immediate submission to Christ, and the hazard of remaining impenitent, always the guilt of unbelief increasing, as well as the power, and always the gulf widening between the soul and heaven. A man living on in sin under the gospel, lives under the malediction of Hebrews, 6: 4, 5, 6; and every moment is in danger of being shot through with that tremendous impossibility of a renewal unto repentance. There is no safety but in a decisive, hearty, humble prostration of the soul at the feet of the Redeemer.

And here we see how dangerous the habit of indecision, the habit of being half-moved, and yet not changed, beneath the powers of the world to come.

There are multitudes in this undecided condition, up to the last hour. They are always going to believe, going to repent, going to prepare for death, going to begin the work of faith and repentance. They are always, as in the parable of the foolish virgins represented, going to buy, till the great midnight cry, Behold the Bridegroom cometh! Then comes the end, wholly unexpected; death, with the sting of sin in full power, arrests the soul for judgment, and the door is shut, and it is too late forever. There are those, whose whole probationary existence, under the full light of the gospel, seems to be passed in this way, oscillating, swinging, between heaven and hell; raised under the power of Divine truth almost periodically very near to heaven, and then retreating again, like the motion of the tides, swayed by the heavenly bodies, but never lifted beyond a certain limit in their earthly sphere. Just so, there is a certain degree of heavenly attraction experienced, but it never reaches to the point of conversion, and from every successive height to which it is carried, the soul inevitably falls away. At length comes the last power, the last effort, the last opportunity, and then there is no more possibility of a renewal of the soul to repentance.

Often it happens that men are disappointed of an eternal good, and defraud their own souls of a salvation which was very near at hand, for want of a little additional effort, or an earnest effort at decision in a timely hour, at the moment of a merciful visitation. He smote thrice, and staid, is the record of many a soul. And the man of God was wroth with him and said, Thou shouldst have smitten five or six times. For want of this decision and perseverance there is many a shipwreck, every week, of bright hopes for eternity, bright promises. Every Sabbath day, the work of the last Sabbath, forgotten and gone like the tracks upon the sea-shore, has all to be done over again. With many persons, it is just like raising a huge rock to the top of a declivity. You get it up by great toil and patience, almost to the summit, but there you have to leave it for a season, with props to secure it, till you can return and finish your work. So is a serious soul, on the verge of the kingdom of heaven. Meantime, the world, and the God of this world, are busy; He comes, and gradually undermines your props, or steals away the checks with which you sought to keep the rock in its position, and down it comes, prostrating in a moment the toil perhaps of years. Just so the spiritual work of the Sabbath is undone by the Satan of the week. The God of this world is busy. You think, on the Sabbath, your work is almost accomplished; a lift more will set the rock on a secure basis; if there could be another Sabbath following upon this, the Word of God and the powers of the world to come, would not lose their grapple; the soul might be saved. But Monday morning the undermining work begins, and soon again the rock falls, and by Saturday night it is down lower than ever. Then the whole work has to be done over again. Such is the process, repeated again and again, between God and the world, heaven and hell, the conflict in and for the soul, the strife and the labor for it and against it. And such is the history of religious impressions in many a soul, especially amidst the worldliness of great cities; Sabbath evenings, near to heaven, but if not decided for Christ, then from Monday morning launched again upon the tide of worldliness, whirled in the vortex of consuming earthly anxiety and care.

At this stage of our investigation let us consider from how many quarters the artillery of heaven's argument on this subject advances upon us. What an overwhelming array of demonstration! The Word of God—the powers of the world to come—the character of Christ—the work of atonement—the nature of the soul—the nature of sin—our already experience of its power and its misery—the activity of angels—the very joy of heaven! What could we ask, what could we conceive, in the way of added proof or demonstration! From every direction, eternal truth marches in upon us. By every avenue of logic and of feeling the conclusion is forced upon the soul that the mighty conflict which agitates the universe is a conflict for eternity, a conflict between two eternities, a conflict between the power of an endless life, and the power of an endless death. Nothing less than this could put all worlds in motion. Nothing less than this could range the Son of God incarnate on the one side and Satan on the other. Nothing less than the certainty and dreadfulness of an endless death, could bring from heaven a Divine Redeemer, the Lord of Eternity, to take upon Himself our flesh and blood, that through death He might destroy him that had the power of death, even the devil, and deliver those, who through fear of death were all their life-time subject to bondage. Nothing but this would permit that Divine Saviour, on any occasion, under any circumstances, to say of any sinner, even the most incredible, that it were good for that man if he had never been born.

The Church's Stewardship.

Now, in view of all these revelations, demonstrations, and elements of excitement and of power, the voice of the Lord our God speaks to His church, His people, collectively as well as individually, "Wherefore gavest not thou my money into the bank, and then at my coming I might have required mine own with usury?"

The true spiritual view of this text is one of great solemnity, power, and glory. The grandest, mightiest, and most responsible stewardship on earth, is that with spiritual elements, spiritual possessions, spiritual agencies. The possession and the use of truth is the greatest of all responsibilities. What a man does with his wealth is of almost no consequence, in comparison with what he does with his knowledge. The houses, or lands or stocks he holds, are dead lumber, and have no power of usury, in comparison with the accumulating, energetic, vital power of truth. This is not the ordinary conception; men feel very little responsibility for their use of the truth with which they are entrusted; but when they stand in judgment before God, then will they see and know that their knowledge constituted the overwhelming preponderance in their stewardship, that it was their use or abuse of truth, that determined everything else in time and eternity, and that where they wasted one talent of silver, they misapplied, or buried, or laid away to rust, ten thousand talents of truth, ten thousand demonstrations of God, ten thousand convictions of conscience. Truth for eternity has such vitality and preciousness, that its stewardship is either of death unto death, or life unto life. It may be held in idleness and insensibility, and that is to bury it in a napkin, and defraud both God and man. It may be held in unrighteousness, and with a reprobate mind, and that is to make it unfit even for the world's dunghill. It may be held in distortion and denial and deceit, and that is to make the world's medicine the world's poison, as if a man could make the rivers of a land run Prussic Acid, or the clouds rain down arsenic.

We have been dwelling on the powers of the world to come. We must consider now the responsibility and stewardship of the church as invested with them, and why it is that such mighty agencies accomplish, after all, so small results.

God doth with us as we with torches do, not light them for themselves. He created all things by Jesus Christ, to the intent that unto principalities and powers in heavenly places might be known by the church the manifold wisdom of God. The church is a body of His stewards, the repository of wealth for the universe, His chosen and perpetual company, the general assembly and church of the first-born, the commonwealth of Israel, a chosen generation, a royal priesthood, a peculiar people, to show forth the praises of Him who hath called them out of darkness into His marvellous light. It is a commonwealth having a life individual, and a life social, public, mutual, confraternal, incorporate, in Himself, to carry on the administration of the vast, yea infinite estate, which He has committed to the whole body, in trust not only for men on earth, but principalities and powers in heaven. For the execution of this trust He has prepared this living spiritual body, which indeed is His body, the fulness of Him that filleth all in all. There is one body, and one spirit, even as ye are called in one hope of your calling; one Lord, one faith, one baptism; one God and Father of all, who is above all, and through all, and in you all. The preparation of this body for this stewardship is first of all individual, and "unto every one of us is given grace according to the measure of the gift of Christ." The church is called and composed first of all in its members, not its officers, in Christ. After that He saith, "when He ascended up on high, He led captivity captive, and gave gifts to men. And He gave some, apostles, and some, prophets, and some, evangelists, and some, pastors and teachers, for the perfecting of the saints, for the work of the ministry, for the edifying of the body of Christ, till we all come in the unity of the faith, and of the knowledge of the Son of God, unto a perfect man, unto the measure of the stature of the fulness of Christ." He has done all things on a mighty and glorious scale, and having so prepared the body, the stewardship with which He has invested it is inconceivably costly and glorious.

What, then, are some of the elements of this stewardship? What have we to work with, and what is it that we are to work, what agencies to set and keep in vital operation, for the advancement of God's kingdom, the accomplishment of God's purposes? On a general view, we have the Idea of God, and men's accountability to Him; His holiness and justice, and men's sinfulness; death, and all that may come after death; the undeniable inward convictions of mankind; the whole range of their natural theology of sin and misery; the law written in their hearts, their conscience bearing witness, and in their thoughts accusing or excusing one another; their sense of guilt and their knowledge of retribution, experimental and foreboded. We have the whole disclosures of revealed religion, Immortality, Eternity, the Judgment, Heaven, Hell, the Second Death, Conscience acting with reference to these things, the Plan of Redemption, the Mystery of the Incarnation, the Cross of Christ, Regeneration by the Holy Spirit and the vast law, immutable, unquestionable, *a new creature in Christ Jesus, or eternal condemnation;* the thunder of the Law, the mercy of the Gospel, the awakening Word, sharper than any two-edged sword, and the convincing and illuminating Spirit, searching all things, and revealing the character and ruin of the lost soul. All these elements of knowledge and of power are gathered together, natural and Divine, and concentrated, compacted, and illustrated, in the stupendous mystery of the character, person, and work of Jesus Christ and Him crucified. Not to know anything among men but Him, is to know all things.

But the natural man receiveth not the things of the Spirit of God, but they are foolishness unto him; neither can he know them, because they are spiritually discerned. He knows even his natural theology only by guesses and terrors, and gloomy doubts, fears, forebodings; and the best and most certain of his knowledge, and the best expressed, is but as the shadows of a fire upon the wall in a subterranean dungeon; but of things Divine he knoweth nothing as he ought to know, and receiveth nothing with open understanding and belief. For men in their native state in sin have the understanding darkened, being alienated from the life of God, through the ignorance that is in them because of the blindness of their hearts. And as it is written, Eye hath not seen, nor ear heard, neither have entered into the heart of man the things that God hath prepared for those who love Him, so neither the disclosures by which God demonstrates those things, nor the revelations of the way by which they are to be attained, nor the worth nor the reality of them, are understood or appreciated by a mind beneath the darkness of a sinful heart. To prepare for the teaching of these truths there must therefore be an investiture of the soul with the spiritual life and understanding of them; to render God's church a teaching church, a living, and not mere speculative or technical intelligence, a church wielding these elements and applying them in demonstration of the spirit and of power, there must be a possession of them, and of the life of them, and an understanding of them, as Christ Himself possesses and understands them.

These treasures are treasures in the ore, in the quartz, in veins, in mountains, in precious impalpable dust of sacred truth, as countless as the sands. It must be collected with great labor and skill, you must go down into the mines, you must work at quartz-crushing and sand-washing, you must prove the metal, it must be assayed, and it must be coined for circulation, and the mint is that of the Spirit of God in our own hearts. It is a mint of life, and not of stamp, form, impression merely. There might be the most orthodox die, cutting by rule with metaphysical regularity, and yet the truth be dead truth, dormitory truth, the respectable orthodox furniture of a heart dead in trespasses and sins, instead of the fuel, and the fire, and the light, that warms, irradiates, enlivens and rejoices, and the pure air that refreshes, and the living water and the bread of life. For all these emblems, and more than all, are used, almost in rhetorical confusion, yet with the rhetoric of loving truth, to set forth these powers and responsibilities, and the office of the heart by the Spirit, and the Spirit in the heart, to keep them from mere form and death, and to illustrate and enforce them. Your heart must be the mint of life, or the truth in it is death unto death. Your heart must be the mint of life, or your stewardship is a stewardship of guilt and condemnation.

If the stewardship appointed be the holding of these truths, and the illustrating, demonstrating and enforcing them out of God's Word, there must be a knowledge of them by experience, and a participation of the life of them; and for this God has provided. This is the baptism of His church with power from on high as at Pentecost, and the turning of truth, otherwise merely speculative, into life and fire in the heart. "For God hath revealed them unto us by His Spirit; for the Spirit searcheth all things, yea, the deep things of God. And we have received, not the spirit of the world, but the Spirit which is of God, that we might know the things that are freely given to us of God. Which things also we speak, not in the words which man's wisdom teacheth, but which the Holy Ghost teacheth, comparing spiritual things with spiritual." And where this life is in the heart, this living spirit of truth, it forms itself into tongues of fire for the mind, and leaps from mind to mind, even in the rudest and most unlettered shapes of language, when *in*formed by that Divine all-quickening spirit. Thus God accompanies the investiture of His church in this stewardship with the faculties for its control and management, the spirit of love, and of power, and of a sound mind.

There can be nothing more glorious than this ministry. It is a ministry of the church in general; and then, as a ministry also in particular, in the forms ordained of God, it grows out of the church, out of Christ in and with the church, and is set in the church, a part and parcel, a concentration and particular investment of the life of the church in Christ Jesus. "For the manifestation of the Spirit is given to every man to profit withal. And in all varieties of gifts worketh that one and the self-same Spirit, dividing to every man severally as He will. For as the body is one, and hath many members, and all the members of that one body, being many, are one body, so also is Christ in the Church of Christ. For by one Spirit are we all baptized into one body, whether Jews or Gentiles, whether bond or free, and have all been made to drink into one Spirit." It is the ministry and stewardship of the church. And so Peter commands, "As every man hath received the gift, even so, minister the same one to another, as good stewards of the manifold grace of God. If any man speak, let him speak as the oracles of God speak; if any man minister, let him do it of the ability that God giveth; that God in all things may be glorified through Jesus Christ." It is the ministry and stewardship of the church, prepared and designated as the Sons of God in the midst of a crooked and perverse nation, among whom it is their work to shine as lights in the world, holding forth the word of life.

It is also, as the ministry, more particularly, of the Elders and appointed Shepherds in and of the church, by the will of Christ, the *same* stewardship, and an instrumentality prepared and established of God for the *fulfilment* of that stewardship. "And so," says the Apostle, "our sufficiency is of God, who hath made us able ministers of the New Testament; not of the letter, but of the Spirit; for the letter killeth, but the Spirit giveth life. Now, the Lord is that Spirit; and where the spirit of the Lord is, there is liberty. And we all, beholding as in a glass the glory of the Lord, are changed into the same image from glory to glory as by the Spirit of the Lord. For God, who commandeth the light to shine out of darkness hath shined in our hearts, to give the light of the knowledge of the glory of God in the face of Jesus Christ. And He that hath wrought us for the self-same thing is God, who also hath given unto us the earnest of the Spirit. All things are of God, who hath first reconciled us to Himself by Jesus Christ, and then given to us the ministry of reconciliation. And as we are allowed of God to be put in trust with the Gospel even so we speak, not as pleasing men, but God who trieth our hearts. And as we have this treasure in earthen vessels, it is that the excellency of the power may be of God, and not of us, and that all gifts and graces might redound to the glory of God."

Thus, then, the gift of the ministry itself to the church of Christ is a gift for the fulfilment of its great stewardship, the gift of an agency prepared of God, and kept in vital activity, that the Word of God itself may have free course and be glorified. And the commonwealth of Israel are commanded to take to their hearts, and bear upon their hearts, those who thus labor among them, and are over them in the Lord, and who admonish them, and to esteem them very highly in love for their work's sake, and to pray for them, that utterance may be given unto them, and freedom and victory in preaching the word. And all are exhorted and commanded, even the whole body of believers, to have the Word of Christ dwelling in them richly in all wisdom, and circulating from soul to soul in life and power. They are commanded to walk in wisdom towards those that are without, to walk as children of the light, to walk in the wisdom of winning souls, and to put on the whole armor of righteousness, and to use the Sword of the Spirit which is the Word of God.

And there is a special and personal discipline, of which we can only glance at the outline, but which God bestows, and which it is the responsibility of the Christian, the individual steward, to keep up, since thus only he can keep his talent out of the earth and the napkin, and God's money in circulation and at usury. It is individual experience by the Spirit of God, which alone can fit the believer for the work of God. Accordingly, this is vouchsafed, just according to the fervor of desire and earnestness of prayer with which it is sought. The great prayer of Christ for the disciples was a consecrating prayer for the illumination and sanctification of His church by the spirit. "Sanctify them through thy truth; thy Word is truth. As thou hast sent me into the world, so have I sent them into the world, and the glory which thou hast given me, I have given them. I have given unto them the words which thou hast given unto me. I have manifested unto them thy name; keep them through thy name." "When the Comforter is come, whom I will send unto you from the Father, even the Spirit of truth, which proceedeth from the Father,

He shall testify of me. He will guide you into all truth. He will show you things to come. He shall glorify me, for he shall receive of mine, and shall show it unto you. And if ye abide in me, and my words abide in you, ye shall ask what ye will and it shall be done for you. These things have I spoken unto you, that my joy might remain in you, and that your joy might be full."

Such joy in the Lord is a Christian's great strength in this stewardship. And God's discipline by his Spirit is kept up in the soul, that the truth of God may be constantly realized by it. The soul is admitted to behold the Saviour's glory, and is baptized with His constraining love, and is taught to rejoice in Him with joy unspeakable and full of glory. What the scene of the transfiguration was to Peter, James, and John, what the entrancement into the third heavens was to Paul, that, the teaching and the discipline of the Holy Spirit with Divine truth is to every believer. Christians are taken down into hell, they are carried up into heaven, they are made to feel and to know that the powers of the world to come, and the scenes of redemption in this world, are no cunningly-devised fables. They have the earnest of the Spirit given to them, and the Spirit of Adoption, and the witness of the Spirit in their hearts, and the earnest of the inheritance of heavenly glory. They have not received the spirit of bondage unto fear, but the Spirit of adoption, crying Abba, Father. And the Spirit beareth witness with theirs that they are the children of God, and if children, then heirs; heirs of God and joint heirs with Christ. They have the spirit of hope, and the spirit of patience, and the spirit of faith, and the spirit of prayer, and the peace of God that passeth all understanding, keeping heart and mind in Christ Jesus. They have the Spirit helping their infirmities, and inasmuch as they know not what they should pray for as they ought, they have the Spirit Himself making intercession for them with groanings which cannot be uttered. Being chosen and sealed by that Holy promised Spirit for God's work, they are baptized with the spirit of wisdom and revelation in the knowledge of Christ, the eyes of their understanding being enlightened, that they may know what is the hope of His calling, and what the riches of the glory of His inheritance in the saints, and what the exceeding greatness of His power towards us who believe, according to the working of His mighty power which He wrought in Christ, when He raised Him from the dead, and set Him at His own right hand in the heavenly world. According to the riches of Christ's glory, they are strengthened with might by His Spirit in the inner man, that Christ may dwell in their hearts by faith, that they, being rooted and grounded in love, may be able to comprehend with all saints what is the breadth, and length, and depth, and height, and to know the love of Christ which passeth knowledge, and to be filled with all the fulness of God. And all this is done on purpose that they may be good stewards of the manifold grace of God, that they may be strong in the Lord and in the power of His might, that they may be no more children, tossed to and fro, and carried about with every wind of doctrine, but speaking the truth in love, may grow up into Him in all things, who is the head, even Christ, from whom the whole body, fitly joined together, and compacted by that which every joint supplieth, according to the effectuul working in the measure of every part, maketh increase of the body unto the edifying of itself in love.

All this is done, that they may be filled with the knowledge of God's will in all wisdom and spiritual understanding, that they may walk worthy of the Lord unto all pleasing, being fruitful in every good work and increasing in the knowledge of God; strengthened with all might, according to His glorious power, unto all patience and long-suffering with joyfulness; giving thanks unto the Father, who hath made us meet to be partakers of the inheritance of the saints in light; who hath delivered us from the power of darkness, and hath translated us into the kingdom of His dear Son. From the experience of such a translation, as from the flying chariot of Elijah, they can speak to a dying world. It is the dispensation of God, not with Paul only, but with the whole church of Christ, to fulfil the word of God, which for that purpose is made manifest to His saints, to whom God would make known the riches of the glory of this Divine mystery of salvation, even Christ in you, the hope of glory.

In addition to all that mighty range of truths and influences, through which we have now rapidly glanced, that go to make up the vast stewardship of the church of Christ, God has also given those simple ordinances appointed in His word, and connected with it, of which the Sacrament of the Lord's Supper is most prominent and important. It is a scene of solemn and affecting remembrance, and a source of most impressive thought and feeling. In it the wandering heart may meet the Saviour, and the tempted heart, as Peter's, behold His reproving look, and the heart that has been mourning after Him may have Him again made known in the breaking of bread. It is the place of renewed vows, renewed mercies, renewed and renewing grace, compassion and forgiving love on Christ's part, and renewed penitence and faith on ours. It is a landing place of rest, refreshment, survey, and setting forth again upon the Christian journey. It is an ordinance for gratitude and love enkindled and increased, and strength administered, as well as sins deplored. It is a mount of vision, where the glass is held to the eye of faith, and we may take a view of our fair and bright inheritance in heaven, and for the joy set before us, be prepared to endure the Cross, despising the shame, and in the light of our Saviour's sufferings, be made willing to go forth and work for Him, and suffer for Him, in behalf of the salvation of a world of dying sinners.

Out of this stewardship, conducted from such experience, comes a great revenue of praise to God in the salvation of dying men. Preached out of this living experience, in the majesty and life of all those heavenly endowments and preparations by the spirit, the Word of God is irresistible, and the result is described by Paul in the Thessalonians, "For our

Gospel came not unto you in word only, but also in power, and in the Holy Ghost, and in much assurance, and ye became followers of the Lord, having received the word in much affliction, with joy of the Holy Ghost. For this cause also thank we God without ceasing, because, when ye received the word of God, which ye heard of us, ye received it not as the word of men, but as it is in truth, the word of God, which effectually worketh also, in you that believe."

Now, the powers of the world to come, the truths of God's word, and the ordinances appointed therein, are elements of motive, energy, and influence, immeasurable, and capable of every increase and expansion; but yet they depend on the state of the heart to be proved living or lifeless, to develop strength or weakness. If the church were wholly in a right state, with the vital electricity from the Cross of Christ poured through it and around it, and charging the heart of its individual members, it would be a governing magnet upon this earth, and a central spring, impelling the whole world's movements. And just let us consider, on the other hand, how great the guilt, if such be at any time the condition of the church of Christ, that all these mighty elements shall be neutralized, fettered, palsied, shall be held in it as it were in weak solution, and not in vital energetic composition, shall be held invisible and powerless, instead of manifest and effective? Does not God justly demand, in reference to any such hiding of His power, "Wherefore gavest thou not my money into the bank, and then at my coming I might have required mine own with usury." Is it possible to conceive of any so great treachery as this? Can there be any imagined breach of trust that approximates to any comparison with it? To have a power committed, on which depends the advancing redemption of the world, to have it mysteriously thrown upon the state of spirituality in the church of Christ, (and mysterious alike the responsibility and the power,—the power of mischief by indolence and delay, and the power of good by wakefulness, and fervor, and activity) to have this power committed and this trust betrayed,—suppose it be by worldliness, by indifference, by neglect, by prayerlessness, by wealth, by all seeking their own instead of the things that are Jesus Christ's—what shall be said concerning so vast a betrayal of our stewardship? Is it not incredible that such a thing should take place, could be possible? What would be thought of a corporation with only a million of dollars vested in trust for only a thousand orphans, if through selfishness and carelessness they kept it so tied up, or so wastefully expended, that nothing of it should ever come to the use of the absolutely needy? Now, the church of Jesus Christ are guardians in trust, and the powers of the world to come are means put into the hands of Christians, with which they may work efficiently for the redemption of lost souls. And what shall be said of a church of Jesus Christ, what of individual Christians, put in trust with these treasures for eternity, invested with these elements of glory and of power, if they bury, or waste, or neglect, or throw away, such responsibilities, capacities, possessions? And they do bury them, they prevent their efficacy, they defraud God and the world, if they neglect the means of realizing and improving them.

What then *are* the means of realizing them? How may they be made accumulating and productive for God and eternity. What are the peculiar personal responsibilities of duty, with which Christians are invested, or to which they are held, by the nature of their stewardship? They are bound to fervent prayer. They can do nothing without this. Everything languishes and dies for want of this. The insensibility of soul so prevalent, the indifference to eternal things, the apathy under the most vivid disclosures from the world to come, are the result just wholly of the neglect of secret prayer. There can be no feeling, while that prevails; lukewarmness will grow upon the soul, till it settles in the sluggishness, the torpidity, preparatory to the horrors of an awakening in eternal death.

But fervent prayer can produce a resurrection even from the death of winter. It shall cover the lifeless trees with new foliage, and then they shall yield and move at every breath of God's spirit. It shall clothe dead truths with beauty, and inspire them with subduing persuasiveness and life. It shall move even upon unconverted hearts and minds, with an influence of solemnity and power, which they knew not, preparing them to be powerfully wrought upon by the truths of eternity. And the same presentation of truth, that before had no effect, shall now, under the supplications of anxious, yearning, heaven-beseeching hearts, under the united pleadings of a church awakened and at work, prove irresistible, by God's grace, with those who till then were heedless and insensible. Except in the atmosphere of prayer, spiritual truth cannot be living truth; it may remain as a dry and dead speculation; but it cannot *live* and *give* life, without prayer.

But again, Christians are bound to an attendance and sustaining of the social means of grace. Except Christ be in such means, there is indeed no life in them. But the special promise of Christ is given forth to just this duty, just this labor of social prayer. "Where two or three are gathered in my name, there am I in the midst of them." Where Christ is, there is life, there a blessing. The mere form of a social gathering is indeed nothing; but the disciples of Christ are bound to be there in heart, bound to go there from the throne of grace, carrying the spirit of prayer, and of compassion for souls to the communion of saints.

How criminally regardless are Christians of the element of power contained in that promise, "Where two or three are." From the too frequent appearance of the prayer meetings in our churches, one might suppose that the promise meant and was understood to *prohibit* the assembling of *more* than two or three at any one time. Let it be remembered that the forsaking of the assembling of themselves together was one of the earliest symptoms of declension and decay in Apostolic churches, that at length died by the visitation of God in their own corruption, spewed out by the indignation of the Saviour, for their lukewarmness, being neither cold nor hot. Let the members of our churches neglect their prayer-meetings, and they ensure the abandonment of God.

They are bound to keep their own hearts with all diligence, for out of *them* are the issues of life. There is no life anywhere, if it be not there. And if they take no interest in the Redeemer's kingdom, what evidence, either in heart or life, of an interest in Jesus. There is no power but life-power. You cannot move a dying world by speculation, by eloquence, by majestic thought, by argument, by persuasion, except it be kindled, inspired, and accompanied by the Holy Spirit, except it be set on fire of love. This is that requisite which you must gain, if you would fulfil your trust. "Restore unto me the joy of thy salvation, and uphold me by thy free spirit; *then* will I teach transgressors thy way, and sinners shall be converted unto thee." If we would speak of Jesus to others, we must have been with Him ourselves. If we would speak of heaven to others, and of God, and of sin, and of hell, with the tone and power of reality, with the vividness and fire of one thoroughly in earnest, we must be much with Christ in secret. A Christian can no more be a fervent messenger for God, while running on his own errands, with heart and mind absorbed in the things of this world, than he can serve God and mammon.

We cannot interest others, except as we ourselves have this living interest and experience. If a man should undertake to lecture on Australia, to give us an account of the gold mines there, and of the manners and customs of the natives, he would scarcely get an audience to pay for his lights of an evening. But if a man should come from Australia, bringing a great quantity of the gold in its virgin state, a man who himself has worked in the mines and gained a fortune, men would listen to him with eagerness; the people would crowd to hear him; and the plainest bare unadorned recital of facts, and from his own experience, would be received with deeper interest than the most elaborate and perfect rhetoric from the other. No exquisiteness of description could equal the reality of life, or of truth the product of life.

As the crowning work, Christians are bound, having thus prepared their issues of God's wealth, to go forth distributing them through the community. They are to put God's truth in circulation. They are to be employed in conveying and applying it to men's hearts and consciences. This is the one grand business for which God has entrusted His church with such grand and costly possessions.

THE END.

VIII.

The Lamp and the Lantern;

Or, Light for the Tent and the Traveller. By JAMES HAMILTON, D.D. 18mo. 40 cents.

IX.

Hetherington's History of the Westminster Assembly of Divines.

12mo. 75 cents.

X.

Christian Progress.

A Sequel to the Anxious Enquirer. By JOHN ANGELL JAMES. 18mo.

XI.

The Christian Father's Present to his Children.

By JOHN ANGELL JAMES. 16mo. 75 cents.

XII.

The Powers of the World to Come.

By the Rev. GEORGE B. CHEEVER, D.D. 12mo. $1 00.

XIII.

The Missionary of Kilmany.

A Memoir of Alexander Paterson. With notices of Robert Edie. By the Rev. JOHN BAILLIE. 16mo.

XIV.

Wardlaw on Miracles.

12mo. 75 cents.

XV.

The Self-Explanatory Reference Bible.

The Holy Bible, the authorized version, with marginal readings and original and selected parallel references. PRINTED AT LENGTH. 8vo. Turkey morocco.

XVI.

Infidelity.

Its aspects, causes, and agencies. Prize Essay By the Rev. THOMAS PEARSON, Eyemouth, Scotland. 8vo.

XVII.

Scotia's Bards.

Comprising the choicest productions of the Scottish Poets, accompanied with brief sketches of each. Elegantly illustrated. Cloth, $. Full gilt, $. Turkey morocco, $.

This work comprises the most exquisite effusions of Thomson, Ramsay, Blair, Falconer, Beattie, Ossian, McNeil, Bruce, Logan, Burns, Graham, Scott, Hogg, Tannahill, Leyden, Knox, Campbell, Cunningham, Pringle, Pollok, Motherwell, Gilfillan, Bethune, Nicoll, More, Wilson, Mackay, Aytoun, Smith, and others.

XVIII.

Jay's Morning and Evening Exercises.

New edition on large type. 4 vols. 12mo. (Preparing.)

XIX.

Kitto's Daily Bible Illustrations.

Vol. VIII. and last. The Apostles and Early Church. (Preparing.)

XX.

Memoir of Richard Williams,

Surgeon in the Missionary Expedition to Patagonia, Terra del Fuego. By the Rev. JAMES HAMILTON, D.D. (Preparing.)

XXI.

D'Aubigné's History of the Reformation.

Vol. V. 12mo. half cloth	.50
" full cloth	.60
" fine edition, cloth	.75
8vo. paper	.38
The five volumes, 12mo. cloth	$2.50
" " " fine edition	3.50
" " in one, 8vo.	1.50

XXII.

John Owens' Works.

16 vols. 8vo. Subscription price, $20 00.

This new edition, now completed, comprises all the writings of this prince of Theologians, except his work on Hebrews, which will shortly be issued uniform with the above.

XXIII.

Charnock on the Attributes.

With Life by Dr. Symington. 2 vols. 8vo. $3 00.

Morning Watches and Night Watches.

16mo. 60 cents.

"Daily grace for the soul is as needful as daily bread for the body. This volume seems well adapted to lead the reader to meditate upon God's 'loving kindness in the morning,' and his faithfulness every night. Active piety will flourish under its guidance."—*Christian Advocate.*

The Martyrs, Heroes and Bards of the Scottish Covenant.

By GEORGE GILFILLAN. Illustrated. 16mo. 60 cents.

"This is a book that we have looked over with great delight. The theme is one of the noblest that modern history has furnished, and it has found a fitting delineator in the polished pen of the brilliant author of the Literary Portraits, who has done his work with some of the fire and unction of a genuine child of the Covenant."—*Watchman and Reflector.*

The Revelation of St. John.

Expounded for those who Search the Scriptures. By E. W. Hengstenberg, of Berlin. Translated by Patrick Fairbairn. 2 vols. 8vo. $3 50.

"No living theologian is better acquainted with the Old Testament than the author of this able and elaborate work. He is, consequently, well prepared to expound those parts of the New, the imagery of which is borrowed from the Old. He has brought to his task, in the present instance, great learning, deep piety, and unquenchable ardor in the investigation of truth. That he has, in everything, written wisely and correctly, is more than can be said; but he has produced a work of great research, and of unquestionable value to those who search the Scriptures."—*Central Christian Herald.*

The Bible Companion.

Designed for the Assistance of Bible classes, Families, and Students of the Scripture. With an Introduction by the Rev. Dr. Tyng. 12mo. 40 cents.

Elegy written in a Country Churchyard, and other Poems.

BY THOMAS GRAY.

Illustrated by Gilbert. Small 8vo. Cloth, $1; full gilt, $1 50; Turkey morocco, $2 50.

"To praise Gray's poems, and especially the Elegy in the Country Church Yard, would be little less than an insult to the intelligence of our readers. But there are some things about the book which we may afford to speak of, as they are not altogether a matter of course. The critical observations at the commencement, are a fitting introduction to the work, as they tell us who the poet was, as well as what he did. The illustrations are just about as beautiful as art can make them. The typography and the paper are both exquisite; and the copy which we have at least, has tasked the skill of the bookbinder to the utmost. It is every way a beautiful book."—*Puritan Recorder.*

Kitto's Daily Bible Illustrations. Vol. 7th.

The Life and Death of our Lord. (Just ready.)

Vol. 8th and last, on the Apostles and Early Church, soon to follow.

The Young Woman's Friend,

And Guide through Life to Immortality, by John Angel James. 16mo. 75 cents.

Historic Doubts regarding Napoleon Bonaparte;

And Historic Certainties regarding the Early History of America. 16mo.

A Stranger Here.

By the Rev. Horatius Bonar, author of the "Night of Weeping," &c.

The Bible Hymn Book.

By the same author.

The Gospel Glass.

Representing the Miscarriages of Professors, or a Call from Heaven to Sinners and Saints to Repentance and Reformation, by Lewis Stuckley, 1669. 12mo.

Living to Christ.

A Mother's Memorial of a Departed Daughter. With an Introduction by the Rev. Asa D. Smith, D. D. 16mo. 60 cents.

"This is an interesting memorial of a beloved daughter, called in her youth to join the angelic throng in that 'better land,' where sin and death are known no more."—*Chr. Observer.*

Daughters of China.

Or, Sketches of Domestic Life in the Celestial Empire. By Eliza J. Gillett Bridgman. 16mo. Illustrated. 75 cents.

"This is the very book which we need to become well acquainted with men and things in China. It is a lady's introduction to the family circle, where, if you observe carefully the principles and habits of the mothers and daughters, you will know what the men are."—*Chr. Observer.*

The Course of Faith.

By JOHN ANGEL JAMES. 16mo. 75 cents.

The Young Man's Christian Year.

By the REV. J. C. RYLE. 18mo. 15 cents.

Memoir of Mrs. Harriet N. Cook.

By MRS. SIGOURNEY. 16mo. 75 cents.

Memoirs of the Lives of Robert Haldane,

Of Airthrey, and of his Brother, JAMES ALEXANDER HALDANE; comprising Notices of many of the most Eminent Men and the most remarkable Religious Movements, from the last Century to the present time. By Alexander Haldane, Esq., of the Inner Temple, Barrister. 1 vol. 8vo. $2.

"This is in all respects an extraordinary production. British biography presents nothing to be compared with it. * * * It is a book of facts, great and varied; it is a book of principles, most of them sound and important; it is a book of examples, shining and impressive; it is a book of lessons, full of encouragement and of caution; it is a book which will, in a future age, be considered as deserving a chief place in the biography of the first half of the nineteenth century."—*British Banner.*

The Spring Time of Life.

Or, Advice to Youth. By Rev. Dr. Magie, of Elizabethtown. 16mo. 75 cents.

"We rarely meet with a volume prepared for youth, in this age of light reading, at once so attractive in style and so rich in evangelical truth. For purity, perspicuity, and beauty of expression and force of thought, it would be difficult to find its superior. It is just what we would wish to see in the hands of every apprentice, clerk, and student in the land."—*Newark Daily Advertiser.*

The Faded Hope.

By MRS. SIGOURNEY. 16mo. 75 cents.

"We have in this little volume a most touching account of the life and death of a highly promising youth, from the pen of his bereaved mother. Everything about the book bespeaks the smitten and yet submissive heart. With the breathings of maternal love, it combines excellent taste, deep pathos, and exalted Christian feeling."—*Puritan Recorder.*

www.ingramcontent.com/pod-product-compliance
Lightning Source LLC
LaVergne TN
LVHW020119110826
845151LV00001B/209

* 9 7 8 1 4 2 5 5 4 1 9 0 3 *